The City of Coventry

The City of Coventry

A Twentieth Century Icon

ADRIAN SMITH

I.B. TAURIS

LONDON · NEW YORK

Published in 2006 by I.B.Tauris & Co Ltd
6 Salem Road, London W2 4BU
175 Fifth Avenue, New York NY 10010
www.ibtauris.com

In the United States of America and Canada distributed by Palgrave Macmillan
a division of St. Martin's Press, 175 Fifth Avenue, New York NY 10010

ISBN 10: 1 84511 034 X
ISBN 13: 978 1 84511 034 5

A full CIP record for this book is available from the British Library
A full CIP record is available from the Library of Congress

Library of Congress Catalog Card Number: available

Printed and bound in Great Britain by TJ International Ltd, Padstow, Cornwall
From camera-ready copy edited and supplied by the author

CONTENTS

To schoolboy role models:
David Duckham for the Corinthian spirit,
and Bob Carlton for the Bohemian

1

INTRODUCTION
Surrealism, Sky Blues, and Specials AKA

While the odd excursion takes the story almost to the present day, this is a book about Coventry in the middle decades of the twentieth century, a uniquely positive period marred only by that pivotal moment in the city's history, the Blitz. The book was prompted by a mix of authorial ego and filial duty. On the one hand I wanted to unite a set of essays written intermittently over two decades but sharing a common theme; and on the other I needed to acknowledge a passing phenomenon: my parents' generation, now in their seventies and eighties, or even older, share a keen sense of urban identity and a deep-rooted affection for their city. This much-battered bond between the individual and the wider civic community was cast in the Depression and steeled by war. The postwar years encouraged a deeper sense of achievement and respect, albeit tempered by increasing disappointment and ultimate disillusion. That disillusion was – and is - invariably expressed in terms of regret for a long-lost era of social citizenship and communal solidarity. There never was a golden age in Coventry, but elderly people mourn the passing of a (superficially) more homogenous society rooted in the nuclear family and located in a compact, clearly defined urban landscape. In 1936 my mother, displaying remarkable maturity and self-confidence for a sixteen-year old, left the west coast of Ireland to seek work in Coventry. With scarcely a trace of Galway left in her voice, she constitutes a triumph of cultural assimilation. The fierce pride she feels for her adopted city (clearly distinguishable from the

scorn with which she views its elected representatives) is shared by
most if not all of her fellow pensioners. It's worth repeating that the
legacy of 1940-41 can never be under-estimated when endeavouring
to pin down the nature of this unique and fast-disappearing civic
psyche.

Unfortunately, my mother has only a walk-on part in the
essays that follow, and the absence of gender is a marked, and indeed
regrettable, feature of the book.[1] Not that scholars have ignored the
role of women in manufacturing industry and local politics, witness
for example the work of James Hinton.[2] The steady stream of men
and women who left the fledgling Irish Free State to find work in
Coventry highlights the enormous contribution 'economic migrants'
and displaced persons have made to the life of the city, both at the
height of the Depression and more recently. Mid-century arrivals,
whether from poorer parts of the British Isles or from continental
Europe, today all too often bemoan the refusal of Caribbean and
Asian families to embrace total assimilation at the expense of multi-
culturalism; even assuming that the colour of their skins would
facilitate such a drastic suppression of ethnic and racial identity. In
so doing, these earlier entrants in to a one-time tightly concentrated
and uniform industrial workforce ignore their own lasting
contributions to the cultural diversity of the city. To take just two
examples: a staid ultramontane Catholicism was energised and
humanised by the arrival of Irish and Polish worshippers, while
between the wars sport and schools benefited enormously from an
influx of Welsh miners and teachers demonstrably proud of their
Valleys heritage.

My parents met in 1939, dancing their way through those
final difficult months of peace – Hitler was a growing threat, but an
IRA bomb in Broadgate strained relations between the indigenous
low church/nonconformist population and the growing Irish Catholic
community.[3] As the next two essays confirm, the war changed
Dad's life for ever. Apart from a brief and bruising return to the
shopfloor in early 1947 (was there ever a worse moment to leave
behind the creature comforts, and above all the warmth, of the
mess?), his experience as a platoon commander and staff officer
guaranteed him entry into middle management. He was aspirational
but not ambitious, perceiving his role as transport manager for
Armstrong Whitworth to be not that different from the sort of jobs he

had enjoyed immediately before and after the German surrender. He maintained a close and paternalistic relationship with his drivers and mechanics, the garage foreman acting as a de facto company sergeant major. It was a world of uniformed chauffeurs driving company directors from one site to another, 'Queen Mary' low loaders in a ceaseless shuttle between Baginton and Boscombe Down, 'Lorry Driver of the Year' contests at Fort Dunlop, and most glamorous of all, convoys laden with display missiles and giant model aircraft en route to Farnborough or Paris. AWA was part of the mighty Hawker Siddeley group, Britain still seemed to be at the cutting edge of avionics, and the Smith family were living a comfortable and untroubled middle-class lifestyle. We exemplified upward social mobility and relative affluence in 1950s Britain. Similarly, my father's employer exemplified the best and the worst of manufacturing industry at that time: brilliant R and D (most notably, the 1947 AW52 'Flying Wing'), and relatively harmonious industrial relations given a growing dependence on highly skilled, well-paid fitters and technicians; yet at the same time excessive pre-production costs, with over-generous procurement deals subsidising outdated management methods and high overheads.

Wartime production at Armstrong Whitworth's Baginton factory

Even before the election of a Labour government in 1964, everything started to change. By 1965 aircraft production in Coventry was doomed, the cancellation of the AW681 V/STOL transport carrier sealing Baginton's fate (again, a revolutionary concept, but frighteningly expensive when compared with a low-tech American alternative). Yet with tragic irony my father's fear of being laid off was to prove unfounded. As fate would have it, from the late 1960s through to the early 1980s Alf Smith's career mirrored the fate of manufacturing industry in the West Midlands, and beyond. When not placating the trade unions at Bitteswell, the refit airfield outside Coventry where he was now based, or masterminding the newly nationalised British Aerospace's transport system, Dad closed down aircraft factories. The cynicism of his bosses was breathtaking. Here was a fundamentally nice chap, retaining the finest qualities of an officer and a gentleman. Most important of all, as far as the board was concerned, the shop stewards trusted him. The trade unions knew my father would get the best deal he could for their members once the redundancy notices went out – after all, once upon a time he had been one of them, serving his time in the tool shop. Dad was part of the last pre-graduate cohort to climb the middle and upper management ladder. In 1982, with Mrs Thatcher's praise for Bitteswell's contribution to the Falklands war effort still ringing in his ears, he was asked to delay retirement for twelve months in order to close his own plant down. A year later Alf Smith finally retired, with a paltry lump sum and a bill for an ageing company car. By that time Coventry was an industrial desert, with scant opportunity for Bitteswell's highly skilled workforce to secure comparable jobs. My father was never bitter – that wasn't his way, even when he saw his immediate bosses secure large golden handshakes and official honours. Yet he was clearly worn out, and psychologically scarred. Less than ten years after leaving work he was dead. His story is Coventry's story.

Compared with other English cities Coventry has attracted more than its fair share of academic research over the past half century. The establishment of two universities in the course of that time has ensured a steady stream of researchers, with Warwick's late, lamented Centre for the Study of Social History in the vanguard of inquiry in to Coventry's recent past.[4] In particular, Tony Mason, James Hinton, and Nick Tiratsoo pioneered and promoted study of the city in the twentieth century, focusing their attention on postwar reconstruction. Tiratsoo's doctoral thesis and subsequent book provided the first informed analysis of Labour's role in rebuilding the city after 1945.[5] Here was a long overdue rejoinder to a familiar, uncritical unfolding of events in which a disciplined party, encouraged by its shopfloor allies in the transport and engineering unions, drove through a comprehensive programme of urban renewal, and in so doing revolutionised town planning and community housing. In this scenario sympathetic and enlightened advisers such as the Chief Architect, Donald Gibson, worked in close partnership with dynamic municipal leaders such as Sidney Stringer, Pearl Hyde, and above all, George Hodgkinson; at the same time a direct line to Transport House, and later Downing Street, came from the city's two most prominent MPs, Maurice Edelman and Richard Crossman.[6] Latter day politicians are seen as pigmies by comparison, a view seemingly confirmed when the Audit Commission listed Coventry as one of the worst performing councils in England and Wales. Interestingly, the AC's 2002 report focused upon poor front-line services, praising the quality of educational provision, economic development, and inner city regeneration as consistent with the standards established in the late 1940s and 1950s.[7] While acknowledging the postwar Labour Party's undoubted achievements, Tiratsoo tested this triumphalist version of urban renewal, and found it wanting. In his original analysis and in subsequent essays he argued that: neither the party machine nor the municipal edifice were as well-oiled and efficient as they purported to be; that Labour's electoral grip upon Coventry was not as firm as was popularly assumed; and above all, that much-publicised successes such as the pedestrian Precinct scarcely compensated for very real failures in meeting or maintaining housebuilding targets and ensuring adequate facilities on new or expanding estates.[8]

Tiratsoo refused to endorse critics of either right or left, the one denouncing top-down social engineering, and the other complaining of an unhealthy partnership with big business that pursued prestige projects at the expense of local needs. He acknowledged that, while the city centre was a demonstrable testimony to urban vision and social democratic idealism, there had been a systemic failure to provide a suitably supportive infrastructure, particularly in the city's newer and/or less affluent areas. Perhaps, as left-leaning social commentators like Jeremy Seabrook implied, there had been an enervating lack of nerve on the part of Hodgkinson and his comrades. Yet in difficult circumstances they had done the best they could.[9] Thus, wartime radicalism had

Late 1940s artist's model of the Upper Precinct

Upper Precinct c.1960

been tempered, firstly, by repeated battles with Whitehall, even before an ostensibly sympathetic administration left office in October 1951, and secondly, by a growing awareness inside the Labour caucus of an absence of grassroots support. At a surprisingly early date it became clear that Labour's natural supporters, whether working-class 'Coventry kids' or more recent arrivals, were largely indifferent to a collectivist agenda that placed the common good far beyond short-term material advancement. In other words, rising affluence and incipient consumerism in the early 1950s – already obvious prior to the war when cars and rearmament fuelled rapid recovery from the limited impact of the Depression – encouraged political apathy and a sharp focus upon the wellbeing of the immediate family at the expense of the wider community. Tiratsoo was careful not to accuse affluent workers and their dependants of rampant materialism, endorsing contemporary observers' insistence that a significant improvement in living standards and quality of life had to be a good thing. He simply concluded that the 'rather disappointing outcome' of the Labour majority's herculean efforts was partly, and perhaps primarily, attributable to 'local citizens... [who] could have demanded the radically refashioned city that had been suggested, but for the most part opted instead for immediate material gain.' In consequence, Gibson and his political masters found themselves 'operating against the grain'.[10]

This bleak yet balanced judgement was largely endorsed by Junichi Hasegawa in his comparative studies of postwar British reconstruction. Making favourable comparisons with other cities designated by the wartime Coalition as priorities for rebuilding, such as Southampton, Hasegawa agreed that Labour councillors were initially successful in mobilising popular support. For example, the October 1945 exhibition, 'Coventry of the Future, was visited by over a fifth of the population. Demonstrable enthusiasm by the general public, qualified support from the local press, and continued success at the ballot box, reinforced the majority party's resistance to local shopkeepers' demands for a restoration of the status quo (in marked contrast to Southampton retailers' insistence on the retention of high street shopping). Similarly, Labour was emboldened to deal confidently with cautious ministers and their officials. It was central government's preoccupation with unfettered economic recovery that forced social and cultural objectives down the priority list, especially once the Cold War demanded maximum output from the region's armaments and aircraft manufacturers.[11]

Having said this, only the harshest critic can dismiss the local authority's efforts to foster a fresh civic vision of challenging, community-based art in the face of cheap entertainment, escapism, and a vibrant, expanding popular culture. As is evident from the essay on John Hewitt, founding director of the Herbert Art Gallery and arguably Ireland's premier poet prior to the emergence of Seamus Heaney, Coventry in the 1950s was a tremendously exciting time for the arts. Hot on the heels of a new art gallery and museum came the Belgrade Theatre, from the outset a hothouse of post-*Anger* drama.[12]

I like to imagine a cinema in north Belfast in the spring of 1941, and John and Roberta Hewitt are sitting eagerly awaiting the main feature film. Their flat in University Road is already becoming well known as a convenient meeting place in which culturally-starved service personnel can recharge their intellectual batteries (and where, ironically, a decade later Philip Larkin will occasionally turn up to drink tea and exchange gossip). A senior post in the Belfast Museum and Art Gallery constitutes a reserved occupation, and anyway Hewitt considers his patriotism 'more provisional than headlong'; but he is doing his bit by giving talks in army depots the length and breadth of the province, and by volunteering to join Northern Ireland's woefully inadequate Civil Defence force. He is even prepared to sit through the obligatory Ministry of Information films everybody has to endure before the main feature is finally screened. I like to think of the Hewitts sitting in the gloom - almost certainly not holding hands (far too public a demonstration of affection, even in the dark), but perhaps sharing in the wartime luxury of a small bag of Bluebird toffees - and watching *Heart of Britain*, a film for too long overshadowed by its director Humphrey Jennings' next major project, his masterpiece *Listen to Britain*. Jennings, surrealist painter, co-founder of Mass Observation, and iconic documentary film-maker, had much in common with Hewitt, not least a shared conviction that poets really could change the world.

In early 1941 the *Luftwaffe* had still to target Belfast, and the cinema audience would unknowingly be previewing an imminent conflagration, albeit not as comprehensive as that experienced in Coventry on the night of 14-15 November 1940. Picture Hewitt –

before the war a regular visitor to England, and thus familiar with the Midlands, if not Coventry - quietly reflecting upon the sad irony of so much death and destruction creating a unique opportunity for urban renewal at some point in the dim and distant future. We know that at this time, ever the polymath, he was immersing himself in the work of town planning's two most visionary pioneers, Patrick Geddes and Lewis Mumford.[13]   However, we also know that, with imminent defeat a very real possibility, Hewitt had to struggle hard to maintain optimism and vision. In December 1940 he recalled how:

> In easy days I joined my voice with them
> who prophesied a new Jerusalem,
> nor dreamed the outcome of the years should be
> a far more terrible Gethsemane.[14]

While the chances of Hewitt having seen *Heart of Britain* are quite high, clearly he had no opportunity to view *A City Reborn*, a short film specially commissioned in 1945 to accompany 'Coventry of the Future'.[15]   Almost certainly, however, he would have seen *Face of England*, shot fifteen years later and originally intended for Commonwealth consumption. Given that the film was made for the Central Office of Information, it seems inconceivable that an invited audience would not have had an opportunity to view the final cut. In fact *Face of England* was only ever shown on Canadian television, there being no obvious audience for *A Tale of Four Cities*, a series intended to cover all four corners of the United Kingdom. In 1959 the Belgrade Theatre had commissioned South African writer John Wyles to write a play about Coventry. The result, *Never Had It So Good*, portrayed the city as a 'gigantic money-grubbing machine', and the film, in the words of the COI:

> ...investigates the truth of this. How democratic, energetic, successful the people of Coventry are, and how representative of modern England, is frankly analysed in this exhilarating programme.[16]

Regrettably no print of *Face of England* appears to have survived, which is a great shame as the shot list and script suggest that it must have offered a revealing insight into late 1950s and early 1960s consumerism and relative affluence. There are, for example, interviews with car assembly workers who had been effectively deskilled but were earning far more than they had as toolmen. Everybody without exception is very positive about Coventry, with numerous references to the Blitz and the city's reconstruction. Yet none of those interviewed in the foyer of the Belgrade have a good word to say about Wyles' play. The theatre itself rightly attracts great praise, as does the Herbert Art Gallery and Museum. One 'Citizen' articulates his civic pride in a suspiciously stilted manner. Paying tribute to Sir Alfred Herbert's ostensible generosity in going the extra mile to ensure the museum would include an art gallery, he insists that, 'all the experts who have seen it agree that it is really outstanding for a provincial town'.[17] Hewitt surely took quiet pleasure in those words. Indeed, *Face of England* must have seemed like a personal vindication: firstly, of his insistence that the art collection should respect and reflect the desires and aspirations of local people; secondly, of his original decision to cross the water and realise a long-held vision of community and popular culture in an English city he saw as *the* testbed of social democracy.[18] It is that vision which the essays in this book keep returning to, most obviously when contrasting Larkin's indifference towards Coventry and Hewitt's all too obvious enthusiasm. Remarkably little of Larkin's mature verse focuses upon his native city, but then, contrary to popular assumption, Hull is rarely more than a backdrop. Hewitt on the other hand, while never for one moment forsaking the 'glens of Antrim', wrote a good deal about and indeed *for* Coventry.

      Hewitt's move was partly because here was a rare opportunity to exploit the coming together of civic enterprise and capitalist philanthropy. Sir Alfred Herbert, whose machine tool empire came to embody both the best and the worst of British manufacturing industry in the middle of the twentieth century, enjoyed a love-hate relationship with the Labour council, but it did produce an end result. The jury remains out as to whether Hewitt's arrival at the Herbert Art Gallery marked the commencement of a self-imposed exile from parochial, sectarian Ulster or a sharp career move. Whatever his real motives, he would have known that, unlikely as it may seem, Coventry had proved fertile ground for both uncompromising Modernism and the 'ruminative Romanticism' that for much of the previous two decades had been such a dominant feature of English cultural life.[19]

The city witnessed predictable tensions between the old and the new until both traditions fused so spectacularly in the decoration and physical structure of the new cathedral. In this respect the architect, Basil Spence, and Graham Sutherland, designer of the massive 'Christ in Majesty' tapestry behind the high altar, represented both a bridge between modernity and four hundred years of Anglican decorative art *and* a bold commitment to 'the new'. Fittingly, Jacob Epstein's uncompromisingly aggressive and yet consciously realist portrayal of St Michael slaying the satanic dragon (a celestial melodrama that seems to defy gravity) stands adjacent to John Piper's Baptistry Window, the sheer scale and dazzling colour of which reminds us that here was a project where for once even the accountants acknowledged that only the biggest and best would do.[20] Not that Piper was unfamiliar with Coventry Cathedral. He was an early recruit to the Recording Britain Scheme, a 'phoney war' initiative to capture on canvas the architectural heritage that might be lost as a consequence of intense aerial bombardment. This state-funded fillip to English Romanticism explained Piper's presence in the ashes of the cathedral on the morning of 15 November 1940. Amidst the ruins of the city centre Humphrey Jennings shot reel after reel, Philip Larkin searched fruitlessly for his parents, and John Piper sketched furiously, all three ultimately producing their own unique depictions of a city on its knees and reeling.[21] Piper rode a postwar tide of 'Romantic retrospection', culminating in the Festival of Britain and the coronation two years later. Predictably, Coventry's contribution to the nationwide festival programme was to resurrect the Victorian re-enactment of Lady Godiva's ride through the streets of the city.[22] Such a well-known feature of local, and even national, popular mythology demanded more permanent recognition, hence the location of Godiva's commemorative plinth and stunning black statue at the centre of the rebuilt Broadgate.[23]

Prior to the opening of the Herbert Art Gallery exhibitions of fine art took place in a variety of venues. Predictably, the local press – the *Coventry Evening Telegraph* and the then weekly *Coventry Standard* – championed the safe and familiar. Unashamedly populist reviewers pandered to their reader's prejudices and lambasted those postwar artists who championed 'the provinces', not because they deemed London too *avant-garde*, but because few in the capital shared their fascination with the wilder reaches of continental surrealism. Michael Remy has convincingly portrayed the West Midlands as an unlikely outpost of surrealism, with the 'Birmingham Group', focused around Conroy Maddox, Oscar Mellor, and John Melville, more dynamic and more politicised than London-based artists such as Roland Penrose and indeed Humphrey Jennings. In the late 1940s and early 1950s exhibitions organised by the Coventry Art Circle were of an exceptionally high standard. Bold and Bohemian, these shows exposed a small but voraciously culture-hungry intelligentsia to the work of evangelical surrealists and tyro abstract expressionists. A high watermark of English surrealism in austerity Coventry was November 1947 when Oscar Mellor opened the CAC's autumn exhibition, and even a sceptical *Standard* acknowledged that there was genuine talent on display. Sadly this view was not shared by bemused visitors to the show, whose loud complaints left Mellor and Maddox bemoaning the city's 'artistic ostrachism'.[24]

While understandable, this complaint was unfair, not least because even before Hewitt's appointment, the city council was commissioning work which rarely played safe. Thus the local-born sculptor Walter Ritchie largely eschewed his Arts and Crafts roots when completing a large frieze for the Upper Precinct in 1957. Relocated to an exterior wall of the Herbert Art Gallery and Museum a decade ago, the power of 'Man's Struggle' (Eric Gill meets Pablo Picasso *circa* 'Guernica') can now be appreciated in all its glory. In its original location the frieze was in heavy shadow most of the time and easily merged in with its surroundings – familiarity did not breed contempt, simply indifference. Arguably the same was true for the ceramic mural commissioned in 1958 by Arthur Ling, Gibson's successor as Chief Architect. The Lower Precinct mural was the work of Gordon Cullen, a leading commentator on urban planning whose 1961 polemic, *Townscape*, coined a shorthand term for 'urban environment' and made an eloquent plea for traffic-free city centres. In a minor classic of post-Festival late 1950s design, the mosaic tableaux depicted Coventry from its pre-history origins to the 'Post-war Masterplan'. Cullen's non-artistic background, and his involvement with Ling, suggests that the newly-arrived Hewitt could have had no more than an advisory role.[25] Nevertheless, the contribution of Ritchie and Cullen in enhancing and humanising the main shopping centre confirmed Hewitt's idealised perception of Coventry as an affluent conurbation where the more basic instincts of avarice and ambition could be tempered by 'ordinary people's' fundamental decency and inherent good taste. Thus, a harmonious and visually attractive 'townscape' would foster a genuine sense of citizenship, exemplified by a common respect for and appreciation of the first fruits of this new civic/public art form.[26] Hewitt incidentally would have been delighted that engraved quotations from his work form an integral part of Cathedral Square in Belfast, an open space very much in the spirit of Gibson and Cullen.[27]

The Godiva Cafe – listed example of modernist invention

Hewitt's idealism remained intact for over a decade, but his perception of Coventry as a bedrock of democratic socialism was based upon an initial misreading of the Labour Party's standing and support across the city as a whole. As Nick Tiratsoo has demonstrated, prosperous suburbs such as Stivichall, Cheylesmore, and even Earlsdon rarely reneged on their Conservative loyalties, even in 1945; while Labour never established a culture and depth of core support comparable to that sustained in traditional manufacturing and mining areas throughout the immediate postwar era. Thus the Labour Club was rarely the heart of the immediate community, even in working-class areas like Foleshill and Hillfields, witness the popularity of works-based sports and social clubs explored later in this volume. With the number of marginal wards growing year by year, Labour's demise was only a matter of time. It came in 1967, exactly three decades after the party first secured control of the council.[28]

Ten years earlier Hewitt was on a steep learning curve, although, as shall be seen, he had an agreed agenda and a clear idea of where he wanted to go. Surprisingly, the antennae failed to pick up the affection Terry Frost retained for the West Midlands, particularly in the years of peripatetic teaching and ambitious, non-representational painting that preceded his return to Cornwall in 1974. Frost was born in Leamington Spa and worked in Coventry prior to joining the Commandos and, as a POW from 1941, learning to paint. Obituarists pointed out the delicious irony of an artist synonymous with sunbursts and swirling circles who before the war had painted RAF roundels on aircraft rolling off the production lines at AWA's twin plants of Baginton and Whitley.[29] I can only fantasise that in the canteen at Armstrong Whitworth my Dad regularly discussed the finer points of derailleur gears with an ex-bicycle repairman from Leamington boasting an encyclopaedic knowledge of gloss, chip-free paint.

Someone else who knows a great deal about metallic paint is George Shaw, who achieves miracles of colour composition with a palette of Humbrol oils previously the preserve of dedicated modelmakers. Shaw's first major exhibition opened the week Frost died, and, while they were two very different painters, there was for me a real sense of the baton changing hands. Neither man had any obvious advantages at the start of their careers, with both singularly lacking in pretensions. But whereas Frost was almost forced to embrace the wider world, from Stalag 383 to San Jose, Shaw still paints out of his parents' back garden. George Shaw is the very antithesis of John Hewitt's aesthetic vision, painting semi-privatised, demi-pulverised council estates as stripped-down Gothic nightmares where an unholy alliance of teenage ennui and revengeful nature is intent on destroying the last vestiges of postwar civic idealism. The critic Richard Dorment summed up the court painter of Tile Hill perfectly: 'in Shaw's eyes, the natural world is locked in mortal combat with architects from the council.'[30]

Looking back on early postwar Coventry, the cultural historian Peter Bailey heard ringing in his ears a ceaseless soundtrack of 'exhortation and congratulation': 'These models of civic renewal and the engineered life were the official narratives of a rational and orderly modernity, devoid alike of risk and romance.'[31] As Bailey, long domiciled in Canada, points out, here was a predictably homogenous industrial workforce, overwhelmingly male and white: the end of mobilisation saw a large proportion of married women either choose or be expected to remain at home; families of relatively high-earning workers became first generation homeowners, their new suburban lifestyle 'domesticated and inward looking'; while the first major influx of economic migrants from the Caribbean and the Indian sub-continent was still several years off. More contentious is Bailey's claim that this 'largely one-class city...seemed classless.' Here was the son of an electrician attending, courtesy of the direct grant system, an independent grammar school located at the very point where urban reality met 'leafy Warwickshire', in other words, those prosperous suburbs Tiratsoo labelled the last redoubt of Tory resistance to the New Jerusalem.[32] While questioning the familiar charge of philistine materialism, Bailey concedes that here was a one-dimensional concept of modernity, rooted in domesticity, and with scant exposure to the more cosmopolitan, challenging, exciting, and down right risky aspects of life in the urban fast lane. 'For the young in particular, American film and music projected a countervailing pulse of freedom, adventure and pleasurable behaviour,' hence the centrality of jazz and later skiffle to a (predominantly male) generation who, courtesy of the 1944 Education Act, were ur-meritocrats.[33]

Bailey describes a far tamer urban lifestyle to that which emerged a decade later. Yet his emphasis on the importance of jazz for bright, bored, and above all sexually frustrated, male adolescents in a pre-Elvis era warrants further examination.[34] Until the 2-Tone phenomenon took off in 1979, Coventry was a backwater of rock'n'roll and pop music. Having said that, the beat boom of the early 1960s, let alone the vibrant DIY punk ethos after 1976, belie the notion that here was a desert of creativity. Similarly, the city, as befits a focal point for Celtic migration, has always boasted a healthy folk scene. As for classical music, the premiere on 30 May 1962 of Benjamin Britten's *War Requiem* was clearly a major event. Despite the new cathedral's poor acoustics, the Third Programme's live broadcast of Britten's ambitious choral and orchestral work generated a hugely enthusiastic response. The two concerts marked the climax of the Coventry Cathedral Festival, a major celebration of internationalism and regeneration which took over four years to plan.[35] Nevertheless these performances remained very much a one-off event until Warwick University's arts centre began to encourage a wider engagement with new, and often difficult, music.

In retrospect it was jazz that by the mid-1960s fostered a fresh, looser, and more adventurous cultural outlook. Duke Ellington conducting in the cathedral was in its own way as seminal a moment as Britten's sombre celebration of the new building's consecration. Ironically, *First Sacred Concert* had more in common with another pacifist composer, Michael Tippett: Ellington's tribute to the King James Bible drew heavily upon his 1940s orchestrations of African-American spirituals. Standing in front of Sutherland's tapestry 'the Duke' insisted to a friend that, 'This music is the most important thing I've ever done or am ever likely to do. This is personal, not career. Now I can say out loud to all the world what I've been saying to myself for years on my knees.'[36] The Lanchester Polytechnic's student union enjoyed remarkable success in attracting star names; a predominantly rock audience embracing what would soon come to be known as 'fusion music'. Thus, from the West Coast Sun Ra and Roland Kirk revealed the true meaning of *avant-garde*, and Larry Coryell played alongside a post-Cream Jack Bruce eager to restate his jazz credentials. The same gig saw a one-off performance by the New Jazz Orchestra, a rare gathering of the British jazz scene's Young Turks.[37] Some of the latter soon returned as part of an expanded Soft Machine, en route to a historic performance at the 1970 Proms.[38] Primarily by accident, but partly by design, jazz enthusiasts kept the flame alive, whether in local pubs, or via a hip polytechnic convinced Coventry really could see the birth of the cool. Thus, drummer Jon Hiseman recalled a crowd of over 2000 responding to the NJO's dense and demanding music with a standing ovation: 'That so-called "idiot" audience didn't clap and rave like pub audiences do – at the loudest, fastest number. The piece that got the best ovation was an arrangement by the late Mike Taylor of Segovia's composition *Study...*'[39]

While initially endeavouring to fuse punk and reggae, albeit with ska as the ultimate ingredient in 2-Tone's potent brew, Jerry Dammers clearly drew on the city's latent jazz heritage for the Specials' final album.[40] Arguably the same is true for Coventry's most famous contribution to popular music, the chart-topping 'Ghost Town'. Whatever the cynicism and rude boy image, the multi-racial, seven-man Specials were a quintessentially Coventry band. They recorded locally, stayed loyal to home at the peak of their careers, envisaged their label as a genuine community venture, and most significant of all, played music that was rooted in – for Coventry – a fresh, multi-cultural, unequivocally political agenda. There is a double irony about 'Ghost Town' in that the band's original line-up had all but split by the time it was recorded, and that Dammers was inspired to write the song by a visit to Glasgow. Nevertheless, the single captured perfectly the impact upon the West Midlands of the collapse in manufacturing industry – a process that preceded the election of Mrs Thatcher but was undoubtedly accelerated by her first administration's adherence to monetarist dogma re control of the money supply. With unemployment at 2.5 million, having risen by a staggering 82% among ethnic minorities in 1980-81, the lament that 'Government leaving the youth on the shelf/No job to be found' articulated the experience of second and third generation families in Foleshill, Lockhurst Lane, Holbrooks, and Hillfields. An insistence that 'Can't go on no more/The people getting angry' seemed even more apposite: 'Ghost Town' was released on 10 July 1981 in the wake of the first Brixton riots; it reached number one a month later, by which time serious civil disturbances had occurred in no less than thirty different boroughs, towns, and cities. The song was a running commentary upon events as they unfolded, hence its iconic status as a three-minute snapshot of the state of the nation. Its application was universal, and yet for Coventry in particular the record was a defining moment – it signalled that the postwar experiment had been brave, honest, idealised, well-intentioned, yet ultimately flawed. 'Ghost Town' signalled a nadir in the city's fortunes, as confirmed by subsequent events in Wood End, a sink estate where sustained rioting suggested a perverse case of life imitating art. For Coventry in the early 1980s, the only way was up.[41]

Two decades on, the same would be true for sport in Coventry – with the notable exception of speedway. David

Moorcroft may be his sport's senior administrator, but local athletics is in the doldrums: Godiva Harriers' glory days are long gone, few schools are fostering talent, and lottery-sourced development funding has all but dried up. A once great rugby club hopes the new Butts Stadium will attract players capable of mounting a genuine push for promotion, but the chances of rejoining the elite are frankly remote. Coventry is no longer a hothouse of rugby in the way it was half a century ago, but the potential remains to attract large crowds. However, the level of investment necessary to break in to the Zurich Premiership, and then stay there, is way beyond the club's current resources. For a fourth season the football team languishes in the Championship, the old Second Division, more focused on avoiding relegation than an end-of-season place in the promotional play offs. In this respect the wheel has come full circle.

All postwar Coventry lacked was a successful football club. The messiah turned out to be the President of the Professional Footballers Association. Having secured the end of the maximum wage, and the retain and transfer system, Jimmy Hill launched the 'Sky Blue revolution' in November 1961. Hill saw football, not as a cheap working-class spectator sport, but as a commodity, to be modernised and repackaged as popular – family – entertainment. Over the next six years the media-savvy Hill brought fun and glamour into football, with pre-match entertainment ranging from pop groups to the manager himself riding his hunter round the pitch in pursuit of an imaginary stray fox. Supported by a sympathetic and imaginative board, Hill initiated a long-term transformation of the Highfield Road ground, and most important of all, took his team from the then Third to the First Division. Success on and off the park brought energy, enthusiasm, and above all, excitement to the city. If there has ever been a golden age for Coventry City Football Club then, notwithstanding a one-off FA Cup victory in 1987, it was the mid-1960s. What is so striking about this period is Hill's ability to anticipate the fundamental shifts experienced by elite football three decades later.[42] Long before the first style guru identified the importance of corporate identity and promoting a universal upbeat message, Hill was submitting a drab provincial side, still firmly rooted in a 1930s mentality, to a complete makeover. The 'Bantams' became the 'Sky Blues', facilitating a comprehensive image change, from team strip to club logo. While much of what he achieved is today taken for granted, specific aspects of the club's identity remain very much Hill's invention. He was a master of invented tradition, witness the longevity of the 'Sky Blue Song', lifted directly from the 'Eton Boat Song' and swiftly assimilated into club mythology. Unlike later in his career, as a manager Hill never wholly broke with football's working-class roots, witness the modest cost of standing on the terraces. While success saw Spion Kop and the West End crowded with spectators, in a pre-sponsorship era redevelopment of the stands was the key to maximising revenue. Comfortable seating could attract a more middle-class (respectable?) audience, as would a half-decent restaurant and an early experiment with executive boxes. Both manager and board saw the commercial - and PR - potential of encouraging families, particularly mums and daughters, to come along on a Saturday afternoon. Hill was an undoubted pioneer in remoulding football as a mass spectator sport in tune with wider social and cultural changes, not least the range of choice and opportunities facilitated by rising levels of disposable income. For an all too brief period he persuaded over 30,000 men and boys, plus a not inconsiderable number of their wives and sisters, that alternate weekends in winter and spring meant watching football rather than DIY, shopping, or a myriad of other domesticated activities.

Hill could only do this of course because his team kept winning. The climax came in 1967 when 52,000 crammed in to Highfield Road to see the Sky Blues secure the Second Division Championship at the expense of arch-rivals Wolverhampton Wanderers. As a manager rather than an impresario, Hill bought shrewdly, particularly when it came to goalscorers. As a coach he fostered young players, and brought out the best in those lower league journeymen he chose to retain. Crucially, his man management skills were not found wanting when forced to bring in maverick players with the technique and ball skills vital to any title-winning side. What the team lacked in flair, it made up for in hard work and a rock-solid defence, built around an uncompromising centre-half and Hill's one expensive signing, an international-class goalkeeper. Once arrived in the First Division the manager announced his departure for London Weekend, the start of a long and seemingly endless career as TV commentator and pundit. In later years his brief returns to Highfield Road as either a consultant or a director invariably ended in tears. Amazingly, despite on several occasions avoiding relegation by a point or even goal difference, the Sky Blues stayed in the top flight for the next thirty years. Yet, apart from that one glorious May afternoon at Wembley in 1987, the excitement that Jimmy Hill brought to the club was noticeable by its absence.[43]

Tommy Hutchison – voted by supporters all-time favourite Coventry City footballer

Football, however, is wholly overshadowed by rugby in the essays that follow. Why should this be? Firstly, and most obviously, because much as I love football, and readily acknowledge rugby union's many faults, there is an emotional investment in the latter which I can scarcely articulate. Suffice it to say that for me no other sport can bring a lump in the throat and a tear to the eye, whether it be Lansdowne Road defiantly chorusing 'The Fields of Athenry' or an All Blacks *haka* silencing the Twickenham mob. In other words, my affection for the game has little in common with late arrivals on the England bandwagon attracted solely by the notion of supporting the one national side with serious pretensions to be the best in the world. Secondly, because, shameless romanticism notwithstanding, as a historian I have a professional interest in the game; and anyway over the past twenty years soccer has generated an impressive body of scholarship[44]. Thirdly, and most contentiously, the history of rugby (both codes) in Coventry and Warwickshire is more interesting than that of football, offering greater scope for speculation and reflection. My first essay on Coventry was prompted by the belief that, contrary to the familiar assumption that the fortunes of the football club mirror those of the city, in this particular case it was the rise and fall of the once-might 'Cov'. With football as the dominant focus of fan loyalty, Coventry could never be a Bath or a Gloucester. Nor is the potential for spectator sport so great as to match Leicester, a unique instance of a large catchment area supporting complementary fan bases. Yet Coventry does boast a rich rugby heritage. 'Cov' is the proverbial sleeping giant waiting for the adrenaline rush of promotion to the Guinness Premiership to bring back the crowds and dissuade ambitious home-grown talent from moving to a top team like Leicester Tigers. Rugby is 'the other' in Coventry, reinforcing my own impression that, unlike say Southampton, where the Saints are very much at the heart of the local community, this is not a 'football city'. The fickle nature of the fans, and the marked drop in attendance since the team's relegation in 2001, suggest that success determines the level of support for the Sky Blues, and that the size of the fan base, as measured by genuine affection and unequivocal loyalty, is actually diminishing. The club needs more than the odd cup run and a bank holiday derby with Wolves to fill the Ricoh Arena week on week – only Premiership football can guarantee big gates.[45]

The city's most consistently successful sport since the Second World War must be speedway, with the Bees' 2005 title confirming half a century at the very stop. Equally prominent in recent years have been basketball, and most especially, ice hockey. Both sports – appropriately located in a multi-entertainment complex - have carved out fresh fan bases, marketing their appeal to both a teenage and a family market. Also new to the city, but with more modest aspirations is rugby league. A speculative essay on the future of the Northern Union, had its pre-Great War outpost in the Midlands proved permanent, was prompted partly by student interest in counterfactuality, and partly in response to the demonstrable shift away from a more familiar, largely empirical mode of historical investigation. Counterfactual history still attracts considerable opprobrium, and yet enthusiasts defend the intellectual validity of reflecting upon what could have occurred as opposed to what actually did. Advocates of 'virtual history' insist that the variables must be minimised in the interest of plausibility. This prerequisite suggests sporting events are ideal for positing credible alternative outcomes, or signals their total unsuitability. However, perhaps the history of sport(s) - as opposed to actual competition - can generate plausible consequences significantly different from the real outcomes. An individual sport, such as rugby league, lends itself to positing a counterfactual scenario – notably one in which the Northern Union established a firm foothold outside its industrial heartland. Notwithstanding the wider national and even international implications, what would have been the longer-term impact upon local communities if Midlands clubs expelled or fined by the RFU before the First World War for illegal payments had established the professional game on a permanent basis? Back in the 'real world', the penultimate essay briefly explores official and unofficial attitudes towards rugby league in Coventry and Leicester before union went open in 1995, and suggests that the six man scrum has recently come full circle.

It's increasingly evident that British sports historians welcome a more sustained engagement with cultural theory and a wider discourse re methodology and epistemology, witness the enthusiastic reception given to Jeffrey Hill's skilful fusion of empirical inquiry and postmodernist scepticism.[46] At the same time 'mainstream historians' now perceive sport as 'one of the most powerful of England's civil cultures'; a belated recognition that, as Martin Polley insists, 'Sport is not passive; it co-exists with its society, and, for post-war Britain, it is an important component of that society.'[47] The centrality of spectator sport to life in Coventry across the whole of the twentieth century is reflected in a two-part lament for the present state of the rugby club, as well as the brief foray into 'what if' history. The significance of participatory sport is confirmed in an overview of works-based recreation from the Great War to the collapse of the city's manufacturing base in the course of the 1970s and early 1980s.

For permission to include essays previously published in *Literature and History, International Journal of the History of Sport* and the *Journal of Film, Radio and Television History,* my thanks to their respective publishers and editors. The latter – Roger

Richardson, Gareth Williams, and David Culbert were all exceptionally helpful and encouraging, as was the late Melvyn Lasky who on a couple of occasions allowed me to write at length in *Encounter*. I haven't approached the magazine's liquidators for permission to republish, albeit in expanded form, the essay on my father in France as technically I am a creditor — CIA munificence notwithstanding, the cheque was always in the post. Thank you also to holders of copyright, especially Coventry City Council and Associated Sports Photography, for all the photographs that appear here; those organisations which never replied should note that every effort was made to secure permission to publish. Dilwyn Porter has proved the perfect collaborator in writing about sport, and Mike Hammond's outsider view of British cinema makes him the ideal neighbour and colleague. Ian Herrity, as well as all too briefly proving every supervisor's ideal research student, did an excellent job ensuring that all the original articles conformed to a uniform house style; and Angela Tubb, Edd Read, Elizabeth Munns, and Anne Curry were all extremely helpful in the final stages. This work was originally facilitated by the research support fund at New College, the University of Southampton's short-lived faculty dedicated to lifelong learning and widening participation. I tip my hat to the RSF committee members, and indeed to all former colleagues in that brief but brave attempt to demonstrate that a Russell Group university can have an agenda which looks beyond how many 4*s can be scored in the next RAE – permanent revolution can breed a remarkable *esprit de corps*.

Most of these essays originated in papers and talks delivered in a variety of venues, including the ultimate challenge of a Belfast lecture theatre at nine o'clock on a Sunday morning; my thanks to the seminar and conference convenors who gave me the opportunity to think aloud about sport, leisure, and literature. One occasion worth a special mention is the talk to my mother's Thursday Club on filming the Blitz. I relished the feedback re *Heart of Britain*, not least the division concerning Humphrey Jennings' portrayal of Pearl Hyde, the *femme fatale* of municipal politics.[48] It was illuminating that no-one present could recall seeing the film, and disappointing that nobody recognised any of the 'Coventry kids' making their way to work amid the smoking ruins or building medium-range bombers at Baginton. Discussing wartime Coventry with its most senior citizens was a one-off, but year after year I have benefited from the views of my students when comparing the impact of the Blitz on the Midlands with on the south coast – as early as November 1940 comparisons were being made between the respective experiences of Coventry and Southampton, usually to the disadvantage of the latter.[49] I hope that in lectures and seminars I have been able to explode a few myths and prejudices, after twenty years arriving at a relatively detached view of how both cities responded to intense aerial bombardment. That view is expounded in the final essay, which, from a personal perspective, looks forward as well as back: recent ventures in to the field (more often, minefield) of local history have concentrated upon Southampton, not least because it makes sense to focus upon where one works, and where so many of one's students reside. The preoccupation (obsession would be too strong a term) with Coventry is most definitely over. Henceforth the one-time Detroit of the West Midlands is synonymous solely with the fortunes, or more likely the misfortunes, of the rugby and football clubs, and the continued well-being of my Mum. Mary and Adam should take this as a firm promise, and I am eternally grateful for their patience on those occasions in the past when I have waxed lyrical about my home town's radical tradition, its history of adopting women novelists from George Eliot to Susan Hill (via Angela Brazil), and its remarkable capacity to produce world-class rugby players.

One final point – when compiling this volume I was faced with the issue of whether or not to update the original articles. While all have been subject to some editing and modest rewriting where appropriate, only the *Encounter* essay has been significantly altered. None of the pieces suffer from providing a clear idea of how I perceived the 'condition of Coventry' at particular points in time over the past two decades: as, hopefully insightful, commentaries they have not as yet been overtaken by events and rendered obsolete. In this respect the volume is intended to be both informative and illuminating, irrespective of whether the reader has a general interest in the direct application of social democratic ideas in postwar Britain, or is a keen observer of great events and everyday life in her/his native city. Whatever your qualifications, enjoy.

2

CARS, CRICKET, AND ALF SMITH
The place of works-based sports and social clubs in the life
of mid-century Coventry[1]

The academic is by instinct suspicious of mixing personal reminiscence with historical and sociological investigation, authorial intervention invariably remaining the preserve of either the preface or the footnote. Yet, as Malcolm Smith has pointed out, British modern historians of a certain age increasingly find themselves reconstructing their own lives: 'we have become for younger people the object of historical curiosity in our own right. We are all walking historical texts in some sense.'[2] While studiously avoiding any charge of nostalgia or prejudice, what follows makes no apologies for mixing the public and the personal, prefacing an overview of sporting and leisure provision in Coventry before and after the Second World War with a pen portrait of my father at the peak of his sporting prowess. Alf Smith thrived in a culture and environment which fostered and encouraged talented sportsmen (and to a far lesser degree, sportswomen). This was a labour force cultivated by paternalistic - but rarely altruistic - employers eager to retain skilled and semi-skilled workers: manufacturing industry in the West Midlands half a century ago endeavoured to accommodate the needs of a new, more diverse consumerism and at the same time meet the growing demands of the 'liberal militarist' state.[3] As volume production came of age in the late 1930s, rolling off the track came both radiograms and radar devices, Morris 8 saloons and Alvis armoured cars.

As acknowledged in the Introduction, Coventry is a city which over the years has attracted considerable scholarly interest. My intention here is simply to signal the considerable scope for researching into the activities, the organisation and structure, and above all the impact on factory, family, and community, of works-based sports and social clubs during a forty year span of mass membership, from the 1920s through to the early 1970s.[4] Twenty years ago Jeremy Crump identified the key role these clubs had played in terms of mass recreational provision prior to the Second World War; but their centrality to the day-to-day experience of the industrial workforce and its dependants is most obvious in the immediate postwar decades - years of recovery, reconstruction, and for an unprecedented number in the city (though by no means all) prosperity.[5] Not that the clubs' wartime importance should be overlooked, not least the role they played in consolidating Ernest Bevin's efforts as Minister of Labour to ensure a national standard of working conditions comparable to that already deemed the norm by major employers in the 'sunrise industries' of the late 1930s.[6] Extended discourse on the changing face of the urban environment, not least how cities respond to the challenge of rapid shifts in the pattern of industrial (and ultimately post-industrial) developments, requires detailed inquiry into specific facets of civic and community life, not least the provision of organised leisure, whether via the public or as in this case the private sector. This essay suggests a broad area for just such inquiry, drawing upon the personal experience of one individual by way of insight in to a way of life few sports enthusiasts today could easily identify with.

A decade after his death my most immediate memory of my father has him in his prime – lean, slight, and much younger than I am now, executing a cover drive with textbook perfection. That memory is in fact a fiction rooted in press cuttings and other people's recollections of Alf Smith's cricketing prowess. By the time I was old enough to appreciate the finer points of the game he had all but stopped playing – to state that he retired would be too pretentious, suggesting a standard Dad was well capable of obtaining had it not been for the war. From the mid-1930s through to the summer of 1940 he played league cricket in and around Coventry, opening the batting and keeping wicket for a succession of colliery sides.[7] Press reports confirm that here was a batsman who played hard and scored fast.[8] I can imagine him as a shy young man, non-drinker and non-smoker, slowly gaining the respect of hard-drinking, chain-smoking collierymen.   His nickname was 'Tiger' after the veteran Warwickshire wicketkeeper, 'Tiger' Smith, with whom my father had precious little in common other than an obsession with fast fifties and serial stumpings.   Like his namesake, Dad was on Warwickshire's books, and every week he would trek from Coventry to the county ground for nets and coaching.[9]

Escape to Edgbaston was my father's dream, swapping the tedium of the tool room for life as a professional. Serving his time at the Triumph he dreamt of century stands at Taunton and Tunbridge Wells, Bob Wyatt signalling from the pavilion to play on until tea.[10] Dad's single-minded determination to be a county cricketer earned him a healthy respect from my grandfather, whose obsession with the game was legendary among family, friends, and workmates. Wherever he was taken on, within weeks he had appointed himself scorer and chief baggage handler. Not that he himself ever had to spend much money on kit – my father's scoring feats had within a few seasons secured him a succession of glittering prizes, from a Gunn & Moore bat to a striped blazer so loud even Bertie Wooster would have blanched.[11]

My grandfather, Jack Smith, at his beloved Triumph Works

Jack Smith basked in the reflected glory of his son's cricketing prowess, every Monday morning boasting to the other old sweats on the track of our Alf's latest headline appearance in 'The Pink' - Griff and Coton would have set some hapless opponent an impossible target to meet, their tyro 'keeper crouched and chomping at the bit.[12]

1939 was the apotheosis of my father's cricketing career. Just as the previous summer's fears over the fate of Czechoslovakia had faded into insignificance while Dad agonised over his batting average, so a year later the prospect of protecting Poland from the onslaught of the Nazi hordes counted for little when all that really mattered was impressing the county chairman. My greatest insight in to the worldview of affluent car workers in the era of appeasement came in 1970, on the eve of going to university. Filled with naively romantic ideas about the International Brigade and poets swapping tearooms for trenches, I asked my father whether he had ever thought of going to fight in defence of the Spanish Republic. His total incomprehension spoke volumes, and taught me a valuable lesson. The furthest south he had ever ventured was Bournemouth, let alone Barcelona. In fact, of the approximately 2,000 British volunteers who fought in Spain with the International Brigade only 71 came from the Midlands (as opposed to, say, 437 from Scotland). Throughout the Spanish Civil War the British Institute of Public Opinion recorded consistent support for the Republic, but a similar proportion of those polled fully endorsed maintaining non-intervention as part of the National Government's overall policy of appeasement. Ernest Bevin was notoriously contemptuous of left-wing claims of a high level of political consciousness and proletarian solidarity. Fellow sceptics quoted George Orwell's 1942 assertion that 'To the British working class the massacres of their comrades in Vienna, Berlin, Madrid, or wherever it might be, seemed less interesting and less important than yesterday's football match', conveniently ignoring the next sentence: 'Yet this does not alter the fact that the working class will go on struggling against Fascism after the others have caved in.'[13] In Normandy in June 1944 my father and his mates proved Orwell absolutely right, but five years earlier, while Molotov and Ribbentrop quietly plotted an ideological bombshell, he cut, drove, and swept his way into the minor league record books. The holy grail of a county contract beckoned, but then Hitler intervened.

Alf Smith (first from the left, front row) and team mates

Workplace clubs gave my father and his mates the opportunity to go on playing cricket after leaving school. With most boys entering the world of work aged 14, church teams played a useful transitional role prior to the better players progressing to the local league sides.[14] The relentless tide of secularism ultimately put paid to most urban church-based initiatives, but what is striking about the works-based sports and social clubs is how resilient they proved. Their structure, support, and culture easily accommodated the onset of postwar affluence, thereby postponing any crisis of identity until the late 1960s. These were clubs with their origins in the aftermath of the First World War which, by virtue of their location in a city that successfully rode the worst effects of the Depression, provided leisure opportunities for affluent workers, both skilled and unskilled (the latter often deskilled if forced as a consequence of redundancy to take a job working on the track in a car assembly plant).

In less prosperous, more traditional industrial areas the larger clubs would have been seen as a distinctly postwar phenomenon. Here was organised recreation and entertainment for those workers in regular employment and with a growing proportion of disposable income, and whose lifestyle Ross McKibbin described so persuasively in *Classes and Cultures*.[15] They were of course the same families that supposedly experienced 'embourgeoisement' in the course of the 1950s, but whose lifestyles and quality of life in practice displayed a remarkable degree of continuity from the late

1930s. In other words, the travails and austerity of the Home Front and the late 1940s constituted an interruption and a setback, rather than a watershed. Coventry on the eve of war had the largest number of car owners outside London, and the highest concentration of working-class owner-occupiers in the UK.[16] The Blitz, and in particular the devastating raid of 14-15 November 1940, had a shattering effect upon the city, but seen from the perspective of sixty years later it was by no means a knock-out blow. By comparison with most industrial areas other than the East Midlands, reconstruction took place upon surprisingly firm economic foundations, not least because of the unexpected ease with which companies such as the vehicle manufacturer Standard adapted to peacetime requirements. A powerful Labour administration, cruelly assisted by the *Luftwaffe*, speeded up a process of civic renewal initiated following the party's success in wresting control of the Corporation from a self-serving 'shopocracy' in the 1937 municipal elections.[17] As explained in the preceding essay, Labour's success in rebuilding Coventry was automatically assumed until around twenty years ago when Tony Mason, Nick Tiratsoo, and others began to question the myth.

Yet throughout the 1940s and 1950s local party leaders such as George Hodgkinson and Sidney Stringer readily conceded that rapid growth in interwar Coventry's size and prosperity had not been matched by commercial *and* municipal provision of adequate leisure and recreational facilities: these could range from a repertory theatre to a decent pavilion for the Memorial Park pitches.[18] All these gaps local government successfully filled in the course of the 1950s, having been forced to delay those private-public partnerships agreed immediately prior to the war, most notably the art gallery. The latter was, as has been seen, partially funded by Sir Alfred Herbert, at that time head of the largest machine tool company in Britain.[19] The workplace clubs helped fill the gap, and after the war continued to cater for the many people who, notwithstanding the self-proclaimed social democratic ideals of the Belgrade Theatre and the Herbert Art Gallery and Museum, felt excluded from the more high-minded of the city's fresh initiatives.[20] They also of course compensated for Coventry City's inability to attract interest in Third or Fourth Division football at Highfield Road, and the rather smug exclusivity of the largely middle-class crowd watching the then highly successful rugby club. As later essays demonstrate, the social composition of the spectators at Coundon Road never quite seemed to match that of the team itself, with the success of the mighty 'Cov' dependent upon both the two grammar schools *and* the elementary - after 1945 secondary modern, and ultimately, comprehensive - schools.

It should be noted that, despite the workplace clubs covering a remarkable range of sports and games, provision for rugby union was very much a secondary concern. This was largely because the Warwickshire RFU was only really interested in autonomous rugby clubs, most of which pre-dated the interwar broad-based workplace clubs and had their roots in old boys and church/chapel organisations.[21] This reinforces the impression that Coventry is very much on the cusp of any north-south divide, witness the physical difference between the south of the city leading into semi-rural Warwickshire and the terraced Edwardian streets in the shadow of the M6. Thus, despite the public school origins of the rugby club's founders in 1873, Coventry rugby – like Leicester – always had more in common with the north than the suburban, middle-class south. As the final essay explains, before the First World War, suspension from the Rugby Football Union provoked an abortive attempt to establish the Northern League as a major presence in the city. This point is worth emphasising because it would be a mistake to assume rugby union had little to do with workplace clubs because of middle-class sniffiness – teams like Broad Street Old Boys and Barkers Butts were not for the faint-hearted.[22] Outside the city, rugby clubs like Newbold had more in common with northern colliery sides, and, as we have seen, in cricket the most uncompromising teams were based in the local pits. Thus dad played with the hard men of Griff and Coton for one reason only – they were the best. Only after he was demobbed did he opt to play for the Sphinx Club, jointly administered by Armstrong Siddeley and Armstrong Whitworth (AWA), the city's aero-engine and aircraft manufacturers.

The Sphinx Club was unusual in taking off after the Second World War, and was a consequence of the two companies' rapid wartime growth and peacetime retention of a large workforce: AWA employed around 10,000 in the 1950s. The majority of workplace clubs were well-established by the mid-1930s. Companies like Coventry Chain had responded to industrial upheaval between 1917 and 1922 by complementing the slap of firm management with recreation and welfare initiatives. However, the real spur was the rapid growth of the machine tool industry and volume car production from the mid-1920s, led by Alfred Herbert and William Morris respectively, followed a decade later by the direct impact of rearmament.[23] By 1939 migration had swollen the city population to well over 225,000, and rising. There followed a consolidation of club life as new arrivals often came from traditional industrial areas with a strong tradition of CIU, Labour, and trade union-based clubs (sport similarly benefited, especially rugby given the large numbers of Welshmen finding jobs in the car factories, and, among the better educated, the schools).[24]

A continued growth in the working population was to prove a major factor in the workplace clubs prospering for so long, with manufacturers continuing to employ huge numbers until the early 1970s. Thus, to take just three companies which between the wars pioneered the provision of recreational facilities, in the mid-1960s Standard employed 14,000, GEC 18,000, and Alfred Herbert 7,300. It is no wonder then that out of the city's 200 plus football teams, no less than 63 were playing in the Works League.[25]

Lord Rootes with Bishop Cuthbert Bardsley and Richard Crossman MP

But to return to the years leading up to the Second World War. The larger the workforce the more industrial grandees such as Sam Courtauld, Sir Alfred Herbert, William (later Lord) Rootes, and the Standard's Sir John Black insisted that a healthy workforce was synonymous with increased production and higher productivity. Thus, they either shared the cost of improving the companies' sports facilities (for example, GEC in 1938) or they paid the full amount, witness medical provision and bigger, better canteens.[26] The rearmament programme brought a shortage of skilled labour, and the clubs were seen as a way of attracting migrants to the city, with the prospect of smooth and easy assimilation via sporting and social events. Black, a former tank commander on the Western Front, was almost unique in Britain in the 1920s in his enthusiasm for innovative, American-style assembly methods.

Sir John Black (right) and Sir Alfred Herbert (left)

In the decade following Black's arrival at Standard in 1928 output and productivity rose dramatically, with car production increasing sevenfold. After 1936 the company proved equally successful in building aero-engines. Although after May 1940 he forged close links with key Labour ministers, notably Hugh Dalton, Black was the embodiment of Baldwin's 'one nation' Toryism. Ruling his Canley plant like a benevolent dictator, he nevertheless worked closely with the trade unions in order to improve local wage agreements and, particularly in 1945-6, to avoid redundancies. This contrasted with GEC and Courtauld which, while embarking on modest welfarist initiatives, remained deeply hostile to organised labour. The managing director introduced a non-contributory pension scheme at Standard in 1936, and facilitated an all-round improvement in working conditions. A keen sportsman, who counted Dan Maskell and Fred Perry among his regular tennis partners, Black prioritised sporting provision for his workforce.[27]

When one looks at companies such as Standard, Courtaulds, and in particular GEC, what is striking is the scale of provision. As

Jeremy Crump has pointed out, by 1939 many of the city's best sports facilities, dance halls, and concert rooms were on the premises of major employers. By 1938 the GEC's social club had an annual turnover of £33,000, with the workforce able to enjoy the varied facilities of the 10-acre Magnet Club and the opulent Connor ballroom; 'the staff' could also relax in the salubrious Grange Club with its 40-acre golf course.[28] Courtauld's Lockhurst Lane ground was sufficiently well-furbished as to host county championship cricket for well over 40 years.[29]

Even before the war many of these facilities were regularly made available to the general public, compensating for the lack of sufficient commercial venues in the centre of the city, let alone in the growing suburbs. Indeed in 1934 the twenty-five major workplace clubs had established an exclusive Coventry Works Sports Association, with its own separate leagues for football, cricket, and so on, largely because other clubs had such poor changing facilities. The CWSA survived wartime suspension, and the predatory instincts of the much bigger, more broadly based Coventry Sports and Social Association, remaining in existence until as late as 1980. Although by the end an empty shell, the federation's real success could be measured in the strength of its constituent sport sections. On the other hand, most companies' first teams preferred to contest the more competitive district leagues, leaving the junior sides to play under the auspices of the CWSA.[30]

Most companies naturally thought that allowing controlled public access to their facilities was good public relations, just as they saw representative sport as important for forging a workforce's stronger identification with the firm – especially important at a time of intense competition for both skilled and unskilled labour. The evidence suggests that company loyalty was not that strong, notable exceptions being AWA and Armstrong Siddeley where sons followed their fathers in to apprenticeships as fitters and engineers. Larger employers struggled to counter an usually high level of labour mobility, both before and after the imposition of wartime constraints. Most employees saw paternalistic initiatives as the consequence of economic necessity not altruism, and acted accordingly. The principal reason why Alfred Herbert retained its workers was because, unlike the car factories, there were never any seasonal layoffs. Yes, the company could claim to be a pioneer of welfare provision, but within the city Sir Alfred Herbert never shook off his reputation for parsimony and harsh discipline.[31]   Although at a company like GEC workers had every incentive to take advantage of the facilities (and continued dancing at the Connor ballroom even if no longer an employee), in some factories the level of involvement was in practice quite modest: before 1940 canteen access was sometimes dependent upon club affiliation, which artificially inflated the number of active members.[32] Those like my Dad who were keen on sport, and were good, could easily be seduced away by a stronger side (although Alfred Herbert and other firms ultimately banned non-employees).[33]   Anyone made redundant rarely retained close links with his former employer's club, hence Crump's conclusion that 'Work and leisure represented related aspects of life for such people.'[34]

Despite a sustained trend of high employment after 1945, with Coventry accounting for over a quarter of Britain's entire car production, redundancy could occur in specific manufacturing areas. This was evident as early as 1949, but the most notable example came much later, in 1965: Hawker Siddeley's closure of the AWA plant at Baginton, and then its Dynamics factory at Whitley in 1968, led to thousands of highly skilled plane makers landing up as car assembly workers, and then progressively losing their new jobs as the motor industry began to shrink at the end of the decade.[35] At the start of the 1960s, despite veiled warnings from Armstrong-Whitworth's managing director about an uncertain future, members of the Sphinx Club could read their bi-monthly *AWA Affairs* and assume that they were living in a golden age – not for nothing did the Christmas 1959 issue depict the new Argosy freighter flying above the rebuilt city's most potent symbol, the soon to be completed cathedral.[36]

What careful perusal of *AWA Affairs* reveals, apart from moving photographs of my parents, is how little the status of women had changed since the 1930s. Prewar GEC had marginalised women when it came to organised sports and social events, witness their absence from any committees, and their patronising treatment in the company newsletter, *The Loudspeaker*: grudging respect for the hockey team was counterbalanced by mocking of the two works and seven departmental women's cricket teams. The existence of women's cricket is striking in itself, particularly given the fact that in its early years the sport was a largely upper middle class phenomenon. But especially remarkable is the number of teams, a reflection of GEC's status as Coventry's biggest employer of female labour (3,450 employees on the eve of the Second World War). The only initiative actively encouraged by a male-dominated sports committee was the GEC Ladies' Physical Culture Club, founded by no less than two hundred women in 1937 under the auspices of the then high profile Women's League of Health and Beauty (my mother has testified to the low status of women at GEC, exemplified by high wage differentials, which if anything increased in the course of the war).[37] Over 20 years later *AWA Affairs* displayed a similarly patronising approach to the female workforce, the editor airily dismissing a 1959 request from four women in the 'Analysis Section, Dynamics Group, Whitley' for a dedicated page and greater coverage of 'the part that women play in the development of AWA'. A promise to provide more of the latter meant in fact highlighting the switchboard and in particular 'pretty telephonist Mrs June McGhee', and the selection of AWA's representative in the final of the Coventry Carnival Queen.[38] Even when a woman employee was seen undertaking a perceived male role, for example, flying solo as a member of the AWA Flying Group, she remained a '29 years old housewife and a secretary at Baginton'.[39]

The same approach was evident in other company journals from the late 1950s and 1960s, all of which demonstrate that works clubs were still operating at an astonishingly high level of activity. Alfred Herbert's *AH News*, for example, covered 27 section activities, each of which was highly competitive.[40] A latecomer was the *Jaguar Journal*, first published in 1960. In the first issue chairman and company founder Sir William Lyons informed his five thousand employees at Brown's Lane that - as well as covering achievement on the Jaguar Sports Field, the 'near 100% attendance at the Jaguar Staff Party', or the visit of the 1,800 'Jaguar Cubs' to the pantomime - the main purpose of the journal was to counter any charges that his workforce was ill-informed. Henceforth the latter would be no excuse for 'unconstitutional stoppages', and in the next issue the Amalgamated Engineering Union's general secretary, the formidable Bill Carron, was given an opportunity to denounce unofficial strikers.[41] Despite the success of its racing cars, Jaguar had experienced a turbulent period in the late 1950s, symbolised by the devastating fire which destroyed over a quarter of the plant in 1957. However, the prestige attached to working for one of Britain's flagship motor manufacturers continued to attract men and women who had risen to the top in their chosen sports. As a result most Jaguar teams benefited greatly from experienced coaching, not least the cricket club, which in 1960 boasted no less than five ex-county players.[42]

Surprise at the healthy condition of women's cricket at GEC on the eve of the Second World War aptly illustrates the dearth of research in this area, notwithstanding Crump's pioneering work nearly two decades ago.[43] Yet the role of workplace clubs is clearly crucial to any consideration of industrial relations in Coventry (and indeed across the whole of the Midlands and beyond) in the final decades preceding the collapse of British manufacturing industry.[44] The nature, function, and diverse activities of these works-based sports and social clubs highlights the remarkable degree of continuity between life in immediate pre-war Coventry and the boom years that followed late 1940s austerity. At the same time, the low priority given to women's sporting initiatives and achievements confirms that affluence and consumerism did not bring in their wake a profound shift in how a still predominantly male industrial workforce perceived their female counterparts (the same being even more the case for managers and directors). The changing fortunes of these clubs, both individually and collectively, deserve revisiting, and thus warrant further research, not least because sport is so central to an understanding of Coventry's rollercoaster history across the past one hundred years.

Coda

Jack Smith's pride in his lad, and readiness to defend him from as formidable a foe as my grandmother, was seen at its best one Saturday evening in the summer of 1939. My father's eldest sister married in Coventry Cathedral, today an empty shell and shrine of reconciliation but pre-war a magnificent testimony to the city's medieval wealth and episcopal power. How such an aggressively 'low church' patriarch agreed to this unlikely venue remains a mystery. However, family folklore records an appropriately sumptuous reception, and that my Dad's absence from this auspicious occasion riled my grandmother and infuriated my aunt.

With the speeches duly delivered, and the bride and groom about to be despatched for the obligatory seven days in Skegness, Dad made a belated appearance carrying the huge cricket bag which over sixty years later can still be found in my mother's loft. With this ill-timed arrival silence fell on the proceedings, and all heads turned to the top table where my grim-faced grandmother turned to her distinctly uncomfortable spouse, and compressed a whole agenda into the single interrogative word, 'Well?'. A long pause followed before Jack addressed his prodigal son:

'How many did you get?'
'108 not out. We won.'
'Get this lad a drink.'

This was the last great family gathering. Within weeks the groom, a Territorial, was with the British Expeditionary Force in France. The next time he met my Dad was in the officers mess at the Palace Hotel, Brussels, some time in late 1945. It was the Second World War, not county cricket, which determined the future direction of my father's life: combat in Normandy followed by a succession of staff appointments ensured a postwar career radically different from the seasonal uncertainty of the journeyman professional. And yet cricket had played its part in his longer-term change of fortunes. In the summer of 1940, like so many young men awaiting their call up papers, Dad joined the Home Guard, leaving work several evenings each week to search for any fifth columnists and German paratroopers lurking in the woods and fields of the Warwickshire countryside. However, throughout the Battle of Britain single-minded committee men like Jack Smith regularly rescheduled fixtures with only one aim in mind, the successful completion of the 1940 season. This unintentional myth-making ensured a regular game for my father, but it also delayed his entry into the army.[45] A severe cruciate injury left him on crutches, and he was still limping when an incendiary bomb blew up in his face early on the night of 14 November. Temporarily blinded and full of shrapnel, it was to be another two years before he was fit enough to be conscripted. A few weeks into basic training he opened the batting in a morale-boosting match for weary recruits still confined to barracks. The stroke-maker effortlessly cruising towards a century caught the eye of his company commander. Paraded before the adjutant the following morning, my father was convinced he was on a charge, yet had no idea what for.

Petrified by the prospect of the guardhouse, he could scarcely make out what the major was saying. To his astonishment it gradually dawned on him that he was being recommended for a commission. As far as the Royal Warwickshire Regiment was concerned he was far too good a batsman to be languishing in the ranks. This was recognition by the county, but with far riskier prospects than an invitation to spend the summer months in the Edgbaston pavilion. The latter would have been life-enhancing, the former was life-changing.

3

'TEMPORARY GENTLEMAN'
My father and World War II[1]

In front of me stands a framed photograph of a country road in Flanders soon after the German surrender in May 1945. I hesitated before writing such an emotive place name: perhaps Flanders will always be associated with an earlier conflict. Yet the winter of 1944-5 saw some of the Second World War's fiercest fighting, across what has so often proved to be Europe's most contested battleground. In Britain before 1914 the Low Countries were synonymous with Marlborough's martial glories and the Iron Duke's greatest triumph. Today, for a nation which in all other respects pursues an unhealthy infatuation with 'our finest hour', Flanders is still stubbornly evocative of a previous, for many seemingly pointless, sacrifice.[2] On television, afternoon repeats of *'Allo, 'Allo* can ridicule the trauma of occupation with scarcely a hint of public protest, but not even *Blackadder* can mock life in the trenches without a final gesture of apology and respect. The glimpse of the Belgian countryside in my photograph scarcely accords with the images that invariably spring to mind when mention is made of the land to the north and west of Mons. Despite the underexposed print, it is clear that the sun is shining, the trees are in leaf, and the fields are hidden from the road by a dense and verdant bank of grasses and weeds. Perhaps there is after all an echo of that earlier conflict: the starkly contrasting landscape behind the lines in Edmund Blunden's *Undertones of War*. Nevertheless, this is the Flanders of a later generation called to arms.

The only hint of discord is a solitary pole, bereft of cable and insulators – the only hint that is other than the large car filling the foreground of the picture. The Humber's carefully tailored canvas lagging is rolled back to expose a radiator grille that, chromed not camouflaged, would befit a Cord or a Cadillac. A huge, billowing pair of front mudguards proudly display the unsheathed sword insignia of the British Army in north-west Europe. This could easily be Montgomery's personal staff car, familiar to me from long Sunday afternoons entertaining my son in the Coventry Transport Museum. Yet the officer posing for the camera is clearly still in his twenties. One highly polished shoe is hidden by the grass verge, its companion still inside the vehicle. A medal ribbon and three pips are clearly visible. With Sam Browne belt and shoulder-strap, his buttons glistening, and a grin on his face, perhaps the young captain is en route to a plum posting at 21st Army Group Headquarters.

In fact he already has a staff job in Brussels, and is enjoying an unexpected break from routine administration. Closer examination of the photograph reveals a leaping antelope on our captain's cap badge: like Monty, his regiment is 'The Warwicks'. He and the Humber hail from the same battered city. Both were born within the same square mile: a network of Edwardian terraced houses adjoining one of Coventry's earliest car factories. The officer so visibly relishing the first weeks of peace is my father.

However relaxed he might appear as the camera clicks, Captain Smith had clearly been assigned vehicle and driver for a purpose. In fact, his destination that warm day in late May 1945 was a ceremony of re-interment for Belgian villagers massacred in an SS reprisal a year earlier. The adjutant had been ordered to deputise for his brigadier as representative of His Majesty's Government, hence the Humber.[3] For us attendance at so sombre an occasion would cast a pall over all other activities, solemnity being the order of the day. In May 1945, still engaged in relentless psychological adjustments, soldiers plunged from euphoria to depression and back again in a few hours.

A community in grief intruded only briefly upon the holiday mood. This was the legacy – and for my father only a brief legacy – of prolonged warfare. The British judged that regular rotation of infantry units could secure up to four hundred combat days before individual soldiers began cracking up. The reality, however, was far different. In the weeks and months after D-Day many of the most experienced troops, often veterans of the Desert War, complained over the length of time spent continuously on the front line.[4] The emotional price of survival was high. Hostilities were at an end, but you continued to take each day as it came. Cynicism and resistance to shock were necessary psychological weapons, the irony being that you were often unaware of any temporary (or for a sad few, lasting) character change. This was doubtless the case for an essentially sensitive man like Alf Smith.

Officers in the British Army were not supposed to have solidly working-class names like Alf, even in 1945. For superiors in the mess he was often Alfred. His brigadier in Brussels preferred the infuriatingly patronising 'Alfie' – a crude and recurrent device for reminding Dad that, however unexpected his elevation in the military hierarchy, he was still on the first rung of the new meritocratic ladder.[5] All his life my father was Alf, but from 1943 to the end of 1946, in messes from Budbrook to Berlin, he was Alfred Smith, holder of the King's Commission, and rare graduate of the shopfloor.

By 1943 the officer corps had been transformed from the relatively homogeneous elite that, Territorials notwithstanding, had taken the British Expeditionary Force to war in September 1939. Having trawled the progeny of the more affluent middle and upper classes, the War Office Selection Board (WOSB) had to look further afield, and from 1942 the emphasis was on aptitude and potential, not simply social background. The system of selection had been regularised, interviews and tests made more demanding, and the value of psychiatric expertise reluctantly acknowledged – a belated but much trumpeted triumph of meritocracy which encouraged a 25 per cent rise in applications for commissions. By the end of the war these more rigorous procedures were responsible for over 50,000 serving officers (predictably, the Guards had insisted on sticking to tradition and the old school tie). The Army gained in both quantity and quality: after 1941 the average passing-out mark at Officer Cadet Training Units rose by 12 per cent.[6]

OCTUs were of course strictly 'for the duration', as were the Army's efforts to recruit its leaders from a more diverse social background. In 1939 84 per cent of the cadets at the Royal Military Academy, Sandhurst, were ex-public school, and of these nearly half were sons of Regular officers. Just as today (although now the Ministry of Defence would strenuously deny it), the Guards, the Household Cavalry, and the most prestigious county regiments were ultra-selective with regard to which particular schools their new subalterns had attended. From the outbreak of war to the introduction of WOSBs, the procedure for gaining a commission ran parallel to the system adopted in 1914: a haphazard and characteristically English form of bourgeois self-advancement, as immortalised by Evelyn Waugh in *Men at Arms*.[7]

At the onset of both world wars, therefore, most new officers shared the same social and educational background as the tiny Regular Establishment. They had the right credentials – family connections, a suitable school (with the obligatory cadet force and character-building sports), varsity perhaps; and, most necessary of all, an obvious proclivity for slipping effortlessly into mess life.[8] Although the First World War generated no less than 229,316 commissions, thus securing diversity by sheer weight of numbers, the Edwardian officer corps proved remarkably resilient in attitude if not in actual personnel (a quarter of them were dead or wounded by the end of 1914). Ian Beckett has suggested that, after four years of fighting, most Regulars appeared even more solipsistic and isolated from civilian society than they were before the war – a disturbing thought given the ambivalent attitude so many officers had displayed towards enforcing Irish Home Rule.[9] Like their counterparts a quarter of a century later, thousands of sixthformers in Liberal England followed a direct path from the house study to the regimental depot – schooling remained the prime determinant of officer potential. Contemptuous of Territorial and New Army officers, the professionals (drawn disproportionately from the

Cavalry) still monopolised senior appointments, moulding the young and impressionable into replicas of themselves.

The public schools were to provide 34 per cent of all 'temporary gentlemen' commissioned during the Second World War. However, the WOSBs' success relied on an even more potent symbol of the new meritocracy, the grammar school. Given the overwhelming preponderance of grammar school boys entering OCTU in the final years of the war, my father's promotion from the ranks seems all the more remarkable. For, contrary to popular assumption, it would appear that the number of officers from a genuinely disadvantaged background were very few and far between; particularly if their promotion was not as a consequence of previous combat experience. Of the 710,000 recruits passing through the General Service Corps in the final three years of the war, only 6% were identified as officer potential. Just 21 per cent of all officers commissioned from 1939 to 1945 were from elementary schools.[10] Not many members of Dad's mess in Brussels, and later in Berlin, had left school at the age of fourteen. How did he find himself in such elevated company? As indicated in the preceding essay, largely thanks to an attractive blend of common sense, self-discipline, practical aptitude, and above all, sporting prowess and good luck. Here was a man with initiative (the only clean-shaven member of his platoon when the barracks plumbing froze – how did he do that?), who could not only strip down and rebuild an engine, but also just happened to be a county-class batsman.

Like so many other temporary officers, Alf Smith's life was transformed by the Second World War. For my father, Tom Wintringham's 'people's war' was both a traumatic and a cathartic experience – it radically altered his perspective on the world, literally and metaphorically broadening his horizons. Upward social mobility, however brief and artificial, created fresh expectations and aspirations, Demobbed and left to fend for himself in austerity Britain, there was no way he could speedily adjust to the harsh realities of civilian life. Of course in many respects he didn't, even though 'Civvy Street' demanded the sharpest psychological adjustment of them all. The defining study of my father's generation is still to be written, and soon it will be too late. All I can do here is reflect upon one man's war, as perceived and interpreted by his son over the ensuing half a century.

Any observations re Captain A.J. Smith, Royal Warwickshire Regiment, would no doubt apply to countless other 'temporary gentlemen': 'civilians in uniform' issued a demob suit and a rail pass, and released by the War Office, Air Ministry or Admiralty into a harsh new world. After the First World War many ex-officers found calm in isolated refuges, where psychological wounds might heal and long-forgotten ideals be revived; BEF veterans on lonely smallholdings were a common event after 1919.[11] Yet the generation that defeated Hitler, however appalling their individual experiences, rarely demonstrated in public a similar intensity of disillusion. What many did share was a reluctance simply to accept whatever work was available, even when their old jobs were waiting for them. However novel his marital bliss, for men like Alf Smith ration coupons, queues, and mortgage repayments on an unheated, sparsely furnished house, were a rude shock after the creature comforts of mess life in occupied Germany.[12] Was there ever a worse winter to move in to a new home than 1946-7?[13] Spurred on by my mother, Dad was determined not to slip back into a married version of his pre-war life – a brief return to the tool room at Armstrong Whitworth was purely a pecuniary measure, and not permanent. He flirted with the idea of a regular commission, but that idea was swiftly vetoed. With the thaw came an upturn in his fortunes. AWA's autocratic managing director, H.M. Woodhams, discovered that within his workforce was someone uniquely qualified to be the company's first transport manager – Dad's bren gun carriers might not have lasted long in the *bocage* but at least he had got them off the beach; nor could Baginton boast too many ex-duty officers fresh from Berlin. With the return of peace thousands of others, in similarly adverse circumstances, shared the same high expectations and the same determination not to waste the experiences and opportunities accrued across the preceding six years. In some cases, like that of my father, those high expectations were met; sadly, for many they were not.

Sebastian Faulks once rightly noted that those veterans most reluctant to discuss their time in uniform are often the ones with the most interesting story to tell.[14] Growing up in the 1950s and 1960s it became clear that, while some of my friends either had no interest in or had been deliberately kept ignorant of their parents' wartime experience, many were in fact unusually well informed. While unborn at the time, we were a generation moulded by 'the war' (it is

remarkable how after six decades the British retain this common
term of reference – are we unique in this respect, by comparison with
say the Americans?). By the time we baby-boomers reached
adolescence, the fascination with an event in which we had not
participated, and yet about which we knew so much, was waning.
Nevertheless, here was a body of knowledge safely stored in the
memory banks, ready to be drawn upon at an appropriate moment
many years hence, whether that occasion be one of nostalgic
celebration or of grieving commemoration. Long before the first oral
history archive, the new tribal legends were being passed down from
one generation to the next: as children we became absorbed in family
folklore, with the legacy of the Blitz *the* dominant domestic and
communal discourse. Given our age we failed to appreciate just how
recent the war had been, and yet twenty years later it remained a very
visible presence. Not all burnt-out houses and bomb sites had been
cleared, and the city centre still retained a number of prefab shops
and 'emergency' civic facilities.[15]

Brought up on a diet of action comics and 1950s war films, in
common with many of my fellow schoolboys I slowly became
familiar with what my father had got up to once in uniform
(predictably, it was only later that I became interested in what had
been happening on the home front). On holiday, tucked up in a
chalet bunk, I would listen attentively to what I now realise was a
sanitised version of the Normandy campaign. Later, on caravan sites
in Mablethorpe or New Milton, I heard again and again the stories of
running a prisoner-of-war camp in the winter of 1944-5. The passing
years brought a sharper focus, so that by the age of twelve, for
example, I was aware of orders to shoot recalcitrant prisoners if the
Ardennes counter-offensive had endangered Dad's camp. Did I
know that the SS were left naked in order to break them?[16]
Thankfully such lurid information did not fuel a perverse fascination
with organised violence. Indeed, if anything, these stories had
exactly the opposite effect, generating by my twenties a deep
antipathy to all matters military. Only in the 1980s did a broadening
of my academic interests, plus direct acquaintance with the Army,
prompt a shift in attitude.

For men like my father travelling abroad in peacetime held no
fears. To 'go to the Continent' in the 1950s (by implication, from
Great Britain – known indiscriminately to the English as 'England' –

to a separate geopolitical entity called Europe) was to revive old memories and revisit old haunts in less trying circumstances. Every spring Dad would lead a convoy of articulated lorries and 'shooting brakes' to the Paris Air Show: an annual invasion of Armstrong Whitworth's first-generation missiles and last-generation aircraft. (Throughout the year Sunday morning dress rehearsals for the trip to Le Bourguet would see Dad oversee the smooth transfer of Argosy fuselages from Baginton to the turbo-prop's final assembly point at Bitteswell, an ex-RAF airfield in the Leicestershire countryside. An abiding memory is a long camera shot of him on the regional news: immaculately dressed in weekend sports jacket and slacks, he is blocking traffic at a busy junction as one of his beloved 'Queen Mary' low loaders crawls past carrying its bulky bulbous symbol of obsolete avionics.)

Negotiating in pidgin French with the local *douaniers* and *gendarmerie*, my father was in his element: ensuring the well being of his unit and its equipment in a republic wracked by crisis and uncertainty. For three weeks the unambiguous officer-and-men relationship re-emerged. Again, a single photograph speaks volumes. Dad and one of his drivers beside the Eiffel Tower, probably in April 1961 at the time of the abortive *putsch* in Algeria.[17] A one-time Welsh Guardsman towers over his slight, wiry companion; yet from the look on their faces it is clear who is in charge. The Welshman (according to my father a genius at manoeuvring monstrous articulated loads through seemingly impenetrable back roads in the Pas de Calais) looks uncomfortable playing tourist with the boss. This isn't just because he is away from home, as his first visit to France was as long ago as 6 June 1944. Dad, however, exudes contentment. Here is a man who is quite clearly in charge, and who knows that things are going well. Dapper as ever, and dressed in a trenchcoat, he is clearly relishing being back in *his* city. The annual three weeks in Paris were the highlight of his year, and when he took my mother and myself to the Hotel Baltimore in August 1963 I began to see why. Needless to say, the drivers and fitters stayed in a less salubrious hotel; an arrangement which, in the light of Britain's post-war industrial record, requires no further comment.

My first visit to Paris confirmed that Dad's claims were all true – he really did know the city inside out. It was to be another twenty years before I finally believed his claim that he had visited the capital while it was still in the process of being liberated. This was so good a story – the equivalent of beating Hemingway to Harry's Bar by a pink gin – that it could not possibly be true.[18] Late adolescence reinforced an earlier gut suspicion. Only encroaching middle age brought belief...

The 59th (Staffordshire) Division, its second brigade partly made up of the 1/6th Battalion The South Staffordshire Regiment, left England on 27 June 1944, the day after Montgomery had launched the costly Operation Epsom against German defences around Caen. A shortage of subalterns saw Dad fighting with the 'South Staffs' alongside his home battalion, the 1/7th'Royal Warwicks'[19] Dempsey's Second Army had consolidated its bridgehead, and was belatedly seeking to break out into the Normandy hinterland. XII Corps, including the newly arrived 59th and 53rd (Welsh) Divisions, provided a final infusion of genuine reinforcements. Britain's reserve of front-line troops was now exhausted, and the size of its armies began to shrink as casualties took their toll. In terms of manpower, XII Corps represented the British Empire and Commonwealth's last great contribution to the destruction of Nazi resistance in the west. Yet no matter how many live ammunition exercises had been undertaken over the preceding two or three years, these were still raw recruits when confronted with the bloody reality of fighting conditions in the *bocage*. Notwithstanding a cadre of Desert Rats among the NCOs, scarcely any of these men – including their platoon commanders – had combat experience. This was one reason for their absence from the initial assault, although of course many who did cross in the first wave were similarly inexperienced.

My father never hid the fact that he did not land on D-Day, and in 1984 he was acutely embarrassed when a newspaper article, recalling that he had led his old platoon along the beach at the first anniversary parade, erroneously suggested his presence on Gold twelve months earlier. (the occasion no doubt left a deeper impression on Dad than on Duff Cooper, who, in order to take the salute, left his Paris Embassy at a delicate moment in Anglo-French wrangling over a future treaty.[20])

The 177th Brigade, of which my father's battalion made up one-third, survived for two months in the front line. A baptism of fire in the battle for Caen was followed by slow advance west and then south of the now pulverised city. On 8 August they crossed the River Orne, and then over the next week moved south-west to take up position midway along the northern flank of the Falaise pocket. With the Americans and Free French to the south, and the British, Canadians and Poles to the north and west, the Allies planned to envelop the Germans by cutting off their only means of escape: eastwards between Falaise and Argentan.

After two days of fierce fighting south of Thury-Harcourt on 17-19 August the Germans were clearly withdrawing, but my father's battalion had been hit hard by the toughest and most experienced of Germany's fighting forces in the west, II SS Panzer Corps.[21] Slit trenches provided precious little protection from Tiger tanks. Each company's casualties were appalling, with a rate of attrition comparable to the worst battles on the Western Front.[22] By the time the Falaise Gap was finally sealed, on 21 August 1944, my father found that the majority of his fellow subalterns were either dead or seriously wounded. In France between June and November around one-third of all rifle platoon and company commanders became casualties each month; each of the seven British divisions lost an average of 341 infantry officers in the first eight weeks of fighting.[23] Despite another German counter-attack, XII Corps could now swing east towards the Seine. By the end of August, for the remnants of 177th Brigade, the battle for Normandy, was over – and so was the Division. As the 'junior and a war time founded division', and owing to the 'present Infantry reinforcement situation', the 59th was cannibalised in order to shore up more experienced battalions desperately short of riflemen. Companies were reconstituted, and then absorbed in to those divisions still in action. The high attrition rate had advanced by six months a crisis of manpower previously forecast for the end of the year. British strategy was rooted in the twin principles of maximising ground and aerial firepower, and minimising direct engagement with a potentially superior German Army. In consequence, from the moment British and Canadian troops landed there had been an acute shortage of front-line infantry.[24] With scarcely a platoon left to command my father had already been pulled out of the front line.[25]

Meanwhile, with American approval, General Leclerc's French 2nd Armoured Division was racing 120 miles to secure control of the capital in the name of Charles de Gaulle. Advance units were in Paris on the evening of 23 August, and by mid-afternoon of the following day the German occupying forces had surrendered. Despite the fighting that still persisted around the Palais de Luxembourg, de Gaulle entered the city in an open car. In a symbolic gesture of continuity and legitimacy he went straight to his old office in the Ministry of War. Twenty-four hours later the three generals of the Free French external forces – Leclerc, Koening, and de Gaulle – led the freed people of Paris in a jubilant march from the Arc de Triomphe to Notre Dame Cathedral.[26] Astonishingly, on that same day – 26 August 1944 – my father was also in Paris. Apprehension, if not outright fear, rendered him oblivious to the historic events taking place just a few streets away.

While Leclerc's tanks were fighting their way in to the city, my father and a fellow subaltern were returning by jeep to Brigade HQ. Still close to the front line, Dad pointed out the proximity of Paris on his Michelin map. His young but worldly companion, a paragon of the self-confidence and 'sense of adventure' ostensibly cultivated by the nation's leading public schools, insisted on spending the night at Claridge's. My father, horrified by the notion of disobeying orders, and petrified by the prospect of street fighting between the Germans and the Resistance, protested. The driver simply turned the jeep east, towards a city which to most residents of pre-war Coventry might just as well have been on another planet. Greeted as heroes, the two 'liberators' finally arrived at Claridge's, where one chap drank vintage champagne until comatose, and the other slept, very lightly, *under* the bed. To be fair to Dad, shots were still being fired from the rooftops, even if more and more they emanated from gun-happy *résistants* than from sniping *collaborateurs* defying arrest. The following morning my father, ever the sound navigator, drove his severely hung-over companion at high speed out of Paris and back to the safe embrace of 21st Army Group.

Dad's behaviour, as recounted in his unconsciously self-deprecating fashion, appeared wholly in character. Yet the story bore every evidence of embellishment and exaggeration – until the occasion twenty years ago when, in a pile of old photographs, we discovered his bill from Claridge's. He really had been present at the liberation of Paris, albeit with the very greatest reluctance. The incident neatly contrasted the 'great jape' bravado of upper-class youth with the (quite literally) sober survival instincts of the older ex-artisan. In fiction Dad would have been the canny staff sergeant deferring to King's Regulations, and then keeping a wary eye on 'the young gentleman'. A cliché scenario, and one wholly at odds with the real-life situation where familiar patterns of class and deference prevailed. Dad would master Paris, but all in his own good time.

On the beaches of Britain in the late 1940s, the knee-length baggy shorts that first saw the light of day in Burma or North Africa were worn with pride. Though too young to remember Army Issue beachwear, I detected at an early age the lingering presence of the mess in my father's clothes sense: the highly polished brown shoes (strangely, not brogues), the sharply creased slacks, the dark paisley cravat, the epauletted short-sleeve shirt, and the suitably coloured (fawn? olive green?) round-necked cable-stitch pullover. Lecturing at Sandhurst in the mid-1980s, I often found myself staring at off-duty cadets looking eerily like Dad on holiday circa 1960. Unlike my uncle (a sergeant in Italy, 1943-5), whose meticulous dress is still worthy of the parade ground, my father loosened up considerably during the 1960s. By the end of the decade a moustache which for twenty years had screamed 'ex-Army' was framed by a pair of fashionable sideburns. The suits, invariably made-to-measure, were no longer always grey. Casual dress was a lot brighter and far less predictable. The company car went faster; and it went a lot farther now that holidays abroad had become the norm. I can only speculate on whether Dad voted Labour in July 1945 (or, indeed, if he voted at all given his absence abroad) – I know my mum did. In an era of Macmillan, Macleod and Heath, masterminding electoral triumphs for Tory councillors scarcely constituted a betrayal of youthful idealism.[27]

The truth was that, after twenty-five years solid slog, Dad and his fellow rankers at OCTU had finally made it: senior management status, or the equivalent – a permanent posting at Civvy Street's equivalent of Brigade HQ. These 'temporary gentlemen', their wartime aspirations finally fulfilled, at last felt confident enough to embrace the contemporary world. The war was still there, but not in the same pervasive fashion. Affluence and achievement – if not always ambition – were of paramount importance. For a few short, middle-aged, years, such men could rest content.[28]

4

SENT TO COVENTRY
Reassessing Humphrey Jennings' *Heart of Britain* (1941)[1]

Introduction: the omission of *Heart of Britain* from the pantheon
On 12 November 1940 Humphrey Jennings was safely ensconced in
a cosy Cumbrian hotel catching up with his correspondence. His
wife Cicely and their two daughters, evacuated to the United States
two months earlier, needed reassurance that Jennings had, at least for
the moment, escaped the capital. London had been bombed every
night since 7 September, but other large cities had yet to suffer
extensive damage and loss of life. Even if she was yet to see the
final film, Cicely Jennings was well aware of her husband's front-
line role in the making of *London Can Take It*, a powerful message
hastily despatched across the Atlantic in order to persuade American
audiences that this really was the British people's 'finest hour'.

Along with co-director, Harry Watt, and two of the GPO Film Unit's most experienced cameramen, Jennings had spent the early weeks of the Blitz capturing on celluloid 'the unconquerable spirit and courage of the people of London'.[2] *London Can Take It* had proved surprisingly successful, (helped by the fact that most New York moviegoers assumed the film to be a personal despatch from Quentin Reynolds, the *Colliers Weekly* correspondent responsible for the commentary).[3] Jennings had informed Cicely in a previous letter that the film, 'has done us a great deal of good *here*: & we are as busy as can be'. Being busy entailed, as we shall see, travelling 'Round the Midlands & the North which are quiet & warm-hearted & practically untouched – believe me!'[4] Writing in his Penrith hotel bedroom Jennings insisted that, despite 'a few exciting nights in the Midlands…The hills and valleys of the North are as quiet as ever & the pubs & dancehalls are fuller & brighter than before.'[5] Yet by the time he came to finish the letter circumstances had changed dramatically, and Cicely had fresh cause to be concerned about her husband's safety: Coventry had experienced the devastating raid of 14-15 November, thereby providing fresh subject matter, fresh inspiration, and above all fresh focus, for 'Backbone of Britain', a project which up to that point had been terribly worthy but somewhat lacking in direction.[6] The final outcome was *Heart of Britain*, a pivotal moment in Jennings' emergence as the poetic genius of British documentary filmmaking.[7]

This essay focuses upon the making of *Heart of Britain*, suggesting that most commentators on Jennings' work have underestimated the film's significance. Attention is given to the director's hopes and ambitions by the autumn of 1940, not least the need to consolidate his collaborative approach to documentary film making; and also, most crucially, the need to demonstrate authority, maturity, and above all, individuality within the complex creative process of reconciling cinematic vision and propagandist need. Jennings' artistic engagement with industrial England occurred against a backdrop of the GPO Film Unit's success in justifying its continued existence (as the Crown Film Unit from the start of 1941), and Jack Beddington's success in getting both feature and documentary film makers to work together following his appointment as director of the Ministry of Information's troubled

Film Division in April 1940.[8] This is a familiar story, but one in which *Heart of Britain* invariably has only a minor role.

Although his admirers tend to depict Jennings as a largely forgotten figure, and an authorised biography is long overdue, there is in fact a considerable body of literature devoted to the man and his work.[9] The fiftieth anniversary of his death – in 1950, aged 43 - generated broadsheet features, a season at the National Film Theatre, a one-day conference at the Imperial War Museum, and a Christmas week documentary on Channel 4.[10] Jennings enthusiasts understandably focus upon his three great wartime films – *Listen to Britain*, *Fires Were Started*, and *Diary for Timothy* – with *Heart of Britain* rarely perceived to be a genuinely seminal work.[11] Ironically, one obvious exception is Dai Vaughan's 1983 biography of Stewart McAllister, Jennings' film editor and creative partner. This labour of love retraces the roots of the 'Backbone of Britain' project, recalls the centrality of events in Coventry to the final shape and structure of *Heart of Britain*, and in the film's powerful combination of music and visual image recognises the Jennings signature so familiar from *Listen to Britain*, the diurnal musical montage generally considered his masterpiece.[12] What Vaughan doesn't comprehend is the degree to which *Heart of Britain* underpinned the myth of the Blitz, fuelling a powerful 'myth within a myth' with regard to Coventry and how its fate was perceived in similarly devastated conurbations, let alone within the city itself.

Vaughan was more concerned of course with re-establishing Stewart McAllister as a key figure in the GPO/Crown team, hence his reluctance to argue the case for *Heart of Britain* at length. This article examines more fully the legacy of the film in terms of Jennings' later work, not least with reference to his use of music and his ambivalent response to German aggression. *Heart of Britain*, far less equivocally than *London Can Take It*, depicts Britain embarking upon a new, offensive phase of the war, marking a clean break with the isolation, defeat, and mere survival of the second half of 1940. Jennings unashamedly restates the need to hit back and wreak vengeance on the Nazis, and yet at the same time he conveys a deceptively simple message with regard to the German people and their cultural heritage (as embodied most publicly via their music). In actual fact, this is a complex discourse regarding the need/readiness/willingness to respect 'the genius of the Germany that was'.

Yes, a case can be made that *Heart of Britain* deserves greater recognition, but this isn't to deny that the film has serious flaws, not least in its depiction of 'ordinary' people. The GPO Film Unit's original, if increasingly contentious, commitment to using real people wherever possible is enthusiastically maintained in *Heart of Britain*. Rather than enhance, might this detract from the film, not least in its depiction of the Women's Voluntary Service (WVS)? Which naturally leads on to a further question – however naïve and well intentioned, is the film demeaning to women (which in itself raises the issue of the film's reception in the spring of 1941, both by the critics, and more significantly, by cinema and non-cinema audiences in the 'heart of Britain' and beyond.)? Did reservations concerning the use of real people talking straight to camera encourage an eventual decision to shoot and edit *Listen to Britain* without dialogue and commentary?

Furthermore, did *Heart of Britain* simply confirm the prejudices of Jennings' fiercest critics on the left, not least those admirers of John Grierson grouped around the *Documentary News Letter* who lambasted the supposedly naïve, romanticised, sentimentalist view of a 'mass observation lad'?[13] Jennings was working on this project at the same time as George Orwell was urging revolutionary change in *The Lion and the Unicorn*, and the common aspirations of these 'lower-upper-middle class' radical patriots has often been noted, not least by Jeffrey Richards.[14] Orwell's often brutally honest observation of working people may have toughened up Jennings' view of a class from which for all his good intentions he remained so detached. More likely, it was trudging the rubble-strewn streets of Coventry or the East End which produced a more realistic, yet in no way less idealistic, view of 'ordinary' people.

By the spring of 1941 Jennings, having tread water in the cutting room compiling *Words for Battle*, was ready for the next project.[15] Similarly, after its last major raids, on 8 and 10 April, Coventry was ready to move on, wrestling with the priorities of short-term accommodation and long-term urban renewal. Four years later, the widely screened *Diary for Timothy* and the highly popular 'Coventry of the Future' exhibition together confirmed just how much both director and city shared a common social democratic agenda.[16] With peace on the horizon *Heart of Britain* already looked dated, and yet its real importance had been demonstrated by the quality of the films that followed, culminating in what with hindsight was an unduly premature valedictory statement.[17]

Coventry, the Blitz, and the refocusing of *Heart of Britain*
In September 1940 the GPO Film Unit, having survived threats of closure or takeover, found itself forced to leave a bomb-damaged Blackheath studio and relocate to Denham, west of London. With his family departed for America, and *Luftwaffe* raids by now a nightly occurrence, Jennings moved close to Alexander Korda's huge studios, lodging with his newly-appointed producer, Ian Dalrymple.[18] Dalrymple, who pre-war had worked for Korda, and thus knew very little about the public sector, proved a highly successful head of the Film Unit. Over the next three years he brought stability, security, and a sense of purpose to an organisation which previously had struggled to define a role for itself within the 'Programme for Film Propaganda' drafted in January 1940 by Beddington's predecessor as director of the Film Division, Kenneth Clark.[19] Beddington himself was fiercely protective of Dalrymple, and his faith in the newly designated Crown Film Unit was amply rewarded. Here was a producer who had a clear sense of direction: although brimming with ideas, he emphasised continuity, and a need to build upon the narrative-documentary tradition established in the late 1930s by the previous producer, Alberto Cavalcanti. The foremost exponent of that tradition, Harry Watt, never warmed to Dalrymple. However, Jennings forged a formidable partnership with a producer ever eager to feed his directors' ideas for new projects, but equally keen to remain aloof from the actual process of making films.[20] Dalrymple saw his job as simply to, 'fight for facilities, conditions and opportunities…[and] act as a buffer between the Films Division and the Unit'.[21]

Dalrymple's first task at Denham was to oversee production of *London Can Take It*, with filming compressed into a frenetic fortnight, followed by seven exhausting days – and nights - in the cutting room.[22] The film's transatlantic success was quickly matched by its popularity at home where a slightly shorter version was distributed nationally under the MoI's five-minute film scheme:

Mass Observation's national panel deemed it by far the best propaganda short screened since the start of the war. Just as in the United States, the key to success appeared to lie in Quentin Reynolds' insistence that he was a neutral reporter (in *Britain Can Take It* he introduces the film on-camera), but for British audiences a further attraction was the film's emphasis upon the courage of, in the words of one MoI projectionist, 'the common people'[23] The film cleverly juxtaposed British understatement – shots of the King and Queen inspecting bomb damage attract no comment – with American flair, Reynolds' commentary proving a skilful blend of comedy, compassion, and commitment. *London/Britain Can Take It* fused traditional images of national resolve (not least the concluding shot of King Richard I's sword-wielding statue in front of a badly scarred Palace of Westminster) with visual confirmation of the 'people's war' (auxiliary firemen, ARP wardens, the shelters, and so on). Echoing Tom Wintringham and 'Cato' in print and J.B. Priestley on air, Reynolds paid tribute to 'the greatest civilian army ever to be assembled…The people's army: they are the ones who are really fighting the war.' Belatedly, official film makers were depicting and articulating a popular mood which, with an immediate fear of invasion gone, had for some already peaked. Nevertheless, the Films Division, and to be more precise the GPO/Crown Film Unit, had at last found a voice *and* a message, laying down a gauntlet for the rest of the MoI to pick up: even stripped of its progressive agenda (courtesy of such great 'English Jacobins' as Priestley, Orwell, Wintringham, and indeed Jennings), there still remained:

> …a vision of Britain's [England's?] historical traditions and contemporary realities which would make sense throughout the years that followed. Britain had an historical tradition in which she could take great pride; it was the values at the heart of that tradition which were at stake in the war and, in its struggle to defeat those who would threaten those values all the people would play their part. This indeed was the People's War, and wartime documentary films paid powerful tribute to their remarkable achievements.[24]

While particular shots in *London Can Take It* are seen as unique to Jennings, not least the more obviously surreal moments in the film, it was very much a collaborative venture. Watt was in many respects the driving force, while McAllister was clearly the key figure in ensuring the project's early completion. Nevertheless, the film does signal Jennings' preoccupation with the dignity and quiet heroism of ordinary working people, all of whom endeavour – in the face of almost but not wholly overwhelming odds - to maintain an air of normality, and, above all, to embody and exemplify a unique combination of communal/urban/national values.

The MoI was keen to emphasise how much *Britain Can Take It* represented 'what is happening in every other British city and town, where resistance to intense aerial attack and powers of endurance are every bit as heroic'.[25]   In mid-October Dalrymple formally proposed a companion film, paying tribute to 'our Northern industrial centres radiating from the Pennines, the "Backbone of Britain".' Jennings had in fact been working on 'a kind of *Spare Time* assignment' since the start of September, when he first visited Coventry, but Dalrymple seized on a Sunday night broadcast by J.B. Priestley as justification for the project. Priestley had characterised his fellow northerners' capacity to match resilience with good humour, as 'Hard work and high jinks'. Jack Beddington was presumably unimpressed by the notion of a film of the same name paying tribute to 'the spirited attitude of the North Country workers'. Priestley's slogan was quietly dropped, and subsequent synopses looked beyond simply focusing upon Lancashire's inspirational 'gusto'.[26] Jennings' influence upon this initial proposal is clear, with a direct line back to the previous year's study of 'the time we call our own'. Although *Spare Time* movingly records the 'chance to be ourselves' among steelworkers in Sheffield and coalminers in south Wales, the most memorable scenes focus upon the cottonspinners of Manchester and Bolton, the latter familiar to Jennings as 'Worktown', the focal point for Mass Observation's study of English working class life on the eve of war.[27] Twelve months later Jennings was insisting upon Lancashire's importance as a role model for the rest of the nation:

The people of these industrial towns have always had the knack of <u>living</u> as distinct from <u>existing</u>, no matter how difficult the times or how dark the immediate prospect. They have it today, and are an example to use. Escapism it may be – but the right escapism, one of the fundamental issues for which we are fighting, the enjoyment of leisure.[28]

The idea of a Blitz-based sequel to *Spare Time* was overtaken by events, but Jennings still wanted due recognition of northerners' capacity to play hard, work hard. Similarly, he held fast to Dalrymple's proposal that the contribution of women to the war effort be duly acknowledged: with full mobilisation of the Home Front still over a year away, the Lancashire cotton mills remained the biggest employers of women industrial workers.

With footage unused from *Spare Time*, and over a month's filming already in the can, Jennings clearly envisaged a more ambitious project than his producer. Treatments drafted in late October drew upon a series of interviews already carried out across the north of England, and in Coventry. A travel schedule for the first fortnight in November was based upon re-interviewing those personalities assigned key roles in Jennings' two lengthy treatments. In successive drafts direct speech is quoted at length, with only odd sentences familiar from the final film - at least four interviews were dropped altogether. A planned sequence of miners exercising whippets, couples ballroom dancing, and families making music, looked back to *Spare Time* and ahead to *Listen to Britain*. Drawing upon the scenes in *London Can Take It* where smoking is clearly intended to signify normality, Jennings planned to film a postman unable to deliver a letter calmly noting the number of a house destroyed the previous night. The intensification of the bombing campaign soon rendered such a scene risible. It also destroyed the credibility of Gill Smith, the left-leaning local government official in charge of training Merseyside rescue squads. Smith's remarks fully articulated the idea of a 'people's war', and one can understand Jennings' initial delight at capturing on film 'a glowing warmth of red flame of love and comradeship for each other which *cannot* be defeated'.[29] However, misplaced optimism was cruelly exposed once the *Luftwaffe* recognised Liverpool's strategic significance. Despite filming Smith in mid-October, and again a fortnight later, the final cut's only direct reference to the port was a shot of rescue workers training in a scarcely recognisable school playground. Night-time shots of Tyneside wherry crews training as fire-fighters, and a Geordie housewife's recollection of a raid, both featured in the

director's original plans. Neither appeared in the eventual film, with
the north-east's contribution to the war effort reduced to a single,
symbolic shot of 'the cathedral towers of Durham'. Jennings had a
clear idea of how the film would end: the congregation of a wrecked
church would sing 'Eternal father, strong to save' with images of
food-carrying convoys projected on to a 'faint magic lantern screen'
in front of the altar, followed by a return to the rural landscape
shown at the start, a final shot of workers pouring into a factory, and
a parting observation that, 'It is not only the crags of the Pennines
but still more the men and women and children of the North who are
the backbone of Britain.'[30]

       This whole sequence comes across poorly in writing, and the
same would no doubt have been true on the screen. However, it is
clear that prior to the destruction of Coventry Jennings had a clear
geographical base for his film, namely his unashamedly metropolitan
conception of what constituted 'the north'. From the outset he
planned a major role for Pearl Hyde, already a leading Labour
councillor in Coventry, and wartime organiser of the local Women's
Voluntary Service. With splendid indifference to northern
sensibility, she was to voice 'the part the women of the North are
playing in this war':

   There are women who work all day in the factories and others
   who keep homes and children going and who are yet members
   of the W.V.S. and who, in the evening, come out to work all
   night: the shock troops of the civilian army. Listen to one of
   their officers:-[31]

       Again, a strong echo of the national mood as evoked in
London Can Take It. Pearl Hyde, unlike in the final film, was
intended to be anonymous, but it would have been clear as soon as
she opened her mouth that she was not from Lancashire or
Yorkshire. Initially, both Jennings and Dalrymple conflated the
Midlands' experience with that of the north-east and north-west,
seemingly ignorant of the immense cultural and socio-economic
differences between traditional industrial communities blighted by
the Depression and the 'sunrise' cities further south. The great raid
of 14-15 November caused both men to change their perception of
Coventry, not least because Jennings now intended to make a very

different film. In consequence, the north-east all but disappeared from the final rushes, as did Merseyside. The Cumbrian shepherds Jennings drove all the way to Penrith to film were swiftly forgotten once news arrived of 'the grim attack on Coventry', and plans were made to motor south.[32]

Coventry Cathedral in the aftermath of 14-15 November 1940

Jennings, along with soundman Ken Cameron and cameraman Henry Fowle, drove their Standard 10 as close to the city centre as they could, and started filming. Neither council nor MoI archives reveal any documented contact with the emergency authorities, although Ministry of Aircraft Production passes facilitated access to the factory of Armstrong Whitworth Aircraft (AWA) on the outskirts of Coventry.[33] However, filming inside the Baginton hangars must have been postponed until Jennings' third visit to Coventry a month later. His priority over the weekend following the Thursday night raid was to record the city's immediate response to the most intensive bombing seen in Britain since the onset of the Blitz.

With no less than seventeen raids since mid-August aerial bombardment had become a familiar phenomenon to the people of Coventry. What was unprecedented was the ferocity and the intensity of the 14-15 November raid. Literally from dusk to dawn around 400 aircraft dropped over 500 tons of high explosive, with delayed-action bombs creating havoc for days afterwards. Even more deadly were the thousands of incendiary canisters which rained down throughout the night, and which in the initial onslaught had set the medieval heart of the city ablaze. The cathedral was gutted, although desperate fire-fighting saved the neighbouring church of Holy Trinity. By morning little remained of Broadgate, the focus of pre-war redevelopment, and the rest of the city centre lay in ruins.

Broadgate, 15 November 1940

Despite its rapid growth between the wars Coventry remained unusually compact, and no part of the city could claim to have escaped lightly. With so many buildings and residents concentrated in such a small area the damage and loss of human life was that much greater, and the psychological shock that much more profound. Over 50,000 residences and 500 shops were destroyed or damaged, with 21 key production plants and numerous smaller factories temporarily put out of action. For once the civilian loss of life matched pre-war predictions, with 568 killed and 863 seriously hurt. Power supplies were disrupted from the outset, and the two hospitals were hit early on, but it was the loss of water and the rapid breakdown in telecommunications which most severely disrupted fire-fighting and rescue operations. The pathfinders' deliberate targeting of public utilities - by dropping the biggest bombs in the first wave - ensured that the incendiary fires would spread rapidly, and that the emergency services would be stretched to breaking point at a very early stage. In this respect the *Luftwaffe* was spectacularly successful.   Not   surprisingly,   the   city   council's   Emergency Committee proved incapable of dealing with the immediate crisis, yet there was no collapse of civil administration such as occurred during subsequent raids on the south coast.[34]

The other most notable feature of the raid was the extent to which, despite initial shock and severe dislocation, the people of the city bounced back. The poverty of emergency provision, the temporary collapse of morale, and the mass evacuation into the Warwickshire countryside, all seemed to signal the medium-term elimination of Coventry as a major contributor to the war effort. Mass Observation recorded the immediate, devastating impact of the raid on a community fearful of an equally ferocious attack on the Friday night. Ironically, given Jennings' eagerness to highlight the value of the WVS, the bitterest complaint was the poverty of support for the survivors, not least the availability of hot food and drinks, and easy access to properly provisioned rest centres. Yet, as early as Saturday morning 'Coventry people were looking calmer and more purposeful. The central area was thronged with sightseers.' Hundreds more were still making their way out of the city, but very few envisaged a lengthy absence. The Germans made a tactical error in not returning the next night, delaying their second major raid until the following April. This provided a significant psychological boost to the local population, and offered breathing space to the civil and military authorities, supported by central government. The absence of sustained bombardment proved to be a key factor in the city's rapid return to full industrial production. 'The crawling rate of social recovery' fuelled popular discontent and undermined morale, but in less than a fortnight Mass Observation could report to the Home Office a strong sense of 'purposeful demeanour [and]…apparent stoicism'.[35]

This then was the shattered city Jennings and his crew discovered on the morning of Saturday, 16 November, timing their arrival to coincide with that of the King. For Jennings and his crew, as indeed for George VI, the scenes that greeted them were all too familiar.[36] Nevertheless, this must have been a formative moment, not just in terms of offering a fresh focus for the film, but in terms of forging a team. Since September Jennings, Cameron, and Fowle had been well out of the firing line, but now they were recording scenes all too reminiscent of *London Can Take It*. The difference this time was the absence of Harry Watt, or any of the other more experienced documentary makers. In Coventry the still relatively inexperienced director demonstrated his capacity to rise to the occasion, engendering trust and earning admiration and (qualified) affection.[37] In so doing, Jennings created the production team responsible for every major project he embarked upon over the next three years: he now had reliable technical support out in the field, and he had Dalrymple and McAllister back at Denham.[38]

Hardened by what they had previously witnessed in the East End, the GPO film-makers did not find Coventry 'as grim as we expected: at any rate the people really were magnificent'.[39] Within a week of their return to London the MoI gave its approval to a sharp change of emphasis: the 'Backbone of Britain' became the *Heart of Britain*, although to be more accurate, with Coventry moving in from the periphery, it was the heart of England that now stood centre-stage. Before Christmas Jennings made a third visit to the city, filming much of the material used at the end of the film. McAllister and Jennings worked on the project over the holiday and into the New Year, and on 22 January 1941 passed two versions of the film on to Beddington's number two, Sidney Bernstein. The Films Division arranged for the domestic version to be available for distribution from as early as the week of 10 February.[40] Meanwhile, a slightly longer overseas alternative, *This Is England*, was acquired by Columbia Pictures and designated a 'Film Broadcast from the War Zone'. Building upon *Britain Can Take It*'s successful use of Quentin Reynolds, the MoI persuaded Ed Murrow, Columbia Broadcasting's high profile London correspondent, to provide the commentary. Murrow's presence on the soundtrack ensured *This Is England*'s popularity when it became available for screening in Britain, and concern was expressed within the MoI about possible audience confusion. Herbert Morrison was so pleased with *This Is England* that he ordered a print be sent to the White House immediately. Less impressed were the censorship authorities in Eire. They refused to authorise the release of *This Is England*, and did so again in March 1941 when the film was renamed and resubmitted: *Undaunted* was thought by Whitehall to be a sufficiently neutral title, but it was still too early in the war for the Fianna Fail government to exercise discretion and sanction a public screening.[41]

Heart of Britain – **the final cut**

It's worth at this point recalling the content and structure of the final film, which at nine minutes in length was significantly shorter than Jennings originally envisaged. *Heart of Britain* opens with a powerful combination of Elgar's *Introduction and Allegro for Strings*, bleak Bronte moorland, and prominent church landmarks. Jack Holmes' solemn commentary offers immediate reassurance:

> The winds of war blow across the hills and moorlands of Yorkshire and Derbyshire. They stir the grasses in the sheep valleys of Cumberland, ruffle the clear surface of Ullswater. They sing in the cathedral towers of Durham, in the tower of Liverpool (still building), in the spires of Coventry. But the heart of Britain remains unmoved and unchangeable.[42]

Solid rock makes way for Sheffield steel, with at least one shot of the furnaces borrowed from *Spare Time* and used again in *Listen to Britain*: 'In the shadow of the hills live the great industrial people, thronging the valleys of power and the rivers of industry. At the end of a shift George Good comes off hot and tired, but nowhere near beaten. He's an air raid warden as well.' By now the commentary has become more conversational in tone, contrasting sharply with a camera-conscious Good telling his mate that after a 'rough shift' he is off home for 'a good dinner', followed by ARP duty. Both footage and commentary move from Yorkshire steel to Lancashire cotton, still focusing upon observation and rescue. In a crowded ARP hut an amiable roof-spotter describes his duties, and the success of the local fire brigade in 'training the youngsters to put out these incendiary bombs'.[43] The tea-drinking Lancastrian is relaxed in front of camera, and the scene works well considering how much of the original interview was cut: McAllister used a brief interjection by another ARP warden to camouflage his splicing, and thereby suggest uninterrupted dialogue. Liverpool's training ground for rescue workers contrasts sharply with the reality of what is to follow – what Dai Vaughan labels, 'an invocation of the documentary image: an insistence that we scrutinise the image for just those properties which will distinguish the Coventry wreckage'.[44] There then follows the part of the film with which modern viewers feel most uncomfortable. Close-ups of women typists and WVS volunteers confirm that, 'Behind this grim work lies an infinite number of patient everyday jobs for the women, dull jobs like typing lists of addresses. Unending ones...'. Shots of the industrial landscape illustrate the fact that, 'the simplest, most difficult task of all is just staying put, with the war round the corner'. Clinging to the obsolescent language of the 'phoney war', the commentary informs us that, 'On a hazy day, Jerry comes droning over about three miles up', at the last minute driving the millgirls down into the shelters. With a raid ostensibly taking place above, they play a game that involves bursting a balloon and laughing hysterically. The audience is invited to, 'look at these Lancashire lassies cowering before the *Luftwaffe*. These are the folk whom Field Marshal Goering hopes to bomb into capitulation.'

At this point the film clearly steps up a gear with Sir Malcolm Sargent conducting the Hallé Orchestra's performance of Beethoven's *Fifth Symphony*.[45] The music continues over shots of, and a very long pan across, a devastated Coventry. Having been told that, 'in Manchester today they still respect the genius of Germany – the genius of the Germany that was', viewers are again reminded of the contribution of the gentler sex. Tea-making WVS volunteers confirm that, 'Here in Coventry, those everyday tasks of the women came right through the fire and became heroic.' As the *Fifth* fades away, we are asked to 'listen to Mrs Hyde':

> You know, you feel such a fool standing there in a crater – pitch darkness of night, and holding mugs of tea - seeing men bringing out bodies. You feel useless, until you know that there's someone there actually in that bombed house who is alive you can give tea to. And then to hear the praises of the men themselves - that tea's jolly good – just washed the blood and dust out of my mouth. And we feel that we really have done a job, and a useful job.[46]

The clear implication is that Pearl Hyde is speaking in the aftermath of the great raid depicted in the preceding shots; but the reason why she appears so remarkably calm is that her contribution was in fact recorded several weeks earlier.

The final sequence is built around the Huddersfield Choral Society singing the 'Hallelujah Chorus' from Handel's *Messiah*

('And even now in Yorkshire the people find the time to sing').[47] The choristers make way for shots of the medieval streets surrounding Holy Trinity church and the charred remnants of Coventry Cathedral. These scenes of people calmly going about their business amid the wreckage were recorded in mid-December when Jennings returned to the city, and they contrast sharply with the film's earlier depiction of the immediate aftermath. As the 'Hallelujah Chorus' thunders towards its climax the tone and delivery of the commentary change, with menace now reinforcing the basic message of grim determination:

> People who sing like that in times like these cannot be beaten. These people are slow to anger, not easily roused. Now they and their mates, their wives and their children, have been subjected to the most savage ordeal ever inflicted upon human beings. But these people have the power to hit back. And they are going to hit back, with all the skill of their hands, the tradition of their crafts, and the fire in their hearts.[48]

Inside the AWA hangars at Baginton, some of Coventry's most skilled workers are seen building Whitley bombers, one of which takes off at dusk on its mission of retribution. As the film switches from the city's still defiant spires back to the moors and rivers where it started, both choir and commentator offer reassurance at home, and warning abroad[49]:

> Out of the valleys of power and the rivers of industry will come the answer to the German challenge. And the Nazis will learn – once and for all – that no one with impunity troubles the heart of Britain.[50]

Heart of Britain – text and sub-text
Did Jennings have Coventry in mind when he later insisted 'that good films could only be made in times of disaster'?[51] The city's destruction ensured a markedly different film from that which he and Dalrymple had originally conceived. In this respect *Heart of Britain* provided a precedent for Jennings' next major project: halfway through shooting *Listen to Britain*, he convinced both McAllister and Dalrymple that the film required a very different approach to that

originally envisaged. Of course one reason why he was able to do this was because so little advance preparation had to be sacrificed (even *Fires Were Started* generated only the most basic script). In the case of the 'Backbone of Britain', Jennings' collaborators could see that there really was no alternative. The footage shot in the Midlands had presented McAllister with fresh images of the Blitz. The power of these distinctly non-metropolitan images was undeniable, hence their propagandist potential. Dalrymple had complete faith in his lodger's capacity to 'liberate the film from its preconceptions'.[52] That faith was strengthened by the prospect of Crown eventually producing two films, with an alternative version capable of emulating *Britain Can Take It*'s overseas success.

By the end of 1940 the MoI had decided to embark on a fresh phase of documentary-based propaganda: as well as highlighting national resilience, future films would emphasise Britain's capacity to take the war to the enemy. This move from defensive to offensive necessitated longer films, invariably with an overtly military theme.[53] In this respect *Heart of Britain* can be seen as transitional. Almost twice the length of the original five-minute MoI/commercial cinema compromise, it heralded the arrival of longer (at least fifteen minutes), more sophisticated documentaries, many of which after 1941 set the agenda for reconstruction. *Heart of Britain* was still designed to boost morale, but the intention was clearly something more than regional self-congratulation. Here was a clear signal that Bomber Command could now give the Germans a taste of their own medicine: the airframes crammed into the Baginton hangar, the Whitley roaring in to the night sky, the triumphant choral music, and above all, the valedictory warning that 'the Nazis will learn – once and for all – that no one with impunity troubles the heart of Britain'.[54] This after all was at a time when even in Downing Street it was assumed that the RAF's precision bombing could produce results – an illusion soon to be exposed, once detailed analysis of photographic evidence exposed a systemic failure to destroy designated targets. *London Can Take It* had similarly highlighted Bomber Command's capacity to strike back, but reassured overseas audiences that – unlike the *Luftwaffe* - only 'legitimate', non-civilian targets would be hit. *Heart of Britain* clung tenaciously to the moral high ground, but not merely to court American public opinion. Jennings would have been horrified by the notion of unqualified retribution, witness his depiction of bombing in *Diary for Timothy*, but six months into the Blitz this earlier film seemed wholly in tune with the national mood.

Heart of Britain contains a story, or to be more accurate, several stories, but the film eschews what would become a dominant narrative mode within the Crown Film Unit. In *Fires Were Started* and *The Silent Village*, his astonishing Welsh reconstruction of the Lidice massacre, Jennings operated within that (fictional) mode, but in *Listen to Britain* he created a film form all his own.[55] Yes it has progression (through 24 hours), and thus structure, but the layers of sounds and images, the symbolism, the celebration, the complexity, and above all the virtuosity, together constitute a remarkable synthesis of formality and experimentation. *Heart of Britain* illustrates just how far Jennings progressed in such a short space of time (as in its own way does the intervening *Words for Battle*). At the same time it clearly signals the direction in which he was moving: both films, in Dalrymple's words, depend for their effect upon 'symbolic, enigmatic or sometimes epigrammatic juxtapositions of image and music'.[56] The centrality of music to *Heart of Britain* indicates what is to come, not least in the final sequence where 'the effect is extraordinary, and the implications obvious. Jennings has found his style.'[57] Lindsay Anderson's enthusiasm is matched by Jeffrey Richards, for whom the music plays 'a vital integral role, contributing to an organic whole [and] carrying the message forward'. At the time Jennings enthused 'that people are singing Handel and listening to Beethoven as never before', but forty years later Dalrymple looked back with distaste upon his protégé's hijacking of the 'Hallelujah Chorus': 'far from a paean of praise, it sounds like a savage war cry'.[58] Had Jennings been merely looking for maximum effect, then surely he would have used 'Rule Britannia', recorded on the same day. The choice of Handel signifies the last of a succession of ironies, some clearly stated, some less so. The English, ever a tolerant people, still respect a culture capable of producing Beethoven, however much it might currently be corrupted by an ideology rooted in irrationality and intolerance. Not only this, but they look back to a brief moment when both nations made common music under a common flag: Handel, court composer of the House of Hanover on the eve of the Enlightenment, is as much 'our' icon of high culture and civilised social and intellectual intercourse as he is that of Germany. Thus, rather than expropriate from the Germans Handel's hymn of salvation (spiritual, and now military), the English view it as an obvious embodiment of the current national resolve.[59]   Jennings would have been well aware that for over a century after his death Handel was largely ignored in Germany. His oratorios only became familiar to German audiences as late as the 1830s, largely thanks to Mendelssohn, who of course was not only a great Anglophile but was Jewish. Mendelssohn composed his own oratorio, *Elijah*, in England at the same time as his countryman, Charles Hallé, moved north to Manchester, bringing with him the glories of Beethoven, Brahms, and Schubert. Thus, the Hallé Orchestra's performance of the *Fifth* was a double reminder that 'in Manchester today they still respect the genius of Germany – the genius of the Germany that was'.[60]

The Hallé's conductor was by late 1940 himself a symbol of resistance to Nazi aggression, his work and reputation bridging the gap between high and popular culture. Malcolm Sargent's much-publicised 'Blitz Tour' with the London Philharmonic Orchestra extended his fame beyond a predominantly middle-class audience of classical music lovers. Just as most filmgoers in early 1941 would have recognised Beethoven's Fifth even if they could not name it, so they would have recognised Sargent's name on the fake poster advertising the Hallé's 'performance' even if they had no idea what he actually looked like.[61]   The choice of Sargent, Britain's best known musician, and the Huddersfield Choral Society, Britain's biggest choir, was clearly deliberate. Both exemplified the way in which the 'People's War' for the first time rendered high culture accessible to all. Jennings applauded and encouraged this temporary breaking down of barriers, witness his readiness in *Listen to Britain* to devote equal time and respect to Dame Myra Hess's performance of Mozart's *Piano Concerto* and to Flanagan and Allan's canteen rendering of 'Underneath The Arches'. In both cases Jennings offered an unashamedly egalitarian perspective on the British at war; and, in overlapping the music with preceding or succeeding sequences, encouraged McAllister to employ the same editing technique which had worked so well in *Heart of Britain*.[62]

Jennings later recorded Malcolm Sargent and the LPO performing Handel's *Water Music*, to accompany shots of uniformed

and civilian Londoners striding forward purposefully at the end of
Words for Battle. This final sequence, and indeed the whole film,
attracted quite fierce criticism.[63]   But again, the man-of-letters'
apparently straightforward call to arms requires a second – or third –
reading, not least because the original intention was to release a
companion film, 'In Germany Now'. Jennings envisaged an actor
such as Anton Walbrook, 'possessing ever so slight an accent',
reciting verse by Goethe, Schiller, Heine, and other great German
poets. The actual film would comprise of clips from *The Triumph of
the Will* and recent Nazi newsreels: 'Most of the illustrations would,
of course, be placed <u>against</u> the sense of the poems: Germany has not
realised the hopes and dreams of her poets: indeed she has surpassed
their   worst   fears…Fundamentally   the   film   would   be   a   simple
criticism of the Third Reich by Germans themselves…'.[64]   In his
homage to Stewart McAllister Dai Vaughan discussed this project at
some length, demonstrating how the conflict between 'the genius of
the Germany that was' in the commentary and the brutal reality on
the screen would have rendered *Words for Battle* ('In England Now')
a very different cinematic experience. The proposal clearly had its
roots in the final stages of editing *Heart of Britain*, but as Vaughan
rightly concludes, early 1941 was not the best time to suggest 'a film
devoted to the humanism of Germany'.[65]

Conclusion: Jennings' shared agenda for reconstruction, and the centrality of *Heart of Britain* to his wartime oeuvre

Jennings'   American   biographers   saw   *Heart   of   Britain*   as   'the
prototypical Jennings war film, blazing the trail for the masterpieces
that were to follow.'[66]   The use of music led directly to *Listen to
Britain*, but the success of Jennings' 'masterpieces' also depended on
a readiness to acknowledge past failure. Even when judged by the
standards and prevailing assumptions of the early 1940s, Jack
Holmes' commentary is flat, unconvincing, dated, and patronising
('Just   look   at   these   Lancashire   lassies   cowering   before   the
Luftwaffe…those everyday tasks of the women came right through
the fire and became heroic.'). How one longs for Laurie Lee's
minimalist commentary to *Spare Time*. 'Wooden performances,
especially when synch speech was required, were one of the banes of
the classic documentary', and in his study of *Fires Were Started*
Brian Winston noted how by 1942 Jennings had learnt the knack of

'directing the undemonstrative English' (multiple takes rendered an exhausted performer far more relaxed and less camera conscious).[67] In *Heart of Britain* there is little to match the convincing dialogue of H.U.1's fire crew, other than the brief exchange between the two ARP wardens skilfully constructed by Stewart McAllister. In the steel mill George Good is painfully self-conscious, addressing his lines directly to an off-camera director. However, worse is to follow: for anyone who knew Pearl Hyde – *the* dominant personality in postwar Coventry, with a remarkable capacity to transcend mundane municipal politics – her terribly proper performance, which contrives to be both gushing and stilted, projects a wholly unrecognisable character.   Mrs Hyde's schoolmistress tone, let alone her hasty embrace of BBC English, no doubt guaranteed hoots of derision whenever the film was shown in the city's surviving cinemas.[68]

Although Jennings was clearly well pleased with *Heart of Britain*, repeated viewings must have left him increasingly uncomfortable with both the commentary and the contributions.[69] Convinced that effective propaganda no longer depended upon direct intervention, Jennings demonstrated in *Listen to Britain* the irrelevance of such artificiality. Henceforth, where commentary was justified then it had to be carefully crafted, and genuinely integral to the film, witness the contribution of E.M. Forster to the making of *Diary for Timothy*. At the same time, supposedly spontaneous, but in fact highly contrived, addresses direct to camera were quietly dropped.

Ordinary people could speak for themselves – or not speak at all, but simply via a gesture, or just their mere presence, stand out amidst the diverse cultural references with which Jennings gently bombarded his audience.[70] Both Kevin Jackson and Jeffrey Richards have alluded to the tremendous respect the director displayed towards his subjects, eschewing a familiar criticism that Jennings sought to capture on celluloid the social behaviour of a class he never remotely understood.[71] Yes he was a romantic, and he was certainly an idealist.   He could also be astonishingly naïve, and yet the experience of the Blitz destroyed any lingering sentimentality. As the film critic Gerald Noxon once observed, Jennings 'was a man of deep sentiment, but he was not sentimental'.[72]   A now familiar comparison is between Jennings' films and Orwell's essays, most especially that remarkable synthesis of quiet patriotism and revolutionary intent, *The Lion and the Unicorn*.[73] Before the war Jennings would almost certainly have baulked at some of Orwell's blunter observations upon the British working-class. Indeed even as late as 1939 he would have been an easy target for a less tolerant Orwell to pick off – 'Wigan Pier' seems a long way from the cosy parlours and tidy pigeon lofts of *Spare Time*.[74] Yet by 1941 both men offered unique and lasting tributes to the resilience and generosity of a nation/family united under fire: not the denizens of Whitehall, Westminster, and St James, but the 'Backbone of Britain'.[75] 'Free born Englishmen' were the sons and daughters of an industrial (and rural) working class whose emancipation was long overdue. Teachers and tank commanders, matrons and managers, were the skilled workers and technocrats around whom would be built a fairer society, rooted in equality of opportunity. This was a view echoed by Tom Wintringham when propagandising the true nature of a 'people's war', and a vision of the future articulated by J.B. Priestley in his 1940 broadcasts. Ironically, none of these radical patriots, with the possible exception of Priestley, could claim affinity with this burgeoning class, the attributes of which they so regularly applauded.[76] If any city in late 'thirties Britain had appeared the embodiment of the new meritocracy then it was Coventry.

Late 1940s competition design for Broadgate

Here was a surprisingly cohesive community given its size where aldermanic social democracy and a boardroom one-nation

Toryism could maintain an uneasy yet potentially fruitful working relationship.

Broadgate construction, 1951

The strength of the trade unions, particularly the engineers and the transport workers (led locally by Jack Jones), and the strong electoral support enjoyed by the Labour Party, forced local employers to collaborate closely with council leaders. Similarly, by the end of 1945 sceptical civil servants had acknowledged the force of public opinion, their ministers endorsing the ambitious plans for reconstruction approved by the city council as early as February 1941.[77] Broadgate's rapid redevelopment, the Precinct's innovative design, and above all, the new cathedral's uncompromising modernity, together ensured Coventry's high profile throughout the 1950s and well into the next decade. A much-publicised programme of municipal rebuilding, industrial renewal, ecumenical revival, and international reconciliation all ensured that the destruction of Coventry at the hands of the *Luftwaffe* remained prominent in the postwar national psyche. The view that the events of 14-15 November 1940 were unique has proved remarkably resilient, witness those New Yorkers who in the aftermath of 11 September 2001 saw the 'Phoenix at Coventry' as a model for reconciliation and recovery.[78] Over the interceding sixty-plus years the city's enthusiasm for commemoration, celebration, and mythologizing has scarcely diminished, however much the elderly bemoan the presumed ignorance of today's multi-ethnic urban population. The

Blitz was – and remains – central to the civic community's collective memory, rooted in a keen sense that of all the *Luftwaffe*'s targets Coventry was somehow unique.[79] Mass Observation reported early resentment elsewhere that Coventry should be seen as somehow special, but *Heart of Britain* nevertheless reinforced and promoted this belief.[80] Similarly, *Diary for Timothy* echoed Coventry's early embrace of internationalism and reconciliation, making 'astonishing interconnections' between domestic and global agendas for postwar reconstruction.[81]

This raises the question of course as to whether *Heart of Britain* had precisely the reverse effect upon audiences to that which was originally intended. In other words, that the film compounded resentment in cities such as Southampton, Portsmouth, and Plymouth that Coventry had been singled out for special treatment, thereby overlooking the ferocity of bombardment experienced along the south coast of England through late 1940 and into the New Year.[82] This seems hard to believe given that, although the bombing of Coventry provided a fresh focus, Jennings' original intention still survived: the 'real' north, both industrial and rural, remains ever present in the film, not least via the music. Today, audience response in the early 1940s is well-nigh impossible to gauge, although there is some evidence to suggest that Jennings' work, and *Listen to Britain* in particular, was well-received when screened in factory canteens, village halls, barrack rooms, and any other locations suitable for the projection of 16mm film. *Heart of Britain* was sufficiently short as to squeeze in to cinema presentations, as well as being shown in those 'non-theatrical' venues serviced by the Films Division's eight regional officers. With factory screenings averaging once a month most northern and Midlands workers would have had the opportunity to view the film some time in the spring and early summer of 1941.[83] Depending upon the number of prints available, workers elsewhere in the country would have seen the documentary later in the year – assuming, of course, that they took the opportunity to do so, content to spend precious spare time sitting in the dark watching government propaganda.

Historians remain sceptical as to the impact of films screened in such uncongenial circumstances, but, even allowing for *Heart of Britain*'s wooden performances and sententious commentary, here was a testimony to regional pride and endeavour capable of touching all but the most cynical or the most traumatised. Not that Jennings' old sparring partners on the *Documentary News Letter* agreed, insisting that, 'Even Americans must be tired now of pictures of raid damage, sparing us nothing, not even the ruined churches with crucifixes gaunt across the sky and the usual defensive commentary.'[84] Interestingly Mass Observation concurred, in so much as most audiences viewed documentary commentaries with a good deal of suspicion, being 'more interested in the pictures themselves' – a finding Tom Harrison could easily have passed on to Jennings in advance of *Listen to Britain*.[85]

Heart of Britain is no masterpiece, a partially hidden cinematic gem awaiting rediscovery. But it is, in a quiet yet forceful manner, inspirational. It exemplifies Ian Dalrymple's insistence in October 1941 that, 'When we make propaganda we tell, quite quietly, what we believe to be the truth,' capturing the war effort on film, and exhorting the hesitant and apprehensive to 'Be of good heart and go and do likewise.'[86] *Heart of Britain* was only one of a succession of GPO/Crown documentaries paying tribute to particular elements of the nation at war – in this case, instead of a specific service or civilian group, the 'Backbone of Britain' was judged to have spent too long in the shadow of a wounded metropolis. Yet in the end the film fulfilled a wider function, both in its peculiar tribute to a devastated city, and in its broader role as a morale booster – a role which, its final section notwithstanding, remained firmly rooted in wartime understatement, an affectation *de rigueur* in Calder's 'Deep England'.[87] *Heart of Britain* signalled a fresh approach for Jennings (and McAllister), its tone, content, and structure identifying it as an obvious prologue to *Listen to Britain*. Yet to relegate the film to little more than an interesting insight in to the maturing of the Jennings style is to under-estimate its emotional power. Furthermore, *Heart of Britain* clearly has its own particular role to play, albeit small, in forging the 'myth of the Blitz'. Where it does loom large is in capturing an urban community on its knees but by no means out for the count – to rediscover *Heart of Britain* is to recall the resilience of the people of Coventry. How ironic, therefore, that today no official record survives of Jennings' three visits to the west Midlands, and that the documentary has had no public screening in the city since the summer of 1941. Here indeed is a film for which reassessment is long overdue.

5

THE COVENTRY FACTOR
Philip Larkin and John Hewitt[1]

In the late 1960s I doubt if many grammar school boys could name
more than one or at best two living British poets, and one of those
would probably be John Betjeman (at least today's average
sixthformer can offer Seamus Heaney). Of course there were always
the Liverpool poets, and, if any of my friends possessed a volume of
verse other than their A-level texts, the chances were that it was *The
Mersey Sound*, sales of which doubtless exceeded the entire print run
for the preceding nine selections of Penguin Modern Poets.[2] But surely
its authors were not *real* poets á la our modernist icons of Eliot and
Pound? Henri, McGough, and Patten acted more like rock'n'roll

journeymen than serious maestros of *vers libre*, with the Liverpool Scene perceived as everybody's favourite festival opener, and not as an advance guard of postmodernist irony: Adrian Henri appeared little more than a raucous Scouse alternative to Viv Stanshall. For those of us observing events on the West Coast, albeit from the safe vantage point of the West Midlands, there were of course the Beats. Yet Ginsberg, Ferlinghetti and Corso, however successful in extending their shelf life courtesy of Dylan and the Dead, were American and - to a late adolescent – ancient. The instruction remained unheeded: name a living *British* poet.

Close scrutiny of school library shelves, and the English department's tiny record collection, could reveal Faber's not so young Turks, Thom Gunn and Ted Hughes, but in my class the only contemporary poet who sprang readily to mind was Philip Larkin. We may not have read *The Whitsun Weddings* in its entirety, but most of us were familiar with the title poem, 'An Arundel Tomb', and 'MCMXIV'.[3] Enthusiastic teachers in tweeds or corduroy would mutter something about the Movement, or recall heady days in wartime Oxford, or simply point out that the great man was one of us - native of Coventry, and distinguished old boy of King Henry VIII School. For some reason, learning that Larkin was a librarian and not a full-time man of letters only added to his appeal, suggesting an attractive eccentricity in a way that Eliot's alter ego as banker and publisher never did. Having read so little of his work, it never crossed our minds for a moment that Larkin's schoolboy memories were no more than luke-warm, and that his feelings towards the city were at best mixed - that in fact he was anything but a fully paid-up 'Old Coventrian'.[4]

Early in 1970 I commenced work as a museum assistant, and even after going to university would return to my humble post every vacation. The then Director of the Herbert Art Gallery appeared a remote and austere figure who rarely emerged from his office other than to appease the more cost-conscious councillors on the Recreation Committee.[5] John Hewitt, bespectacled, white-haired, and with trim goatee beard, had a gravitas and air of professorial authority which left me in awe of him, even though I had no idea he was one of Ireland's premier poets - perhaps in a pre-Heaney era *the* premier poet. The Director appeared to leave running the gallery to his two young assistant curators. I now know he was devoting much of his time to writing about the resurgent 'Troubles', and preparing for retirement in

Belfast. Hewitt and his wife Roberta finally left Coventry in 1972, but three years earlier they had acquired a house back home and commenced a gradual re-engagement in the cultural life of the province. In the winter of 1970 Hewitt joined John Montague in a series of poetry readings across Northern Ireland which quietly announced he would soon be back for good. Not that he had ever really been away, as each year since their departure in 1957 the Hewitts had visited Ireland, and for the first eight years had retained their cottage at Cushendall. Thus, during only three of the fifteen years 'on the mainland' - were John and Roberta not resident in Antrim or 'hill-hooped Belfast'.

Given Hewitt's growing preoccupation with events at home, as reflected in early 1970s collections such as *Ulster Reckoning* and *Out Of My Time*, and his obvious influence upon a later-generation of Northern Ireland poets, the truth is that he had bade farewell to Coventry long before he finally left.[6] Seemingly eager to leave, Hewitt's over-riding preoccupation with poetry and polemics was further fuelled by a growing unease over the paths pursued by modern art during the previous decade. His 1969 'Variations on a Theme', a lighthearted mixture of prurience and Puritanism prompted by musings on the miniskirt and worthy of James Hogg, is explicit - in section 6 - that abstraction has its boundaries. The unashamedly non-metropolitan collector and critic, who 'never braved the oceans' of 'Panofsky, Gombrich, Berenson' but 'safe in shallow rock-pool waded', clearly had little time for pop art, or indeed any other fashion of the day:

> I'm not the only one who wants
> the popping of each non-event,
> and hopes it drops where Dada went.[7]

Doubtless Larkin would have said 'Amen' to that. Yet it is hard to envisage the two men agreeing on very much else, other than the importance of Auden in influencing their early work. Larkin for example would have been delighted that the Conservatives finally controlled the city council in Coventry, whereas for Hewitt this was almost certainly another reason why it was time to go. No doubt there was mutual agreement on the stifling atmosphere of postwar Belfast: in the early 1950s the assistant director of the city's museum and art gallery very occasionally invited Queen's colourful English librarian home for tea, Bushmills, and gossip.[8] Of course, simply by virtue of both being poets Hewitt and Larkin had plenty in common, not least their mutual suspicion of academics prying into their public let alone their private lives.[9] But the two men clearly felt very differently about their respective native and adopted city; and it is their contrasting perceptions of Coventry at a crucial period in its history with which this essay is concerned. As one born and raised in the city, attending the same school as Larkin, and working alongside Hewitt, albeit briefly, dare I offer a fresh insight into two men who while still alive enjoyed, in their respective countries, that rare combination of popular appreciation and critical acclaim?

The popular assumption is that Larkin cut loose from Coventry in the autumn of 1940 when he went up to Oxford, and that thereafter he was clearly indifferent towards 'home'. He never railed against narrow provincialism (living literally at the end of the line, and being the man he was, this was scarcely an option). Yet he rarely displayed anything more than polite interest in a city which was to experience profound changes throughout the remaining 45 years of his life. Evidence to support this view naturally includes 'I Remember, I Remember', but also John Kemp's cathartic visit to the blitzed Huddlesford in *Jill* (again the train journey marks a break with the past), and Larkin's remark to an interviewer in 1965 that his biography could easily begin when he was 21.[10] There are of course plenty more direct and indirect references to support this view of Larkin tacitly disassociating himself from the place of his birth, and no doubt Jake Balokowsky has them readily available on his database. Larkin's real-life biographer encourages the popular view of 1940 as a watershed year but, to be fair, Andrew Motion focuses upon the family and not the community, while also emphasising a clean break with schoolboy poesy.[11]

Clearly it would be absurd to advance a revisionist view of Larkin as a lifelong 'Coventry kid' skillfully camouflaging wistful nostalgia. In 1964 he confided to a friend that 'There is not much to be proud of in being English, and one can assume a similarly dismissive view of civic pride. He had no filial ties, and scant interest in news from either Highfield or Coundon Road - this was a man with better things to do at teatime on a Saturday.[12] Thus, it would take a remarkable re-reading of Larkin's published work to depict him as a writer firmly rooted in the centre of England, and forever toiling in the long shadow of the three spires. On the other hand, to assume that Coventry is of little relevance to any understanding of Larkin's life and work is to ignore the friendships he retained from schooldays, and the extent to which mention of the city occurs in both his published work and his private correspondence. Larkin will forever be associated with Hull, and rightly so, but the journey from Parkside to Humberside was by no means one-way.[13]

Conversely, Hewitt should not be seen as an Ulsterman first and last. Like Larkin, his affection for Coventry scarcely attracts the attention it deserves: the Detroit of the Midlands can never appear as enticing as the Glens of Antrim, nor its politics as exciting as those of Belfast. Yet, contrary to the impression given in the introduction to his collected poems, Hewitt wrote a good deal about and indeed *for* Coventry.[14] If Larkin's references were all too often oblique, Hewitt's fascination with a city rebuilding and rediscovering itself after the trauma of war was overt and overwhelming, particularly in the late 1950s when enthusiasm for creating a genuine people's gallery had yet to wane.

During his lifetime Hewitt did little to discourage the belief that in 1952-3 he was a victim of Unionist bigotry and reaction in not being promoted to Director of Belfast Museum and Art Gallery.[15] Indeed, he actively promoted an image of himself as a man of the left, scornful of sectarianism and Unionist hegemony, forced to pursue both his career and his ideals in a more congenial environment across the water. Only when faced with his imminent return home did he first feel uneasy about being seen as a victim, let alone a martyr. Once back in the bosom of the Belfast literary establishment, the by now grand old man of letters conceded that leaving for a new life among the 'civilised people' of the West Midlands was the best thing that could have happened to him.[16] Nevertheless, admirers of Hewitt, radical and self-proclaimed 'regionalist', perpetuate the myth that he and his wife were forced into exile for espousing views which a generation later would bring the Unionist monolith to its knees.[17] Roy McFadden, close friend and fellow poet, poured scorn on this interpretation of events three years after Hewitt's death. More recently, Richard Kirkland, and in particular Sarah Ferris, have challenged the view of Edna Longley, Declan Kiberd and others that the champion of 'open and open ended' regionalism was 'made a political scapegoat for his socialist and literary allegiances', thus stifling forever a liberal, non-sectarian alternative vision to the Stormont status quo.[18]

Hewitt, his career ambitions thwarted, nevertheless retained complete control over the municipal art collection. Aggrieved and disillusioned, he and Roberta were to remain in Belfast a further four years before decamping to Coventry. As early as September 1957 Hewitt was waxing lyrical in the *Belfast Telegraph* about life in 'this remarkable city ... of surprises and contrasts'. In a scarcely veiled message to the burghers of Belfast that he had landed on his feet, Hewitt delivered his paean of praise to a 'triumph of municipal planning' and urban renewal - a seamless harmonising of past and present, secular and spiritual, privilege and opportunity, country and city. The denizens of east or west Belfast must have found such a model of cross-community cooperation and civic pride scarcely credible. But then most citizens of Coventry would have expressed surprise, to put it mildly, at learning of their involvement in, 'the adventure of social democracy and the Welfare State, of British urban civilisation in the second half of this century, the blue print of the future society'. Learning that Britain's first traffic-free precinct was 'like a piazza in Venice', and on Saturday mornings a 'country fair', would have been hard enough to swallow, let alone being challenged to create a 'true community, not out of work or habitation merely but of the good, the abundant life'.[19]

It is easy to sneer, and to be fair Hewitt rightly identified a dangerous over-dependence upon the motor industry, let alone the urgent need to assimilate freshly established Asian and Caribbean communities. Historians such as Tony Mason and most notably Nick Tiratsoo have in recent years identified serious social tensions already evident in Coventry by the time Hewitt arrived. It's been pointed out that, for all the party's success in supervising the city's reconstruction, Labour's power base in the 1950s was surprisingly fragile.[20] Given that, under the formidable dual leadership of George Hodgkinson and Sidney Stringer, Labour had ruled since 1937, it was understandable that Hewitt took control of a half-constructed Herbert Art Gallery confident that Coventry was a bastion of social democracy.[21] The party was to cling on to power for another decade, but the 1960s confirmed its 'inability to communicate with those groups at the centre of social change'.[22] For all its naivety, Hewitt's letter home demonstrates his initial faith in Coventry as a social experiment: an urban industrial *community* reconciling the needs and pressures of living in an advanced industrial society with those 'ideas for a just organisation of human needs and fulfillments' espoused by an early and enduring influence, William Morris.[23]

The Herbert Art Gallery and Museum, c.1960

Morris's romantic verse may have influenced Hewitt's early poetry, but his 1880s lectures on art and revolution left a more lasting impression. Hewitt embraced the idealism of *News From Nowhere*, fusing in later life the socialist utopianism of Morris's workshop - of truly purposeful labour - with the urban vision of Patrick Geddes, and more especially, of Lewis Mumford.[24] Writing from Coventry in 1957, Hewitt celebrated a city whose wealth was rooted in a craftsmanship unblighted by the darker side of the Industrial Revolution, and where skill and beauty could still be appreciated: the new cathedral offered a unique fusion of applied art and 'the technical resources of this age', with evangelical outposts rooted on new estates 'not imitation-this or revival-that, but made of the materials and in the style of this century'.[25] Nine years later, in a short but revealing history of Coventry, Hewitt devoted almost as much space to local decoration of Basil Spence's three 'utility churches' as to the impact of Epstein, Sutherland and Piper on 'the premier place of pilgrimage for an anxious, searching, hoping generation'.[26]

Not surprisingly, Hewitt's first formal proposals for assembling and exhibiting a permanent art collection embraced a gallery monitoring urban regeneration in Coventry, including construction of the cathedral. His foremost aim was to establish a unique assembly of contemporary work - 'British Life and Landscape' - intended to reflect everyday life and thus attract, 'the factory worker and his family whose thoughts will seldom if ever be caught up in the complicated tangle of aesthetic theory'. This was no green light for socialist realism, despite a deliberate policy to exclude 'abstract and non-representational work', merely confirmation of Morris's insistence on rendering all facets of artistic endeavour available *and accessible* to all. It was also a blueprint for selling modern art to a sceptical council.[27]

Coventrians had always known how to enjoy themselves, but the general consensus by 1945 was that the city was a cultural desert. Thus, a postwar alliance of industrial grandees such as Sir Alfred Herbert and Lord Rootes, council power-brokers and veteran autodidacts like George Hodgkinson, and a culture-starved professional middle class, ensured the presence of the visual and performing arts at the heart of urban regeneration. To appease the less high-minded, provision was made for a multi-floor dance hall - the Locarno - in the centre of the Precinct. From its opening in 1958 the Belgrade Theatre pioneered community, youth, and schools-based work, as well as premiering challenging new plays. Yet Bryan Bailey, the Belgrade's first Director, always ensured that a popular and familiar repertory would appease the more culturally-challenged burghers of the city.[28] Hewitt appears to have found a similar formula for reconciling a personal vision and a populist appeal. Morris, the definitive philanthropic entrepreneur, would surely have endorsed Hewitt's later description of his 'diapered-brick' home as a:

> ... token of our mixed economy, of private benevolence and public enterprise, the Museum with its cars and ribbons and antiquities, the Art Gallery with the challenge of its changing exhibitions.[29]

Hewitt's 1966 celebratory essay, commissioned by the council's public relations department to preface a photographic record of a city basking in the warm glow of postwar prosperity, is well researched, beautifully written, and cleverly constructed (narrative history complemented by a tourist-friendly 'easy-paced stroll' around 'this complicated community'). Larkin appears on the first page, the most neutral lines from 'I Remember, I Remember' ('... watching men with number-plates/Sprint down the platform to familiar gates'), juxtaposed with an earlier traveller's more favourable impression of the city: Tennyson's 1840 visit to the railway station inspired him to write 'Godiva'.[30] Unlike Tennyson, Larkin in 'I Remember, I Remember' is totally disorientated, finding no familiar landmarks (yet, as Hewitt proudly - and ironically? - announces, the 'strikingly-new' station did not open until 1962 - seven years after Larkin's poem first appeared in print):

> Things moved. I sat back, staring at my boots.
> "Was that", my friend smiled, "where you have your roots'?"
> No, only where my childhood was unspent,
> I wanted to retort, just where I started:[31]

Larkin's detachment and disappointment - his inability to fix Coventry in place and time - is further compounded by a counterfactual map of childhood memories and images. We must consider again mention of '... that splendid family/I never ran to when I got depressed'; but for now contrast Larkin's irritation at even considering a necessity for roots in both place and past, with Hewitt's enthusiastic embrace of 'this changing, enduring city ... symbol for the undefeated determination of men of goodwill'.[32]

This was no transfer of allegiance - Hewitt never compromised his nonconformist Ulster roots. Nevertheless, in his early years of 'exile' Coventry matched up to his high expectations, its history running parallel with his own radical agenda, rooted as it was in the Putney Debates, 'English Jacobins' from Paine to Cobbett, Chartism, ethical socialism, and an early flirtation with dialectical materialism.[33] Morris, the Bible, *and* Marx all helped mould Hewitt's understanding of history. Certainly, his portrayal of life in late medieval and early modern Coventry suggests a recent re-reading of A.L. Morton, if not Christopher Hill. Similarly, Hewitt is unlikely to have let *The Making of the English Working Class* pass him by. Yet, whether or not he read Thompson, it is easy to understand Hewitt's enthusiasm: not only did the 'common people' foster Lollardy and shelter John Ball, but succeeding generations rebuffed a Royalist assault, *and* rang out

'Lillibulero' on the cathedral bells to welcome their Protestant heroes, first William of Orange and then the Governor of Londonderry. Nineteenth-century Coventry witnessed Cobbett contest its Commons seat, Joseph Squiers coin the phrase 'Christian Socialism', Feargus O'Connor rally a flagging Chartist cause, and the polymathic Charles Bray exhort a young Mary Ann Evans to exhort reform and defy convention.[34] No wonder 'the Planter in Hewitt could savour a good-humouredly romantic sense of homecoming' when he discovered the family name prominent in the city records (including the 'lavish menu' for Alderman John Hewitt's mayoral banquet in 1755). In the words of Frank Ormsby, his posthumous editor, 'the constants and continuities of Hewitt's philosophy had found a natural home'.[35]

Leading his reader around the centre and suburbs of contemporary Coventry, Hewitt develops at length the ideas and impressions encapsulated in his 1957 article for the *Belfast Telegraph*. Again the optimism - and the naivety - shine through. With the grim benefit of hindsight there is much black humour - Bell Green's 'bold shopping centre' was bleak, grey, and abandoned long before rioting broke out in the summer of 1992, and who today lingers long in Hillfields admiring 'airy blocks of bright flats ... justice being done and being seen to have been done'? To be fair, Hewitt could scarcely have anticipated the full impact of deindustrialisation, not least upon those 'great estates and the other municipal and housing deltas in the suburban segments'. On the other hand, had he not assumed only Labour could be synonymous with effective planning and design, he might perhaps have anticipated the ruling party's imminent demise. He had witnessed enough 'ingrown parochialism' at home not to welcome a destabilising of the municipal status quo.[36] Yet is it not understandable that a man so indebted to the idealism of Morris *and* to the social democratic values of 1945 might fear dealing with an incoming Tory administration:

The strength of purpose which this great undertaking evinces has been obviously informed and directed by a bold social idealism. It is clearly this which has given emphasis to such concepts as the comprehensive principle in education, the insistence on contemporary design in structure and lay-out, the use of the most up-to-date methods in construction; but above all, to a watchful awareness of human needs and aspirations, for childhood, maturity and age. For, while the working out of these ideals in practical form has been in the hands of professionals and experts, the drive has come from the elected representatives of the ordinary people.[37]

Only two years later Hewitt was voicing a suspicion that the art gallery and museum had been built largely to satisfy aldermanic egos: 'Devotion to the arts among politicians is rare, but they do feel that they should be saluted. In my view a gallery exists to make men proud of being men'. The publication in August 1968 of Hewitt's first collected poems had prompted an interview and a review in the local evening paper. Hewitt was surely right to insist that, 'In Coventry writers are invisible men'. Yet, aged 60 and with high hopes of belated recognition as a major force in contemporary Irish verse, 'I can now afford to assume the posture of a poet. ... [and] I never want to lose the capacity for rage and compassion'.[38] However, the 1968 collection attracted remarkably little critical attention beyond Belfast: the disappointed, increasingly detached civic official soldiered on for a further four years, his rage and compassion fuelled by 'each convulsion of that fevered state', that 'island, maimed by history/and creed-infected'.[39]

Hewitt claimed culture shock upon his arrival in England cost him a year of silence, and he does appear to have written no poetry prior to his 'Lines on the Opening of the Belgrade Theatre' in February 1958.[40] Ever eager in his early days to refute the notion that, 'this city breeds prosaic men,/ without tradition, sceptic of the arts', Hewitt not for the last time assumed the post of *ex officio* poet laureate, this role climaxing in a glorious piece of doggerel to mark the opening of the Whitefriars monastery as a museum in May 1970.[41] Hewitt was publicly engaged in the life of the city, and - contrary to popular assumption - privately too. By comparison with Larkin, Hewitt was a prolific poet (and of course by no means as ruthless in discarding inferior work). His immediate circumstances and surroundings were a natural inspiration, witness the number of poems with a local theme in *Out of My Time*. The Warwickshire countryside may be contrasted with 'another country', but it has its own Protestant martyrs, Civil War heritage, and 'labouring folk/ humble, enduring', all duly and dutifully acknowledged.[42] Often oblique references to Coventry occur unexpectedly, and even when the subject is Ireland the reader is sharply reminded that this is a view from a distance.

Perhaps Hewitt's first major poem after breaking his silence, the much anthologised 'An Irishman in Coventry', casts too long a shadow over his subsequent work. Critical attention focuses upon the second half of the poem, with the writer engulfed by a tide of mixed emotions when suddenly surrounded by fellow countrymen - despair at their collective failure to put 'eight hundred years' disaster firmly in the past, elation at this brief relief from the still unfamiliar, and keen but quiet anticipation of eventual return. Yet this is a refugee still exuberant at arriving in an 'eager city', tolerant, aggressively modern, visionary, and free from:

> ... all that flaws the glory and the grace
> which ribbons through the sick, guilt-clotted legend
> of my creed-haunted, godforsaken race.[43]

This is as much a poem of escape as of exile, powerfully expressing the same cultural and ideological certainties which rendered Hewitt's 1957 article and his 1966 essay so persuasive, and yet with hindsight so sad. In an interview to accompany the *Standard*'s 1959 publication of 'An Irishman in Coventry' he confirmed the appeal of a city which, on his arrival from a 'conservative and provincial setting', he found delightfully open-minded and cosmopolitan. Nine years later he was still saying the same thing: unlike Ulster, 'People are so casual'.[44]

For planter Hewitt prosperous, parliamentary Coventry was not so alien a city, as he readily acknowledged in one of his finest poems, 'The Search'. And yet:

> It is a hard responsibility to be a stranger;
> to hear your speech sounding at odds with your neighbours';
> holding your tongue from quick comparisons;
> remembering that you are a guest in the house.[45]

For all the unexpected familiarity and common [Protestant] heritage, 'this is not your abiding place'.[46] Reference to 'the western island' hints at the mode adopted in some of Hewitt's most effective commentaries on Ulster's summer of '69.

The poems that appeared in the booklet *An Ulster Reckoning* were written in the immediate aftermath of the sectarian riots of August 1969, the month British troops were first deployed on the streets of Derry and Belfast.   'The Coasters' is a powerful indictment of a complacent Protestant bourgeoisie for too long salving its liberal conscience with token gestures across the sectarian divide.[47]   Like Tom Paulin a decade later, albeit with less subtlety, Hewitt deploys classical allusions and parallels.   Thus, Ulster becomes an Hellenic hotspot, its discredited oligarchy belatedly appeasing mistrusted Thebans long settled within the city walls: suspicious of compromise, the mob smell blood.   Allegorizing Thucydides, which in 'Parallels Never Meet' Hewitt concedes is a fruitless artifice ("Reality is a of a coarser texture"), nevertheless echoes an earlier poem, 'The Colony', published in 1953.[48]   Here Ulster becomes a wild outpost at the edge of the empire tamed by Caesar's legions and an expatriate 'rabble' of land-hungry *cives*, camp-followers, and clerks, their children and grandchildren ever fearful of a wrathful and revenging dispossessed:

Alone, I have a harder row to hoe:
I think these natives human, think their code,
though strange to us, and farther from the truth,
only a little so - to be redeemed
if they themselves rise up against the spells
and fears their celibates surround them with.[49]

Yet, after centuries of cultivating and adapting to a once harsh and barren land, now 'we would be strangers in the Capitol;/this is our country also; and we shall not be outcast on the world'.[50]

Hewitt returned to the colonial experience in 1971, in 'The Roman Fort'.   The Herbert Art Gallery and Museum's major archaeological project in the 1960s was the excavation and partial reconstruction of the Lunt Fort at Baginton, a village just within the city boundaries, adjacent to the then aspiring 'Coventry Airport'. Field archaeologist Brian Hobley made his name digging the Lunt, enabling him to move on to more ambitious projects at the Museum of London. Hobley persuaded the Royal Engineers to help reconstruct the wooden gateway to the fort, with latter-day legionaries using replica tools and techniques:

> Like the Romans also, they may shortly receive
> further experience in a beleaguered colony,
> for, daily, public prints and moving pictures
> bring evidence of the stubborn barbarians.[51]

Admittedly, engineers rarely find themselves 'Shielded, vague soldiers, visored, crouch alert', but Hewitt makes his point neatly and emphatically.[52] It is a rare occasion when his preoccupations back home and at work are at one; and the poem is arguably as effective and polemical as its much longer, laboured, and ever so slightly priggish antecedent, however laudable 'The Colony's' lesson of understanding and reconciliation.

Belfast may have been 'irredeemably home', and the Glens of Antrim more than a mere R and R refuge from the exposure of the municipal frontline, but Coventry clearly meant far more to Hewitt than has previously been appreciated. There appears to be an orthodoxy of exile, of Hewitt - in Heaney's words - setting 'his lonely present against a rooted past, in terms of a lost community and family'. Hewitt's final editor sees the Coventry poems reflecting, 'the exile's yearning to adapt and an echo of loss that is more than mere nostalgia'.[53] Well yes, but is there not a danger of writing off fifteen years of Hewitt's life, a time when much of his most important work was being produced, as being a mere transitory phase? Am I being unfair and over sensitive in interpreting most critical commentary as, 'In body he was in the West Midlands for ten months of the year, but in spirit he was *always* back here with us'? The Ulster identity is clearly paramount, and yet what is fascinating about John Hewitt is the degree to which in a quiet unfussy way he really did adopt his adopted city. Here is a familiar story of the outsider cultivating a much greater civic pride and a far deeper knowledge of the locale than most of the natives. The irony is that, beyond his immediate circle of colleagues, councillors, and confidants, precious few were aware of Hewitt's efforts to promote the virtues of Coventry *redux*; nor indeed of his qualifications to be a poet wholly appropriate to the 'Phoenix city', fuelled as he was by an intensely personal, secular vision of social justice, community/regional values, and *citizenship* ('... these were the King's horses going about the King's business, never mine.').[54]

Like Hewitt, Larkin was at heart an unequivocally Protestant writer, but of a largely formal Anglican mode far removed from

Presbyterian dissent and respectable sedition. Unlike Hewitt, whose values and politics drew heavily on those of his father, Larkin could never recall his parents with that same mixture of awe and affection.[55] Andrew Motion explored at length the young Philip's uneasy relationship with Sydney and Eva Larkin, his hero seeing himself by the age of eighteen, 'as someone both dependent upon and dragged down from his whining mother and autocratic father'.[56] Not only is Larkin seen as escaping in 1940 from what some today would see as a disturbingly dysfunctional family, but his insistence to Kingsley Amis that growing up in Coventry was singularly uneventful is tacitly endorsed. Larkin of course always encouraged this impression, maintaining that life behind the baize curtains at Manor Road was 'very normal'. Any hint that this might not be the case, such as the suggestion that Sydney was a member of the pro-Nazi, pro-Appeasement organisation The Link, was peremptorily dealt with.[57] Slightly in awe of the supremely confident young Amis, Larkin may have dismissed his upbringing in a sentence; but two holidays in Germany suggests that, by comparison with most Midland schoolboys in the late 1930s, life was anything but uneventful.

'As for school, I was an unsuccessful schoolboy', and yet even before his death the more assiduous student of Larkin would have viewed such a statement with some scepticism: in *Larkin At Sixty* journalist and publisher Noel Hughes questioned his old school-friend's unhappy recollection of life at King Henry VIII, offering a bland if nevertheless revealing insight into young Philip's extra-curricular activities.[58] One-time artist Jim Sutton's posthumous essay on the adolescent Larkin has far more resonance and *joi de vivre*, particularly regarding the role of jazz in his fellow sixthformer's rite of passage.[59] Even before Motion's biography appeared it was clear from *Collected Poems* that Larkin had written literally volumes of poetry while still at school.[60] More importantly, for all the heavy debt to Keats, and by 1939 to Eliot and Auden, Larkin's early verse is fresh, evocative, and - with the benefit of hindsight - signals what is to come.

The influence of Auden is most obvious in 'Last Will and Testament', drafted with Noel Hughes in Larkin's final term at King Henry VIII. The model is Auden and Louis Macneice's 'Their Last Will and Testament' in *Letters From Iceland*, a rambling, shambling, slightly surreal, and just occasionally very funny series of private jokes and witty aperçus rightly overshadowed by the same volume's more muscular 'Letter to Lord Byron'.[61] *Letters From Iceland*, ostensibly despatches from beyond the Arctic Circle, provides today's reader with a shrewd and often cruel commentary upon prewar England. Larkin would surely have noted Auden's affectionate acknowledgements of his Midlands roots scattered throughout the book:

> It's the most lovely country that I know;
> Clearer than Scafell Pike, my heart has stamped on
> The view from Birmingham to Wolverhampton.[62]

Appropriately, the next stanza recounts an early train journey through the Black Country. 'From a corridor' the infant Auden gawps at:

> Tramlines and slagheaps, pieces of machinery,
> That was, and still is, my ideal scenery.[63]

Larkin the sixth-former was already writing about railways (see 'Ultimatum' and 'Out in the lane I pause'), and appropriately King Henry VIII lies adjacent to a main line - the short journey to and from school entailed passing the station.[64] He and Hughes had already journeyed south once for interviews and entrance exams by the time their final bequest appeared in the *Coventrian*, the official school magazine they jointly edited and in which Larkin's verse first appeared in print. Motion rightly describes 'Last Will and Testament' as 'relentlessly light-hearted, yet unavoidably elegiac', and the poem clearly signals Larkin's bitter-sweet feelings towards his schooldays: uninspired by dingy science laboratories and dank pavilions, and trapped within a system of rigorous streaming and compulsory sport, he tread water until entry to the sixthform brought liberation and opportunity.[65] Although Larkin and Hughes range widely in wreaking gentle revenge for past indignities, the war is never far away, 'On this 26th of July 1940':

> Next (now the troops have taken their departure)
> With ever-grateful hearts we do assign
> To our French master, all the Maginot Line.[66]

Larkin's defeatism is well-documented, although a generous interpretation might be that much of the time he was simply out to shock. As late as April 1942, admittedly at a time when defeat in the Far East and North Africa had severely dented national morale, Larkin was insisting that, 'England *cannot* win this war; there's absolutely no *spirit* in the country [his italics]. I feel everything is in a mess ... '.[67] Personal experience from even before September 1939 had encouraged a feeling of organised chaos, whether it be his father's half-hearted involvement in municipal ARP planning, or King Henry VIII's ill-fated endeavour to maintain business as usual. During the 'Phoney War' Larkin observed the complement of staff and pupils slowly diminish, adding fire-watching and shelter supervision to his list of prefectorial duties.[68] Never a pillar of the school establishment, the unattractive prospect of participating in King Henry VIII's finest hour could only strengthen a great feeling of release when in July 1940 he crossed the Warwick Road railway bridge for the very last time. However, more than once that summer he must have speculated on whether the Germans would in fact get to Oxford before him. They did not, and arrival at St John's signalled a break - but by no means a clean break - with the past.

Introducing the 1964 edition of his first novel, Larkin emphasised how, although *Jill* is rooted firmly in the Michaelmas Term of 1940, it is only autobiographical in so far as it draws heavily upon general recollection rather than direct experience: John Kemp, the definitive naive working-class boy up at Oxford, is most definitely not Philip Larkin. Trawling the novel for obscure autobiographical references, which only someone familiar with Larkin's school and birthplace might recognise, proved a frustrating and rather pointless exercise (with the exception, as we shall see, of the climax of the book). Kemp and Whitbread are acutely aware of being grammar school boys, but ironically it transpires that Warner and his circle only attended a minor public school (yet, like Old Etonians, they play football, as it is the grammar schools which in practice forge the rugby tradition - Warner acts like a 'rugger bugger', but literally and metaphorically he is neither).[69] In 'Not the Place's Fault', Larkin confirmed that 'no pipe-lighting dominie' played a similar role to Joseph Crouch, although the latter's descent into mediocrity clearly reflects young Philip's view of his own teachers.[70] Mrs. Warner presumably owes something to Jim Sutton's mother, the schoolboy Larkin appreciating the 'natural hospitality' of a family prosperous, relaxed, and visibly at ease with one another. In other words, an atmosphere and environment wholly at odds with Sydney Larkin's understanding of domestic bliss.[71]

The one occasion when John Kemp comes near to being Philip Larkin is of course when he goes back to a now devastated Huddlesford ('What you mean a real air raid - like Coventry?').[72] There are significant differences in that Kemp travels by train and alone, whereas Larkin hitched home with Noel Hughes on Sunday, 17 November, forty-eight hours after Coventry had been subjected to what was up until then the most concentrated aerial bombardment of the war.[73]   Once in the city the two friends remained together, first searching for Larkin's family in the environs of Manor Road, and then bisecting the centre to secure news of Hughes's parents.   With a prearranged return lift, they were back in Oxford by early evening.[74] However, Larkin did draw directly upon this brief but traumatic visit when describing Kemp's attempt to cross the centre of Huddlesford and find out whether the family home is intact.   The Kemps live in 'King Edward Street - by the Stadium', and Larkin would have known King William Street, leading up to Highfield Road football ground, had, like so much of the Hillfields district, suffered severe damage.[75] Kemp's home seems very similar to terraced houses in Hillfields, although the back garden has more in common with 1 Manor Road. His dread as he approaches the front door matches that actually felt by Larkin if Hughes is to be believed.   Kemp finds a note giving an address in Preston, an experience more akin to that of Hughes, who learnt from a cousin his parents were safe, than to Larkin for whom reassurance came in the form of a belated telegram from his father. The description of a blitzed Huddlesford echoes so many accounts of Coventry on that desperate weekend of 16-17 November as a half-empty city came to terms with the scale of what had taken place. For Kemp, 'The town had been so familiar and so intimately wound into his boyhood that its destruction became fascinating.   Dozens of places he knew had been wrecked ... '.[76]   Motion has written of how profoundly unsettling the Blitz was upon Larkin, abruptly bringing home to him the realities of twentieth-century warfare, and destroying for ever the suburban stability which, for all the mockery, he still at this time needed.[77]

Nothing would ever be the same again, and indeed by June 1941 the Larkin family had left Coventry for good, Sydney commuting from Warwick for the last three years of his working life.   For John

Kemp his hurried trip to Huddlesford is a truly cathartic experience, as he himself recognises when safe and secure on the train heading back south.[78] In late 1940 Larkin himself traced this change of mood in 'New Year Poem', two stanzas of which capture the still, chilling atmosphere of shattered suburbia:

> These houses are deserted, felt over smashed windows,
> No milk on the step, a note pinned to the door
> Telling of departure: only shadows
> Move when in the day the sun is seen for an hour,
> Yet to me this decaying landscape has its uses:
> To make me remember, who am always inclined to forget,
> That there is always a changing at the root,
> And a real world in which time really passes.
>
> For even together, outside this shattered city
> And its obvious message, if we had lived in that peace
> Where the enormous years pass over lightly
> - Yes, even there, if I looked into your face
> Expecting a word or a laugh on the old conditions,
> It would not be a friend who met my eye,
> Only a stranger would smile and turn away,
> Not one of the two who first performed these actions.[79]

Contemplation of death and afterlife necessitates, ' ... The bells/That we used to await will not be rung this year', yet ' ... life will again move forward/Implicating us all; ... '. With 'the voice of the living' calling in chorus for an individual and collective reaffirmation of hope and love, the poem ends on an unusually positive note, at variance with the unbridled cynicism ever present in Larkin's letters at the time - a time when he was still, for all intents and purposes, in late adolescence, and surprisingly immature.[80]

For all the intermittent correspondence with Old Coventrians, and sporadic exchange of memories, Larkin was gone for good. Via Wellington, Leicester, and Belfast, he finally found a new home, and in many respects a new identity. Aging masters at King Henry VIII might have kept the flame alive, but for the rest of the nation - including most well-read residents of his native city - Larkin was synonymous with another community rebuilt from the ashes of the

Blitz, Hull. Coventry forgot about him, and he appeared to have forgotten about Coventry. Was Larkin privately flattered, or was he genuinely irritated, when in early 1978 the city council awarded him the newly instituted 'Coventry Award of Merit'? Although he conveyed the impression to Barbara Pym that the award ceremony was tacky, parochial, and a bit of a bore, Larkin found himself in distinguished company: a high profile former bishop, a pioneer of comprehensive schooling, and the general secretary of Britain's largest trade union.[81]

I suspect that, for all the curmudgeonly remarks about his fellow recipients, and having to take a day off work, Larkin was actually rather flattered. What better way to have one's ego massaged than to sit in civic splendour enjoying a good lunch, and have compliments showered upon you by the leader of a council which had employed your father for 25 years?[82] Many memories must have come sharply back into focus that day, even if the physical environment appeared so very different from that of his childhood - the Larkins' cheerless, gloomy abode had long since been bulldozed in the interest of rapid traffic flow, and the centre of the city wholly rebuilt. Only in the narrow streets behind the Council House, Sydney Larkin's second - or perhaps even first - home, were there remnants of the compact medieval community which had grown up around the cathedral and had survived remarkably intact until November 1940. Briefly, as he entered St Mary's Hall to receive his bauble, Larkin could recall passing along those same streets to visit his father or to plunder the central library.[83] But everything else had changed, just as he knew it had to after that symbolic return in the aftermath of the Blitz: the *Luftwaffe* wiped out the heart of the city, and in so doing conveniently wiped out uncomfortable childhood memories. The student Larkin had no time for nostalgia, and anyway, in his mind there was precious little to be nostalgic about. The adult Larkin had even less time for family sentiment and 'the good old school', hence his reluctance to gain a wider audience for 'Not the Place's Fault', a rare occasion on which he had let his guard drop.

Larkin's verse has a constant engagement with 'the past' - twentieth-century England's 'past', whatever the postmodernist historian may wish to define that as actually being - but not in terms of shallow wistfulness. 'I Remember, I Remember' is more concerned with the process of recollection than the actual memories: 'Coventry' as a geographical and social construct, as a particular place at a particular time, had gone - in the case of Larkin's most familiar landmarks, quite literally. A tarmaced, stressed concrete landscape of ring roads, precincts, and elevated walkways was both alien and anathema. Yet what Larkin walked away from, John Hewitt warmly embraced as a realisable vision of urban renewal. Hewitt, by the time he returned to Belfast for the last time in 1972, had become disillusioned. Yet the commitment to Coventry, and more specifically its people, had never wholly flagged, even after control of the council changed hands, and the endless round of finance meetings and committee briefings became ever more arduous. The poetry confirms this continuing fascination with a radical past and with a future where rampant consumerism can at least be tempered by genuine *community* values of tolerance and social justice. Thus Hewitt had an affection and a *concern* for postwar Coventry which the native son rarely displayed.

Larkin's qualified indifference contrasts sharply with Hewitt's fascination. But this should scarcely come as a surprise: Larkin left Coventry for Warwick/Oxford at the age of nineteen, while Hewitt spent his middle years at the heart of his adopted city's efforts to carve out for itself a new and distinctly contemporary identity and purpose. The 1960s were boom years, but signs of incipient decline were evident even before the end of the decade: like Larkin, Hewitt chose the right time to leave. Looking back across more than a quarter of a century it is equally clear that in 1957 Hewitt chose the right time at which to arrive. His public and private contribution to Coventry at a vital moment in postwar recovery was unique, but is still largely unrecognised - unlike, ironically, Larkin's identification with *his* adopted city. John Hewitt was first and foremost always an Ulsterman - and as such a key figure in modern Irish poetry - but for 15 years he lived and worked in the heart of England, often writing about distinctively English topics and themes: the Warwickshire of Joseph Arch, but also the Coventry of Dick Crossman. 'Regionalism' could cross the Irish Sea: John Hewitt was a poet of his times *and* of his place, wherever that may be.

6

AN OVAL BALL AND A BROKEN CITY
Coventry, its people, and its rugby team, part 1[1]

In England the 1993-4 rugby season saw the once-mighty Coventry club face up to life in Division Three of the then Courage Championship. For 'Cov' supporters over the age of 35 this was, in footballing terms, the equivalent of Manchester United facing up to a weekly diet of Aldershots and Peterboroughs. When the English leagues were first conceived, few questioned placing Coventry in the premier echelon. The city had always boasted a strong and skillful side, with its players dominating county and then club cup competitions in the 1960s and early 1970s. Coventry schools bred a unique blend of powerful forwards, halfbacks who could both kick and create, *and*, in an era that stretched from 1950s legends like Peter Jackson to David Duckham in the 1970s, some of the finest backs ever to don a Lions shirt.[2] Few clubs could boast so many internationals. Yet, as early as the mid-1970s, there were signs that the glory days were over, particularly when a misconceived policy of attracting to the Coundon Road stadium big names with no real love of club or city ultimately backfired. Ironically, today's team suffers from sides in the top division recruiting young local talent eager for international recognition. The decline of industrial towns mirroring the fall from grace of their football clubs is a familiar story; but Coventry is unique in that the glories and then the travails of its rugby team tell us much about the changing fortunes of its citizens over the past forty years. At a time in the early 1990s when the city became synonymous with an Iraqi-owned relic of a once-great machine-tool industry, the rise and fall of Coventry RFC offered an unusual insight into how a community rooted in civic pride and a manufacturing tradition has been brought to its knees.[3]

Although the 1991 World Cup brought English rugby a new audience of armchair followers for whom Guscott was as familiar as Gazza, the game retained – and still retains - a doggedly middle-class image.[4] Perhaps it was the location of modern rugby's most successful clubs; but for every Bath and Harlequins there was a Leicester and an Orrell. At the very top it was no longer how you spoke and who you knew, but how you played, witness England's then championship-winning back row.[5] Indeed exceptional talent had invariably made it to the top, whatever their social background. Back in the Edwardian era rugby outside the south had rarely conformed to the popular misconception of an overwhelmingly middle-class pastime, on a par with tennis or golf. In its capacity to conform to an imposed 'gentlemen and players' persona, and yet in reality cut straight across conventional class divisions, rugby union in large parts of the Midlands and the West Country had much in common with the make up of colliery and village cricket. In the 'Heart of England' the game avoided being hijacked by the old boy network of the Rugby Football Union and its Scottish equivalent. Nor was its cohesion undermined as in the north by the 1895 split: the row over compensation for workers' loss of wages which led ultimately to the creation of the Northern League, from the 1920s better known as rugby league. As the penultimate essay explains, before the First World War Leicester and Coventry incurred the wrath of the RFU for illegal payments, but both were too far south to abandon the amateur code. Midlands rugby had more in common with the game as played and administered in the Borders and in south Wales than with the more 'gentlemanly' version that had evolved out of the public schools and established itself in the home counties. A major difference between the more remote Welsh and Scots sides, and most Midlands clubs, was that the latter faced stiff competition from modestly successful football teams. Unlike its Midlands rivals, in the west of England Gloucester's industrial and commercial expansion came too late to support professional football. The rugby club has always enjoyed undivided loyalty from its supporters and the same was true of the players so long as the game remained amateur. Gloucester - like its Munster equivalent, Limerick - is undoubtedly unique. Yet, in keeping a team at the top that champions the wider community's keen sense of regional identity, what some would regard as a rather dull, over-grown market town exudes a spirit of survival that contrasts sharply with the Coventry experience.

Although a manufacturing centre, Coventry prior to the First World War was not that dissimilar to Gloucester. The city had not experienced the same intensity of suburban expansion by then synonymous with industrial growth and prosperity. The new industries, notably in transport and man-made fibres, were rooted firmly in the trades, skills, and factories that had transformed a medieval town into a model of Victorian ingenuity, entrepreneurialism, and industriousness. Coventry enjoyed an unusual concentration of both male and female skilled workers. The presence of an adaptable workforce of trained fitters, mechanics, lathe-operators, and the like facilitated product development *and* product diversification; hence the ease with which local companies improvised during the two world wars. Until the creation of the 'shadow factories' in the late 1930s, Coventry experienced only modest peripheral development. Despite a steady rise in population, partially the consequence of Celtic immigration as the local economy emerged early from the Depression, the city remained surprisingly close-knit. Individual areas acquired their own identities, but work and play still focused strongly on the city centre. Coventry people cultivated the belief that everyone still knew everybody else's business. The city's sportsmen, its eccentric personalities, and above all the evening paper, all acted as common points of reference. Individual families were known either for their sporting prowess, or for their notoriety. All families were proud of their city, and of their own particular localities. Factory development and the workers' homes that came in its wake tended to be on the northern side of the city; middle-class suburbs to the south. (As noted in the introduction, even today, the north-south divide seems to run through the middle of Warwickshire, with Nuneaton at one extreme and Leamington at the other.) Industry, amenities, and housing were all within walking or cycling distance of each other, and all roads led ultimately to Broadgate. It was possible, for example, to work the Saturday shift at the Humber, nip home for a late dinner, and get to Highfield Road in time for the 3.15 kick-off without having travelled more than two or three miles.[6]

The pride of my parents, and of earlier generations, soon becomes evident when they recall life in Coventry before and immediately after the Second World War. Nostalgia is invariably laced with bitterness over the disappearance of the environment in which they grew up. In their view, the destruction of 'our city' was not the sole responsibility of the *Luftwaffe*, nor the postwar idealists who made the Precinct and the new cathedral realities; rather, a later generation of planners and social engineers who by the mid-1960s were busy creating a new urban landscape in which car finally triumphed over community. The consumer product that made a reconstructed Coventry prosperous ultimately proved the instrument of its downfall. Thirty years after the Blitz a circular freeway completed the divorce of Broadgate and its immediate environs from the rest of the city. Swathes of Victorian terraces were cut down to make way for flyovers. Former residents, many elderly, found themselves in blocks of flats, or obliged to decamp to bleak new council estates bearing little resemblance to the pioneering projects of the 1930s and early 1950s. On the edge of what by 1970 was a conurbation little different from any other messy urban sprawl was poorly-designed and equally poorly-built high-rise accommodation, the surrounding estates wracked by social deprivation and already labelled 'problem areas'. What was surprising about the 1992 riots on the Bell Green and Wood End estates was that they had not occurred years earlier.

The transport consultants and tower-block architects were all too often public sector professionals with no deep-rooted attachment to the city they were busy redesigning. Their 'expertise' too often over-rode local objections, even when articulated by elected representatives. Similarly, the directors and managers determining the future of Coventry's factories were less and less likely to have been born locally. Older managers, having made their way up from the shopfloor, and held on to their jobs when companies like Armstrong Whitworth merged with large conglomerates, gradually made way for graduate engineers and fast-stream executives who had little in common with their workforce. Industrial grandees like Lord Rootes, Jaguar's Sir William Lyons, and Standard's Sir John Black, all of whom as we have seen pioneered the provision of sports facilities for their employees, were by 1970 either dead or retired. London-based executives had replaced the city's one-time paternalist, albeit authoritarian, benefactors.

The same year, the political career of Coventry's most famous member of parliament and cabinet minister, Richard Crossman, for all intents and purposes ended. The defeat of the Wilson government, and the Tories' control of the council after 1967, marked the end of an era for Labour. The local party had rebuilt Coventry after the war, riding on the back of manufacturing industry's seemingly inexorable growth; and in the process tightening the party's grip on at least two of the three parliamentary seats. MPs like Crossman and writer Maurice Edelman notwithstanding, Labour in Coventry was a genuinely working-class movement, within which women were offered an opportunity to provide leadership. Labour's early success arose out of the party's painful post-1931 rehabilitation, and was consolidated by its role during the Blitz. Having lost power after thirty years, the original party machine began breaking up; the victim of age, complacency, and the increasingly vocal presence of younger, more militant elements disillusioned by the results of Wilson's six years in power. Labour councillors could no longer be guaranteed to be 'Coventry kids'. Family hierarchies were breaking down, with the next generation either apolitical or away. By representing old and new ethnic arrivals, most of whom viewed ageing councillors' nostalgia as an excuse for inertia, the new activists represented a disruptive but at the same time potentially positive force.

Clearly the city's old order was breaking up, and not even the rugby club was aloof from change. Coventry's success had been attributable to a genuine rugby culture fostered, not simply in the two oldest grammar schools, but also in one-time elementary schools such as Barkers Butts and Frederick Birds where sports-mad staff devoted hours of their spare time to fostering young working-class talent. These teachers were often Welsh, reflecting the impact that migration from the Valleys in the 1930s had on Coventry's politics, education, and sporting prowess. The old boys clubs, and the other junior sides in and around the city, constituted a de facto youth programme given Cov's longstanding - and ultimately fatal - reluctance to establish a colts side at Coundon Road. So long as league football either appeared unglamorous or simply fostered an impossible dream, rugby and cricket could rule supreme; a predominance that survived until the arrival of comprehensives and schools soccer at the end of the 1950s. Unlike the London clubs, Coventry brought together players from a diversity of backgrounds, the bar and the bath proving a great social leveller. Teams embraced solicitors, greengrocery wholesalers, teachers, engineers, bank clerks, labourers, and anyone else with the skill and strength, if in those days not always the fitness, to play senior rugby. In a pre-transfer era, players were loyal to their club, *and* to their city. Individual contributions to public life often went far beyond sport, particularly for the more affluent ex-grammar school players. Bablake and King Henry VIII schools' wealthier old boys formed the heart of the city's commercial and professional elite. Although they were often prominent in the local Conservative Party, many were not. Privilege and opportunity meant they had got a lot out of Coventry, but to be fair they had put a lot back in. Players from ostensibly humbler backgrounds found that representative, especially international, rugby brought in its wake better job prospects and social advancement. Thus, the rugby club became a microcosm of the meritocratic society 1950s and 1960s Britain strived for but never attained.

Yet as early as 1970 Coundon Road was already losing its air of invincibility. Gates historically had never been that high, and on the other side of town a hard core of loyal supporters had followed the football club through thick and thin. The 1966 World Cup, and the local side's success in progressing from the Fourth to the First Division, had finally made soccer in Coventry attractive. Jimmy Hill, today a familiar face on TV, but in 1961 a combative leader of the Professional Footballers Association, had been forced to quit the game through injury. He took up management and was a spectacular success, relaunching Coventry as the 'Sky Blues', a club that promised glamour and razzamatazz off the pitch and success on it. By 1967, the year Hill and his heroes entered the top flight, even the reserve games at Highfield Road were attracting gates inconceivable at any regular rugby fixture. Although Warwickshire continued to win rugby's distinctly unglamorous county championship, Coventry had no league or cup triumphs to underpin the club's reputation, and thereby attract fresh support. Local derbies with Mosely or Leicester, and 'grudge matches' with Gloucester or the Welsh sides, were no substitute for the excitement of dominating a division or lifting a trophy at Twickenham. Instead, reflected glory came from the magic of Rod Webb, Peter Preece, Geoff Evans, and above all David Duckham, on the rare occasions when their England colleagues remembered a rugby team has fifteen and not ten players. Cruelly, Duckham had to go to the other side of the world with the Lions in order to demonstrate what he did on his home ground every week.[7]

David Duckham, Coventry, Warwickshire, England,
and British & Irish Lions

In reality, most rugby fans only ever appreciated the city's finest ambassador courtesy of the BBC's international coverage. As well as *Grandstand* on TV or watching the Sky Blues, Saturday afternoons now offered a range of activities, from shopping expeditions to DIY in the new owner-occupier estates eating away at Warwickshire's green belt. But the wealth that the motor car had brought to Coventry also had a downside: the city's over-dependence on an industry inefficient and reluctant to reinvest. Firms such as Rootes were, when seen in the context of the global automobile industry, dangerously exposed, with any hope of harmonious industrial relations thwarted by poor management and tunnel-visioned shop stewards. Coventry had already begun to see the loss of its most priceless asset: the reservoir of skilled engineering workers that had been built up throughout the century, and had survived a depression and two world wars. As signalled in the first chapter, an early indication of this was Hawker Siddeley's closure of the former Armstrong Whitworth's production and development plants, leaving only an aircraft servicing operation in the Leicestershire countryside. In 1982 the remnants of a once highly-skilled workforce, still bound together by company loyalty, family ties, and a love of aeroplanes, were thanked by the Prime Minister for their endeavours during the Falklands war. Twelve months on, all those men and women were out of a job.

Although Mrs. Thatcher accelerated the process of deindustrialisation, even at the height of its prosperity Coventry was already witnessing the demise of manufacturing industry - of *making* and not merely assembling a finished product. The car plants' postwar tolerance of high unit costs in the absence of major import penetration encouraged a deskilling of those assembly workers who had opted for high wages and regular overtime rather than seeking employment in what was already a shrinking engineering sector. Machine tool companies, most notably Alfred Herbert, experienced a loss of skilled labour to the assembly line, and a dearth of major contracts sufficient to fund attractive wage levels *and* reinvestment in state-of-the art equipment. The obsolescence of British machine tool manufacturing had been exposed by the dependence upon American lathes during the war, and by West Germany's export success afterwards. In the wake of a successful onslaught upon an equally out-dated and obsolescent motorcycle industry, came a hi-tech Japanese challenge to the machine tool makers. By the 1980s the industry was all but dead in the west Midlands, and by definition the country as a whole. 'Serving your time' at an Alfred Herbert or a Bristol Siddeley was for too many young men in this apparently booming city no longer a priority - whatever your dad or granddad advised you to the contrary. Jobs at the end of the 1960s were still plentiful and relatively well-paid, and the cost of enjoying yourself invariably more than any apprenticeship brought in. Ironically, the problem of filling vacant apprenticeships never arose as the numbers available were declining in inverse proportion to the rise in the number of suitably qualified school-leavers.

After 1970 it was downhill all the way. Successive reorganisations, rationalization, restructuring, and retrenchment left volume car producers like Peugeot leaner and more efficient, but at what human cost? Seen from Detroit, Jaguar – Coventry's proudest marque - was at the time just another over-manned European division. At least these operations have survived: the list of local bankruptcies and resultant redundancies stretches back far beyond the collapse of a short-lived credit-based boom. If Britain was, as the Tories continued to insist,

experiencing 'unprecedented growth' in the mid-1980s then someone
had clearly forgotten to tell the west Midlands. Shops in Coventry were
boarded up for *all* not just some of the Thatcher-Major era.
Throughout these same years Coventry RFC had been going through
its own painful martyrdom, or, in the more brutal language of a long
discarded *Independent* match report, 'continued self-destruction'.

In 1994 the fate of the rugby club seemed synonymous with the
fate of the city; with no obvious light at the end of the tunnel. Clearly,
what happened to Coventry as a manufacturing centre has to be seen in
the context of wider developments, most notably the economic policies
pursued with such vigour after 1979. Nevertheless, the rugby club's
experience since the mid-1970s offered an insight into what is a
common occurrence elsewhere: the absence of urban regeneration in
terms of expertise and leadership, or to put it another way, the loss of
the best and the brightest. If the 1950s had brought relative affluence
then the 1960s offered, for some if not for all, enhanced educational
opportunities. Like any other city in Britain, Coventry in the second
half of the decade witnessed a dramatic rise in the number of middle-
class eighteen-year olds leaving home to go to college - and never
coming back. Prior to full comprehensivisation, LEA, voluntary-aided,
and direct grant/independent grammar schools totalled six, with the
original comprehensives nurturing small sixth-forms.[8] Far too many
were still leaving school with a few CSEs or no qualifications at all, yet
the number of successful O- and A-level candidates continued to rise.
The post-Robbins expansion of higher education was at its height, and
LEA payment of termly travel made even the most distant campus a
reality. Life in Brighton, Canterbury or York quickly came to seem a
lot more seductive than staid old Coventry. Of course thousands came
to the city in order to study at the polytechnic or at Warwick
University, ultimately the most successful of the 'plate-glass'
campuses; but those graduates who opted to stay could just as easily
have done the same in Birmingham or Leicester. They had no local
roots, and too often their perceptions of the environment and the
community were little different from those of the planners and their ilk.
Indeed, often, they were one and the same.

Just as 'Cov' could no longer be guaranteed the cream of schoolboy
talent, so the city as a whole was left with a vacuum. Yes, a good
number did stay, or returned home eventually; but so many more did
not. Like the car wrecking the local landscape, so those other products

of postwar prosperity - upward social mobility, and greater geographical mobility - helped sow the seeds of urban decline. In consequence, the intervening years all too often saw an absence of leadership and example, and a gut feeling that nobody at the top, in both the city's public and private sectors, really cared.

If, well over ten years ago when first published, this was a lament, then it was a distinctly unfashionable lament: bemoaning the absence of enlightened, progressive, and efficient leadership from those who benefited more than most from the welfare and education systems which came out of the war and proved so beneficial for the baby boomer generation. I went to university in the autumn of 1970. At school and after, the quality of education I received could scarcely be matched thirty years later without having to pay for it. I was both privileged and lucky: those who failed their Eleven-Plus no doubt have a very different tale to tell. It was great fun to be a sixthformer in Coventry at the end of the 1960s, and I always envisaged going back to work there after graduation. Needless to say, I never did. Neither did the brilliant young rugby players of my age who, in a previous era, would have kept Coventry at the top throughout the 1970s, and laid the foundations for continued success today.[9] Instead, they went off to find sex, music, travel, drink or drugs, and a brave new world a million miles from Coundon Road. Monthly trips to see your mum, and checking out the soccer and rugby results on a Saturday night, are no substitute. For me, and for my friends from three decades ago, Coventry made us whatever we are today - and our only thanks to the city has been to abandon it.[10]

7

AN OVAL BALL AND A BROKEN CITY
Coventry, its people and its rugby team, part 2 1995-98[1]

This essay continues the story of a once-great rugby union club and its relationship with a large Midlands city struggling to adjust to two decades of sustained recession and deindustrialisation. It focuses upon the period between August 1995 and July 1998, explaining why the Coventry club was so desperate to secure success on and off the field in English rugby's second season of full professionalism. In the event Coventry RFC ended the 1997-98 season still languishing in the second division, its hopes of regaining financial solvency and recalling former glories stymied by inconsistent performance on the pitch and incompetent management in the committee room. How and why did a club with a history and tradition firmly rooted in the heartland of English rugby, find itself in the summer of 1998 in the hands of the receivers? What insight can Coventry's experience offer into the impact of professionalism upon rugby union in England in the period following the decision of the International Rugby Board (IRB) in August 1995 decision to declare the game open?

Coventry fans have to go back a quarter of a century to discover the last time their team won a major trophy. The club's last appearance in the final of what is today the Powergen Cup was in April 1974, the tournament's last year without sponsorship. The knock-out competition has appeared in a variety of guises (for which read sponsors) since its establishment by the Rugby Football Union (RFU), the governing body of English rugby, in 1971. Introducing an element of competition marked a belated recognition that a season comprised purely of so called 'friendlies', spiced up only by the civilised thuggery of a local derby (say Bristol away at Gloucester), or the odd prestige fixture (say Leicester hosting a New Year visit from that Corinthian flagship of the amateur ethos, the Barbarians), signalled terminal decline for a game seemingly incapable of matching the excitement, attraction and attendances of league football in the decade following England's 1966 World Cup success. In 1974 'Twickers' would only secure a capacity crowd for England's two or three home games in the annual post-Christmas Five Nations Championship and an intermittent autumn visit by New Zealand's All Blacks. Thus Coventry retained the 'Club Competition' trophy in front of a tiny gathering of die-hard supporters, mostly concentrated in the main stand of what was then a cavernous green stadium, with the remainder scattered across the terraces, and comforted only by the fact that they vastly outnumbered any rival fans.[2] 'Cov' beat London Scottish 26-6 in a game marginally more exciting than the dour battle with Bristol a year earlier; but given that fourteen of the side had played for their country, and that the captain was England/British Lion legend David Duckham, an upset was unlikely. With hindsight, Twickenham on 27 April 1974 marked the zenith of Coventry's dominance of English club rugby in the 1960s and 1970s; the final decade of an amateur – and amateurish – game; when the poor performance of the national side (if playing in the Five Nations, yet not, strangely, in South Africa and New Zealand) reflected the complacency of those Midlands and West Country coaches and committees who were more than happy to crush smart society London sides while convincing themselves that defeat by the then rampant Welsh scarcely counted.[3]

Coventry's most recent fixture with London Scottish was in March 1998 at Coundon Road, home to the Midlands club from 1916 to 2004. The match warrants attention in that it offered an insight into the reality of professional rugby for struggling clubs desperate to secure the prestige and *qualified* financial security of Premiership One status – in other words, to be one of today's elite twelve clubs in the Guinness Premiership. The ground, unseated on three sides, looked little different from in Duckham's day, other than for three hospitality portakabins adjacent to the clubhouse. Lack of ground improvements reflected an eagerness to sell the land, clear debts so great that the bailiffs' arrival was imminent, and move to a purpose-built stadium on a green-field site (today's Butts Stadium). A £10 ticket for the terraces was rewarded by an eventful yet uninspiring game, in which Coventry's player-coach Derek Eves led by example, and three players on loan from Cardiff and eager to impress visiting scouts, spurred their new team-mates on to a 37-10 victory. Despite the score the quality of the rugby was abysmal, with poor handling and an ugly mood (a weak referee sent off no less than three players). With hindsight, the game was rich in irony. The Coventry players, enjoying a rare spell of consistency, had in fact not been paid for several weeks. London Scottish were dire and yet at the end of the season secured promotion in the play-offs, leaving the pre-season favourites languishing mid-table. Coventry's failure to secure council support for relocation hastened eventual bankruptcy; yet London Scottish would henceforth play in a proper stadium by signing a three-year deal to share the Stoop Memorial Ground in south-west London with historically the capital's richest side, Harlequins. NEC Harlequins, incidentally, is so far the only club to incorporate the principal sponsor into its name. Other than defacing the jerseys and brightening up an over-priced programme, it was difficult to see what Peugeot offered Coventry's players as they ground out a result against the exiled Scots.[4]

The programme in itself highlighted the two sides of professional rugby in England by 1998. A bulky and very glossy inset, *Allied Dunbar Premiership Weekly Update*, announced the 'English Rugby Charter', which at face value appeared to confirm that, after two years of acrimony and recrimination, the top clubs were now ready to make their peace with the RFU, and 'play their full part in the development of England as a world-class rugby nation at all levels of the game, for the benefit of both spectators and participants'.[5] Such a statement was a reaffirmation that, whereas in the southern hemisphere international contracts and commitments took precedent, in England professional rugby would be firmly rooted in the clubs. This principle had been accepted by the RFU in the transitional season of 1995-96, following the IRB finally ending the increasingly flimsy pretence that rugby union was a wholly amateur sport. The power of the top clubs, increasingly focused upon their representative body English First Division Rugby (EFDR), would fuel an endless succession of disputes between 1996 and 2000.

Coventry's programme warned the few thousand faithful, most of whom looked as if they had also attended the 1974 match, that the following week's friendly against Bristol (another great club in trouble as it wrestled with mounting debts and imminent relegation from Premiership One) was yet to be confirmed. A tannoy announcement at half-time confirmed that the Bristol team was not coming - this was supposedly a professional sport, and fans had to put up with the next match being cancelled because the prospective visitors either could not raise a side or could not afford the costs!

In August 1995, when the IRB had made its historic announcement, most of the senior English sides paid their players only modest cash payments, even if size of ground, level of support, location, and financial acumen, determined just how generous these 'expenses' could be. In this respect, although seemingly stuck in the second division, Coventry appeared a reasonably stable and secure business organisation, the club's modest gate revenue complemented by merchandising and substantial bar takings. The committee, drawn from the local great and the good, its credibility and prestige underpinned by the presence of former players, not least legendary England and British Lion winger, Peter Jackson, enjoyed the trust and respect of club members. Officials supervised gradual decline, grateful only that a humbling sojourn in the third division had lasted only one season.[6] As suggested elsewhere, in terms of social composition committee members running senior clubs differed little from unpaid enthusiasts in even the humblest bars and changing rooms up and down the country. The RFU reflected this grass-roots homogeneity, albeit with an in-built hierarchy of elected officials, usually well-off and with an inherently conservative attitude towards the modern game – as opposed to the ruling body's full-time administrators, who recognised the need for change and the vital role of television revenue to fund English rugby at all levels.[7]

The RFU was sufficiently tuned into the late twentieth century's marketing needs and commercial imperatives as to exploit the higher profile English rugby enjoyed as a consequence of the national team's success in the Five Nations Championship, and the second and third World Cups.[8] From September 1997 the Allied Dunbar financial services group sponsored the 24 clubs in England's top two divisions for the next three seasons to the tune of £7.5 million. The renamed Premiership One clubs received £500,000 and

Premiership Two half as much, with Twickenham endeavouring to reassure smaller clubs that further cash would trickle downwards.[9] Furthermore, inspired by the US$550 million deal Rupert Murdoch's News Corp had signed with the 'Tri-nations' of South Africa, New Zealand, and Australia, in May 1996 the RFU sold BSkyB sole rights to broadcast live for the next five years all internationals, club and representative games in England. The price of £87.5 million dwarfed the £27 million previously paid by the BBC for the three-year contract due to end in 1997. Crucially for Coventry £22.5 million was set-aside for the senior clubs, albeit with a heavy bias in favour of Premiership One.[10] For the next three years controversy dogged a deal which was unilateral, and not part of a jointly negotiated package with the three other Home Nations. Traditionalists were furious at the pace of change, and at not being able to watch England's home matches on terrestrial TV, with the net result that for two years the RFU was wracked by division and factionalism. The rugby unions of Wales, Scotland, and Ireland threatened to expel England from the Five Nations over inadequate compensation, and in early 1999 for a short time actually did so. But although most club and county representatives in England openly endorsed the Celtic view that Twickenham had a moral if not a legal obligation to perpetuate the status quo, the top teams enthusiastically welcomed BSkyB funding. It was clear that even the most successful, stable and secure clubs, such as Leicester and Bath, would only survive if large salaries could be underpinned by central funding, via sponsors and Sky Sports. From the outset even the most poorly supported of the senior sides assumed that generous contracts were unavoidable: high-spending broadcasters would only be interested in club rugby – whether English, or British, or most lucratively European - if assured that star names would be playing. It was equally clear that most TV revenue and corporate sponsorship would go to Premiership One, and that EFDR would have a key role to play in defending the interests of an increasingly exclusive elite of top teams. Commercial viability, and thus medium-term survival, seemingly depended upon first division status, and nowhere was this more acutely felt than at Coventry.

    In October 1995 the prominent north-eastern businessman and inspiration for the revival of Newcastle United Football Club, Sir John Hall, invested heavily in Gosforth, relaunching the club as 'Newcastle Falcons' with the intention creating a team that won trophies and made money.   Success came on the pitch when Newcastle became Premiership One champions in May 1998. However, in March 1999 a disillusioned and embittered Hall relinquished his 76 per cent controlling interest.   The initial investment had been set at £1 million, but by the time Hall sold the club total losses were heading towards £9 million.   Nevertheless, between 1996 and 1998 Sir John Hall was a role model for less high-profile businessmen who in succeeding months persuaded membership-based clubs to convert to company status.   The first generation of millionaire rugby club owners came from a variety of backgrounds and were rarely soaked in the game.   One exception was Nigel Wray, who invested £2 million in Saracens and offered £500,000 of shares for sale.   Another was Gerry Sugrue.   Already chairman of Coventry, Sugrue had initiated a modest restructuring of management and coaching in the belief that professional rugby was imminent.   Like others who thought they were ahead of the game, he anticipated that for a relatively small outlay he could recruit players capable of ensuring promotion.   However, financial rectitude was an early casualty of the rather arrogant assumption that Coventry should get back into the top flight at the earliest opportunity.   The principal difference between these two benefactors was that Wray was executive chairman of an immensely profitable property investment group, and Sugrue the founder of a successful but small computer systems company.   In other words, Wray could personally absorb a sizeable proportion of the cost involved in securing and maintaining success, whereas Sugrue could afford only seed costs (most notably the appointment of Bristol's Derek Eves as player-coach). Coventry's chairman needed early success to ensure additional sources of income, not least the commercial advantage of Premiership One status and membership of EFDR.[11]

The importance of supplementing gate revenue was highlighted by Premiership One attendance in 1997-98.   Admittedly there was a 22 per cent rise in spectators, but the global figure was only 823,446, with a club average of 6,238 (Leicester's 12,589 compensating for 4 out of 12 teams attracting only around 3,600).[12]   Yet because clubs were desperate for success, the new owners were still prepared to bankroll them to the tune of, in some cases, literally millions of pounds. After 1996 wages spiralled, and although the bubble seemed to burst in the summer of 1998, the most ambitious and affluent owners were still prepared to gamble large sums on overseas players who would bring the clubs trophies, and also the much-prized AB supporters.

In the spring and summer of 1998, an alarming number of English clubs began declaring players' contracts null and void. Blackheath, a perpetual also-ran in London rugby, followed another Premiership Two side, Moseley, into administration.   Moseley, Birmingham's best-known team, owed £800,000 and was carrying a weekly wage bill of £120,000. With a track record of illicit payments and income tax evasion, the club had been taken over in 1996 by local businessmen whose indiscriminate recruitment and indifference to average gates of 1,500 guaranteed financial disaster.   A new consortium sold The Reddings, Moseley's ground, to the property developers Bryant Homes in order to clear the club's debts. Moseley's new backers not surprisingly failed to persuade the team's traditional rival, Coventry, to merge and relocate nearer Birmingham, or to convince Warwickshire Cricket Club that their Edgbaston ground was ideally suited to winter rugby.   Moseley would be homeless in three years time, and yet in the summer of 1998 it was successfully relaunched as a cost-cutting semi-professional club. The same proved true of two of Premiership Two's weakest and most poorly supported clubs, Wakefield and Fylde.[13]   Ironically, these mediocre sides proved role models for how, no doubt to the disgust of diverse creditors, clubs could be resurrected in an astonishingly short space of time.

Blackheath (founded 1870) and Moseley (1873) had long histories, but it did not save them going to the wall. Nor did a keen sense of history prompt the RFU to step in and rescue them, as had happened to Rugby Lions (note the location) in 1993.   Five years later not even the biggest names in English rugby could expect sympathy and support from the RFU, as was evident when recently relegated Bristol went into receivership in July 1998. Historically a major force in English rugby, especially in the West Country, Bristol's wage bill was over £1 million for the previous season, thus generating a loss of £500,000 and a total debt of over £2 million. Quite simply, the club's main creditor and benefactor could no longer afford to keep making interest-free loans with no hope of repayment - he simply wasn't that well-off.[14]   This was proving a common scenario: a club owner had to be extremely rich in order to subsidise the shortfall between sponsorship and television income, plus gate receipts, merchandising and bar takings, and the multi-million outgoings. Furthermore, if a club of the size and status of Bristol was refloated as a new company - with players employed on a part-time semi-professional basis, and with wages to match - then this suggested that within two years all but a select group of highly successful, well-endowed clubs would be organised along similar lines.[15]

Bristol intended to regain its sizeable if rather rundown stadium, an asset Moseley had sacrificed to survive. Similarly, Coventry had sold Coundon Road in order to remain solvent. In February 1996 chairman Gerry Sugrue marked the stadium's seventy-fifth anniversary with plans for total refurbishment. Yet by the following September he was insisting that a £1 million deal with Leander, a 'development and investment corporation', meant a move. Before Coventry six similar-sized clubs (including Sale, Moseley and Rugby Lions) had been approached by Leander but concluded the company was only interested in gaining control of their assets. Suspicious committee members at Coventry, hoping that delay would prompt an impatient Leander to withdraw, persuaded the chairman of the city's Premier League football club to declare his interest in merger. The ploy worked, with Leander making unacceptable demands as the price of postponement. With his committee increasingly divided, and his personal assets draining away, Sugrue looked to Bryant Homes, the property developers already negotiating to buy Moseley's ground. Coventry was maintaining a squad and support staff (including a full-time physiotherapist) comparable to a top club like Bath, and paying its player-coach, £130,000 plus bonuses and a car.[16] This was an astonishing amount even if Derek Eves proved in the short-term a resourceful coach and an inspiration on the pitch. He also cultivated a youth policy. With 30 junior clubs in Warwickshire and an immense interest in junior rugby, Coventry needed to match Leicester Tigers in attracting and retaining talented and ambitious young players; in other words, young talent who a generation earlier would have automatically gravitated towards Coundon Road, rather than travel up the motorway to one of the two most successful sides of the previous decade (the other being Bath).[17]

Sugrue and his closest associates within a club already wracked by suspicion and scarcely disguised mutual antagonism gambled everything on promotion at the end of the 1996-97 season. Premiership One status would strengthen the case for selling Coundon Road to Bryant Homes in order to clear the club's debts, and encourage the local authority to confirm the availability of a green-field site for development. Major new sponsors had provisionally agreed to pump money into the club, and most important of all, a number of leading players had been offered lucrative contracts in order to ensure the team was not relegated after only one season at the highest level. On 11 May 1997 Coventry lost its second promotion play-off match at London Irish, while at the same time the football team against all expectations preserved its Premier League status. The following season the Sky Blues were forecast to go down but in fact flourished, and Cov were predicted for promotion but in fact floundered. In February 1998, a leaked fax revealed that by the end of the season Coventry's wage bill could exceed £1 million. Amid much publicity Coundon Road was finally sold to Bryant Homes for around £2 million, with Sugrue claiming a surplus £1 million once debts were cleared - enough to fund a joint development with the city council and other interested parties of the proposed multi-purpose stadium. Completion of the deal was then prevented by rebel committee members securing a court injunction. Succeeding months saw club resignations and recriminations, a fatal break with the city council, and a succession of creditors taking legal action against the club.

With Coundon Road stripped bare by the bailiffs, the team played much of the second half of the season unpaid, their loyalty to Sugrue rewarded once late proceeds from BSkyB cleared the outstanding salaries bill. Being in breach of contract over paying players meant the club's captain and only international, Rob Hardwick, could reluctantly move to London Irish without payment of a transfer fee (an anticipated £75,000). Hardwick was followed by the bulk of the first team squad, while most crippling for the club's long term youth policy was the loss of three schoolboy internationals to Leicester. On 23 July 1998 Gerry Sugrue resigned, leaving a tax bill of over £750,000, plus as much again and more owed to the Customs and Excise, the bank, the brewery, and a variety of smaller yet less patient creditors. Sugrue had mortgaged company and home to keep the cash flowing, but council procrastination, poor results, and personality clashes inside and outside the club, left him with little option but to leave.[18] His had been a worthy but ultimately naive attempt to buy success, starting from far too narrow a financial base. Within a week the club had gone into receivership, with debts of £2.4 million. Coventry appeared yet another victim of the mistaken assumption that professionalism offered a fast if furious means of reviving old glories.

In fact, a consortium waiting in the wings immediately bought the club name and fixtures, and relaunched it as a part-time operation on a players budget of £360,000 for the season. With fresh capital, a new sponsorship deal with Peugeot, a transparent business plan, and an infusion of local expertise in sports promotions, Coventry RFC experienced a remarkable resurrection.[19] Eves began to rebuild his squad and, before he returned to Bristol mid-season, had moulded a team which, if a little more consistent, would have been promotion contenders come May. Renewed negotiations with the city council and the local further education college now focused on redevelopment of The Butts, a run-down inner city stadium, which the club would move to in the autumn of 2000.[20]

Like most middle-ranking clubs in 1998 and 1999 - whether Bedford, Sale or West Hartlepool in the nether reaches of Premiership One, or over half the teams in Premiership Two - 'Cov' had been taught a harsh lesson. Switching to semi-professional status meant a belated coming to terms with financial reality. Unlike the previous regime, Coventry's new directors placed a priority on traditional sources of income as opposed to external subsidy: admission prices were reduced to increase crowd levels and maximise bar takings, and a target set of 2000 season ticket holders in order to boost capital investment. The new stadium and training facilities would cost £4 million, but be built and paid for in phases, making early provision for local community use while later targeting corporate support via executive boxes, reserved car parking, and high quality catering.[21] The Butts was a microcosm of Coventry City FC's Arena 2000 project in so far as both were a model of cooperation with the council (post-Sugrue bridges were rebuilt remarkably fast) and with other interested parties, not least the Department of Environment. The speed with which both projects secured initial planning permission reflected local and central government's shared view that sport, whether spectator or participatory, has a key role to play in urban regeneration and wealth creation. The absence of delay also highlighted the value of community consultation, thereby demonstrating concrete benefits to local individuals and organisations concrete inconvenienced by the presence of a large stadium in a semi-residential area. However, any comparison of the two initiatives can only go so far in that the Premier League side had planning permission for a ground capacity of 40,000, with 6,000 parking spaces, a purpose-built railway station, and a large shopping complex integrated into the stadium/arena. The whole project, located on a brown-field site in a run-down area on the outskirts of the city, was costed at £135 million.[22]

This stark comparison of the two Coventry stadia reinforces the point that in England rugby union at club level is not a mass spectator sport comparable to football, or in the north of the country rugby league. Even a side as regularly well supported as Leicester Tigers has a crowd capacity of approximately 16,000, with clubs like Saracens and Wasps which share football grounds only rarely achieving this level of attendance.[23] Even the Powergen Cup Final, which in recent years has brought large numbers to Twickenham, as recently as May 1999 attracted fewer than 30,000, most of whom were cheering on local side Wasps against a sparsely supported Newcastle Falcons. The poor attendance no doubt confirmed for Sir John Hall that the professional game is commercially non-viable. The reality was that the RFU marketed the match poorly, and grossly over-priced the tickets, thereby attracting none but the competing clubs' most loyal supporters. Spectators will watch the very best of club rugby if it is well-marketed and sensibly priced. Nor need this apply solely to the Premiership sides. A club like Coventry can build upon a core of support, albeit at present still *very* modest. Effective promotion of a successful and attractive team, plus a purpose-built family-friendly ground, is starting to bring back old supporters and create new ones. Drawing heavily upon rugby league marketing techniques, Saracens pioneered ticket discounting and community links, targeting schools, youth organisations, and junior sides. Coventry does not have the cachet of Guinness Premiership status; nor a clutch of household names eager to promote the club in neighbouring schools and sports centres. Nevertheless, success depends upon locking into local community and sporting networks, hence the argument for sharing The Butts, once complete, with the Coventry Crusaders Basketball Club - a well-established and a newly fashionable sport: each sport can target a different audience but minimising their overall costs by sharing facilities. Diversifying in to summer rugby league offers a small-scale yet surprisingly successful precedent for economies of scale.

What is clear from Coventry's unhappy early experience of professionalism is that it is fatal to look backwards, and assume future success on the strength of past glories. Yes, a club like Coventry can draw on tradition, but in modern rugby this counts for little. If anything a keen sense of history inhibited fresh thinking, and anyway 'tradition' needs to be put into context. It is nearly forty years since rugby in Coventry enjoyed parity of esteem with professional football: despite frequently flirting with relegation, the Sky Blues survived in the Premier League, formerly the First Division, for over three decades. The travails of the rugby club seem minuscule when compared with the amount of income Coventry City previously generated via gate receipts, stadium use, merchandising, and above all television coverage. Measured by any criteria, the Premier League has been a rip-roaring success, confirming the centrality of football in the English national psyche and thus in popular culture throughout the 1990s and in to the twenty-first century - with the inhabitants of Coventry no exception to the rule. Few would deny that, despite England's triumph in the World Cup, most boys in 2003 still looked to Beckham not Wilkinson as their sporting role model. In any case - as outlined in the previous essay - it is nearly half a century since Coventry could draw upon a profusion of young local talent: in the 1960s county-class players from the two grammar schools increasingly left home for university, and never came back; in the 1970s complacency meant the club failed to establish a credible youth policy; and in the 1980s low morale and industrial action saw the collapse of competitive rugby in state schools. Outside of the independent sector, many teenagers who want to play the game seriously can no longer do so at school, hence the importance of Coventry linking up with Barkers Butts, a large local club fielding various junior teams from mini-rugby upwards.[24]

The Barkers Butts initiative demonstrates how a sleeping giant like Coventry has much to learn from those up and coming clubs which in recent years have provided the most sensible model for professional or semi-professional rugby. Across the Midlands there are younger clubs that have achieved recent success through a contribution of initiative, imagination, and caution. Sides like Birmingham and Solihull, Newbury, and at a more elevated level the remarkably successful Worcester, have small purpose-built stadiums with up-to-date facilities but low overheads, usually partially funded by the National Lottery. Unlike the more senior sides, from the outset they have understood the importance of keeping unit costs low. A flat management structure, dependent upon the cash and acumen of local businessmen, supports a small core of full-time administrators, coaches, and senior players. The first team comprises of local young talent and experienced imports whose ethos is not all that different from when they trained and played solely for pleasure – in this respect at least Worcester, now firmly established in the Guinness Premiership, are no longer the role model. Aware of the absence of any deep-rooted rugby tradition, but of their location in relatively affluent areas of the country, clubs like Worcester have exploited their own success and that of England over the past decade, in order to raise their profile. They actively encourage the local community, including sponsors, to be aware of and to take pride in their achievements. Worcester maintain important links with local schools and colleges, funding sports scholarships and encouraging players to gain more qualifications. The absence of a major football club renders the task that much easier, with Gloucester and Bath being the two obvious role models. Coventry's use of Worcester's newly-built indoor training facilities in the winter of 1997-98 symbolised the passing of the old order.[25]

The main thrust of the previous essay was that, whereas the fortunes of a football team are often seen as mirroring those of its parent town or city, in Coventry's case it was the rugby club. That analogy broke down in the second half of the 1990s as Coventry RFC's miserable descent into bankruptcy and near extinction took place against a backdrop of a city which slowly, almost painfully, was regaining a self-confidence and relative prosperity not seen for a generation. In this respect the remarkable capacity of the football team to cling on to its Premiership place, and apparently thrive in adversity, more aptly reflected the city's efforts to carve out a fresh profile for itself as something more than a recession-wrecked relic of England's one-time manufacturing heartland. Regional and civic partnerships within and between the public and private sectors enjoyed mixed success in creating a fresh role for Coventry once an injection of fresh investment facilitated a succession of post-industrial initiatives. The city, while still retaining a sizeable - if shrunken - manufacturing base, took advantage of its geographical location, and pool of skilled labour and academic expertise, to refocus upon retail and postal distribution, financial services, and telecommunications. Unemployment remained above the national average, and the level of inner city deprivation remained unacceptably high, but Coventry at the end of the decade boasted an infrastructure and level of economic activity that contrasted sharply with the ravages of deindustrialisation so evident at the time Mrs Thatcher left office in 1990.

Nine years later the football club's Arena 2000 project – today's Ricoh Arena - was being seen as a symbol of Coventry's renewed confidence and optimism. On a more modest level the same was true of The Butts stadium, with prospects remarkably good for a club which the previous summer had faced extinction.   The consortium of ex-players and sports promoters that had relaunched Coventry RFC in July 1998 had a vision for the future, but a vision rooted in realistic expectations, a genuine commitment to the community, a respect for the wishes of members and supporters, and above all, a sound business plan. If the team showed the same consistency, and talented young players came to recognise national and international recognition did not necessitate them joining Leicester, then the future looked bright. Success would build on success, both on and off the pitch, and the prospect of Premiership One rugby would not only boost income from sponsorship and BSkyB, but draw in fresh support eager to see stars previously familiar only from watching international rugby on television - and enjoy access to stadium facilities vastly superior to the portakabins and crumbling terraces of Coundon Road. Like most other clubs three years into professionalism, Coventry had learnt a hard lesson in 1997-98, yet it had emerged contrite and still capable of competing with the best of the then Premiership Two. The club would always have to stand in the shadow of Premier League football, and the same was true of English rugby as a whole; but in its guarded optimism Coventry accurately reflected the state of a sport which it would not be an exaggeration to say had been traumatised by three years of economic mismanagement, internal division, and inflated ambition. There were to be bigger casualties, not least the EFDR's removal of Richmond (and, ironically, London Scottish) from Premiership One in May 1999.[26] But for a generation which grew up wondering not if England would field a Coventry player but how many, bailiffs and bankruptcy in the summer of 1998 was a salutary and moving lesson.

8

"BACK, MOODY, KRONFELD? WE DON'T NEED THOSE LADS AT TREIZE TIGERS"
Sport, counterfactual history, and the twin codes[1]

The debate over counterfactual history: can it be employed in the study of sport?

Hugh Trevor-Roper once famously said that 'history is not merely what happened: it is what happened in the context of what might have happened'.[2] The late Lord Dacre was not especially well known for his interest in rugby league, but he might have found a quaint charm in applying the question 'What if...?' to a familiar topic for British sports historians, namely the persistent failure of the thirteen man game to establish itself south of the Pennines.[3] Were he still alive, E.P. Thompson, who apparently watched neither code of rugby when he had the opportunity to do so in Halifax [league] and Coventry [union], would be scornfully dismissive of such speculative inquiry: in *The Poverty of Theory* he famously talked of 'counterfactual fictions' as being 'unhistorical shit'.[4] Similarly Croce, Carr, and Oakeshott, all in their time denounced counterfactual history as self-indulgent, time-wasting, intellectually indefensible, and even downright irresponsible.[5]

Michael Oakeshott insisted in the early 1930s that any historian reflecting upon alternative scenarios to that which 'the evidence obliges us to conclude did take place' steps 'outside the current of historical thought' in order to foster 'a pure myth, an extravagance of imagination'. This is nothing less than a 'complete rejection of history'.[6] Most recently, Richard Evans has depicted 'what-if' history as reflecting that supposed 'postmodern helplessness in the face of current events' which he critiqued so powerfully throughout his extended historiographical essay, *In Defence of History*. Evans identifies the case for chance and contingency with what he labelled 'the young fogey school': inspired by the heterodoxy of Jonathan Clark, and intent on aggressively challenging the centrality of historical determinism for an earlier generation of Marxist or Marxian historians. Evans accuses Niall Ferguson – ostensible 'young fogey' spokesperson by virtue of his initiating the influential essay collection *Virtual History* - of erroneously depicting determinism as entirely devoid of human will. In fact, insists Evans, 'determinism simply means that historical events and processes are ultimately caused by factors independent of the individual human will.' For Evans so-called 'speculative history' is in its present form an essentially conservative, pessimistic phenomenon, whereby the likes of Ferguson and Andrew Roberts can demonstrate how much better it could have been, had say Liberal England not gone to war in August 1914. Evans rightly points out that the early part of the last century offered a mirror image, whereby popular historians such as G.M. Trevelyan demonstrated that Liberal England would never have come about in the first place had his Whig forefathers not ferociously defended parliamentary sovereignty.[7]

On the other side of this cavernous historiographical divide Ferguson, in the lengthy, scene-setting introduction to *Virtual History*, offers a spirited defence of counterfactuality. He pre-empts his critics' insistence that the volume's essays are simply flights of fantasy, each starting from a feasible premise but becoming quickly subverted by imagination and prejudice.[8] Calling on the ghosts of Gibbon, Namier, Trevelyan, Trevor-Roper, and most especially Isaiah Berlin, the tyro champion of empire and the free market insists that he and his fellow contributors advance an alternative sequence of events and developments rooted firmly in a discernible empirical base. To do otherwise – in Ferguson's own words, 'to rely for inspiration on hindsight, or to posit reductive explanations...to make anachronistic assumptions' - is to produce exactly the sort of 'counterfactual fictions' which Edward Thompson found so offensive.[9]

Ferguson is most persuasive in his insistence that counterfactual history *has* to be rooted in plausibility, in other words, the emphasis upon what could conceivably – probably and not possibly – have happened as opposed to what did actually take place. Thus the counterfactualist has to discard all those questions (and in consequence, all those scenarios) which are quite clearly implausible. For example, 'What would have happened to English rugby after 1895 if all clubs had accepted 'broken-time payments''?' is an absurd speculation as the affluent southern clubs were clearly not going to compromise on their amateur status.[10] On the other hand, the future of rugby league outside the north is worth considering because between 1909 and 1913 there was a very real possibility that the Northern Union would become a permanent fixture in Midlands working-class life. This then is where imagination is tempered by harsh reality – the historian goes back to the point immediately prior to what actually took place, and works through credible alternative scenarios.

In a succession of intellectual assaults upon historical determinism Isaiah Berlin posed as an ur-counterfactualist, emphasising plausibility as the *sine qua non* of any debate surrounding contingency and probability.[11] Ferguson draws on Berlin to support the argument that to ensure credibility, the counterfactualist reduces contingency from diverse (infinite?) alternative versions of the past to a much smaller number of plausible outcomes, each of which – assuming that there is more than one – is rooted firmly in historical probability.[12] The problem with this of course is that men and women are not rational beings, and therefore their behaviour is rarely if ever determined by pure reason – assuming that a rational course of action is obvious anyway.[13]

Of course one of the key problems with counterfactual history is the absence of necessary knowledge, or to use Ferguson's hijacked phrase, 'facts which concededly never exist'. To counter this objection he insists that, 'We should consider as plausible or probable *only those alternatives which we can show on the basis of contemporary evidence that contemporaries actually considered* [author's emphasis].' The argument is that people in the past were invariably faced with a variety of different futures – unlike us, they had no idea what would in fact happen – and the onus is on historians to 'attach significance to *all* the outcomes thought about'. Not to do so is to fail to recapture the past 'as it really was'; assuming of course that such a remarkable historicist achievement is sustainable in the first place.[14] Thus, we need to get a clear idea in our minds what did not take place, but which to those present at the time could so easily have come about.[15] Seemingly this can only be done when there is sufficient documentary evidence to illustrate how and why contemporaries considered hypothetical scenarios, in other words, that which did not actually come about. Notwithstanding an obvious postmodernist challenge, Ferguson's counterfactual paradigm prompts a number of questions. Firstly, how much documentation constitutes a bare minimum of acceptability, and secondly, what about all the primary evidence that hasn't survived? Also, is there not a very real danger of the historian placing too much importance upon those artefacts that have survived, and imposing a pattern of causation upon what is actually a random selection of surviving evidence?

Nevertheless, Ferguson's insistence that counterfactual history starts from the premise of only considering 'the alternatives that were seen at the time as realistic' is a seductive defence of 'virtual history'. Richard Evans argues that working from a particular blueprint at a particular point in time confines the method to a very narrow range of history - primarily political, diplomatic, and military – at the expense of social and cultural. While retaining a healthy scepticism about methodology, should we accept Evans' claim that the current fascination of so many (mainly male) political and military historians with counterfactual history reflects its inappropriateness to the study of 'essentially impersonal' cognate areas within the discipline?[16] Can not, to revisit Trevor-Roper, the history of sport be 'not merely what happened ... [and] what happened in the context of what might have happened'?[17] Arguably the focus should be upon sport *per se*, and not the actual competition. Ferguson's insistence insist that the variables must be minimised in the interest of plausibility might suggest sporting events are ideal for positing credible alternative outcomes ('Well Trevor, with such evenly matched sides the result could have gone either way...'); *or* it might equally signal their total unsuitability ('Well Trevor, anything could have happened this afternoon...'). It's clear that the student of history needs to be especially wary when investigation of pure competition prompts – almost unavoidably - speculation on what might have been.

The Northern Union in the Midlands before the First World War[18]

In the Edwardian period the Northern Union made a concerted effort to establish a firm foothold in Leicestershire and Warwickshire, not least because both counties boasted expanding manufacturing centres surrounded by smaller industrial communities, invariably mining villages, in which families worked hard and played hard. Grassroots rugby thrived, and the two senior clubs were already establishing a reputation for cutting across class barriers in the interest of maintaining regional and even national success.[19]   Thus both Leicester and Coventry paid generous expenses, and turned a blind eye to players who shared the same approach to the game as was by now the norm 'up north'. The Northern Union maintained informal contacts with both players and officials and monitored growing tension between the two senior clubs and the RFU. In 1908 the RFU charged Leicester with 'veiled professionalism', but found the club not guilty. Had the verdict gone the other way then the Northern Union would no doubt have exploited the resulting ill-will, just as it did a year later when the RFU suspended Coventry for three months and individual players indefinitely.[20] Within a fortnight the Northern Union was liasing with local businessmen and embittered fans to organise exhibition matches prior to the imminent establishment of a senior side. The Coventry club was to last three seasons and initially attracted gates of 5000. Feeder leagues were established, including teams from all the major firms in the city, and the impressive Butts Stadium was taken over by the professional game when the now struggling rugby union club forgot to renew the lease. Grassroots rugby league was in rude health, and would have continued to grow had the senior club not folded in June 1913. The demise of the Coventry Northern Union club was by no means inevitable, and seems largely attributable to four key factors.

Firstly, the club experienced an extraordinary amount of bad luck, particularly with the weather. It appears that just about every major fixture prompted a downpour, although the Australian tourists appeared to have escaped a soaking in September 1910.[21] Unfortunately on the day in question the directors doubled the price of admission, thus halving the normal attendance. This short-sighted decision highlights the general incompetence of the board, particularly when it came to signing players (forwards when backs were required, and vice versa, plus a tendency to recruit superannuated league players rather than foster home-grown talent). Crucially, the Coventry side failed to string together a succession of victories, gain momentum, and in consequence retain the large number of spectators originally attracted away from the rugby union and football clubs. Financial projections were based on average gates of 3000, and, while this was feasible in the first year, continued failure saw the crowds melt away: the team finished its third season bottom of the league without a win in 27 matches.[22] Flagging enthusiasm on the part of players and officials combined with the debilitating effect of relying on a creaking rail service to take the side to Lancashire, Yorkshire or Cumbria every other week. It was probably this more than any other factor that led to the decision in June 1913 to wind up the senior club, and subsequently all the junior sides.

Midlands Rugby League and counterfactuality

The point is that rugby league could easily have become established in Coventry in only slightly different circumstances (a few key victories, decent match day weather, a better rail timetable, and so on). The same would probably have been the case in Leicester had not the unusually foresighted RFU commission of inquiry in 1908 realised the consequences of taking a hard line towards a club which seven years earlier had been formally invited to join the proposed Northern Rugby League.[23] In consequence, it is not unreasonable to speculate upon what would have happened had both elite and grassroots rugby league established a foothold in the Midlands, in other words, moved a few steps closer to that elusive vision of a genuinely national game.

What is striking is the speed with which junior sides in Coventry and the industrial hinterland to the north and east of the city adopted rugby league.[24] As might be expected, teams representing the older industries, especially coalmining, embraced the northern game, but so too did the dynamic new vehicle and engine manufacturers – companies like Triumph, Rover, and Humber dominated the Works League established in 1912.[25] It is important to note that these sides only reverted to rugby union because their role as feeder clubs ended when the senior side folded. Even today, a rugby league player coming south to play for, say, Newbold, the 'village' home of Rugby Cement, would experience no great culture shock. Within the city boundaries, clubs like Barkers Butts have a distinctly ungenteel reputation for producing supposed 'hard men' like recent England forwards, Richard Cockerill and Neil Back. The reality is that clubs in Warwickshire, and to a lesser extent in Leicestershire, could – with the notable exception of grammar school old boys sides – transcend class barriers to a degree unimaginable in southern, essentially suburban rugby union. In a pre-professional era this, of course, was the secret of first Coventry and then Leicester Tigers' success as senior club sides.[26] Almost certainly this would not have been the case had rugby league become permanently established. Thus, one can imagine a scenario comparable to Australia where the game would have flourished during 1914-18 because miners and other workers vital to the war effort had not volunteered or been conscripted. An alternative scenario of course is that the enormous authority granted to the RFU as a consequence of rugby union's association with wartime patriotism and endeavour might have enabled the 15 man game to reassert its regional hegemony.[27]

Most obviously, class would have been a far more important determinant of who played what, with education as *the* key factor. Thus one can envisage the elementary schools established under the 1902 Education Act preferring to play rugby league. It would have made sense for children from less privileged areas to learn the rudiments of their fathers, uncles, and brothers' preferred winter sport. Despite leaving school at 14, boys actually acquired far more than the basic skills and a general acquaintance with the rules: they played rugby union for two or possibly three seasons, and no doubt the same would have been true had their schools switched to league.[28] Teachers migrating from Wales between the wars would have simply switched codes – jobs were too scarce to be precious over sporting loyalties. With the passage of the 1944 'Butler' Education Act the elementary schools were mostly redesignated 'secondary modern', for those pupils not selected by examination at 11 for the supposedly more academic grammar schools.[29] From the early 1950s the Leicester, and to a lesser extent Coventry, local education authorities were pioneers in introducing a non-selective

comprehensive system.   Incongruously, both cities' independent
grammar schools still partially operated within the public sector until
the mid-1970s, when 'direct grant' per capita funding from central
government finally ceased.   These schools then reverted to being
fully private, maintained primarily by parental fees.   The elementary
schools would have established a century-long tradition of state
schools playing rugby league, even if from the 1960s football would
have acquired equal and then superior status.   In common with the
rest of the country the much smaller number of grammar schools
would have extolled the virtues of rugby union, the keenest players
progressing to play for their old boys sides.[30]   With no opportunity
for *all* schools to compete against each other, except possibly on the
cricket field, the social divide forged by pre-adolescence selection
and/or middle-class parental choice would have been even greater
than was quite clearly evident before and – ironically - after the
ostensibly meritocratic restructuring of British education initiated in
1944.

Within such a scenario rugby union would have been very much
the poor relation, there being a dearth of junior clubs to foster home-
grown talent and ensure a high level of competition.   Both Coventry
and Leicester would have been a shadow of their actual selves,
unlikely or unable to provide a steady supply of outstanding players
eager to pull on an England shirt.   Pre and postwar Lions tourists
such as Jimmy Giles and Ivor Preece would have remained unknown
given their education and family background, unless of course they
had enjoyed similar success playing for the Great Britain RL team.
In order to fulfil their international ambitions grammar school boys
such as David Duckham or Peter Wheeler would have had to move:
thus English rugby 30 years ago would have focused upon a
Northampton/Bedford   –   Bristol/Gloucester   (plus   Bath)   –
Harlequins/Wasps (plus Saracens) scalene triangle.   Most likely
Leicester and Coventry would have had far more in common with
those northern clubs forever in the shadow of the large, well-
supported league sides – not even a Sale or an Orrell, but more of a
Broughton Park.

In this parallel universe therefore the majority of Warwickshire's
two hundred plus rugby clubs would be playing league, with union
for much of the past century a distinctly middle-class game, with its
heaviest concentration in the south of the county on the Oxfordshire

border. On a more modest scale a similar bias would be evident next door in Leicestershire, albeit with union having a stronger rural base in the east of the county. Leicester's notoriously intimidating Welford Road stadium would boast the 13 man game, hence the absence of those distinguished Tiger flankers listed in this article's title.[31]   Until the footballing renaissance of the 1960s the principal face of sport in Coventry would be the mighty 'Cov', at Wembley crowning the club's golden jubilee season by winning the 1961 Rugby League Challenge Trophy.   Conversely, instead of commencing their club's 1974 centenary season as English champions, union players and officials would be reflecting upon what might have been had their Edwardian predecessors not incurred the full wrath of the RFU.[32]   Of course, just as one can discount several star players who might not have flourished had rugby league been dominant, one can identify plenty more who could still have become household names: on the wing, for example, Lions legend Peter Jackson, probably not, but Rodney Webb or even Rory Underwood, almost certainly yes. From the Wheatley brothers in the 1930s to the Johnson brothers today Coventry and Leicester have fed England teams a formidable supply of big forwards, most of whom by dint of size and background would have achieved comparable success packing down in a six-man scrum. Some of them, of course, did precisely that, switching codes when made an offer they couldn't refuse.

This reminds us that in reality from the late 1940s to the 1980s a steady stream of Midlands players chose 'to go north' and play rugby league. Arguably the most successful was the brilliant, ball-playing, place-kicking hooker John Gray, constantly overlooked by Twickenham except for international sevens. Gray went straight in to the Great Britain side as soon as he moved from Coventry to Wigan, before moving on to two triumphant spells with North Sydney. His loss spoke volumes about English rugby union in the 1970s. Two of the first Coventry players to turn professional were winger Frank Castle and second row forward Ron Tilbury who both signed for Barrow in the late 1940s. Castle later claimed that there was no ill-will when he announced his departure, but such understanding contrasts sharply with the official attitude towards players attracted by the possibility of paying off the mortgage and buying a car. Neither player featured in their former club's centenary histories, which is surprising given that Castle would almost certainly have been selected for England had he stayed. Ron Tilbury's ostracism extended to being banned from talking to his son's team when watching school matches nearly 20 years later.[33] England and Lions star David Duckham turned down several generous offers to move north, yet following the publication of his autobiography in 1980 the RFU banned him from having any further involvement with his old club. Tentative links were restored only after restrictions were lifted in 1995.[34] Past treatment of players who went professional clearly remains a sensitive issue, so it comes as no surprise that Coventry's current chairman and chief executive, ex-England prop and captain Keith Fairbrother, refused an interview to discuss why he left the club for Salford in the early 1970s.

Conclusion

The irony is that Keith Fairbrother is largely responsible for attempting to turn 'virtual history' in to actuality. The six man scrum has wheeled full circle in that after 90 years rugby league returned to the city, first at Coundon Road in its dying days and now at the new Butts Stadium. While the main focus will always be on promotion to union's elite Guinness Premiership, the club can now boast the Coventry Bears, remarkably successful in the Rugby League Conference albeit now struggling in the newly-established National League Three. The Butts offers rugby union in the autumn and winter and rugby league in the spring and summer. With only a brief overlap at the start and finish of respective seasons the opportunity is clearly there to play both codes, assuming of course a player has the motivation *and* the ability to play what remain two very different games. The potential for attracting reasonable gates to watch both codes is clearly there, witness Harlequins taking over the London Broncos in order to bring the south's only Super League side back to The Stoop. Leicester remains a very different story, with plans either to expand Welford Road beyond its current 16,000 capacity, or to incur the wrath of most fans by joining the football club at the still new Walker Stadium.[35]

So how plausible is a scenario whereby the permanent presence of rugby league in the Midlands did in fact generate a continued spread of the sport well beyond the two counties originally targeted by the Northern Union? It is tempting to see the professional game slowly making its way southwards while at the same time finding fertile ground in an admittedly football-mad Black Country, the historic heart of British manufacturing industry to the west of Birmingham.   The reality is that the other east Midlands senior clubs, Northampton and Bedford, were firmly rooted in the amateur ethos, as in the opposite direction was Moseley.   Indeed it was the latter, an early manifestation of Birmingham middle-class suburbia, which first drew the RFU's attention to its two rivals' alleged creeping professionalism.   It is thus fairly safe to assume that rugby union would have remained unchallenged within the nation's second city.   Similarly, while the market towns of Northamptonshire were in their own quiet way hotbeds of radicalism and democratic socialism, the chances of league challenging union, and perhaps more crucially, association football, were remote.   Assuming that Leicester and Coventry would today be Super League sides with strong rugby league hinterlands, the key question therefore is what would have happened in Nottinghamshire and Derbyshire.   Had neither county embraced the thirteen man game at grassroots level, then today's rugby league would in fact have two not one heartlands. Almost certainly the advent of the First World War would have stymied any early initiatives by the Northern Union to as it were bridge the gap; while conditions in the 1920s would have been wholly unsympathetic.[36]   In other words, even in a counterfactual scenario English rugby league's holy grail of a genuinely nationwide and national sport would still remain waiting to be secured.

9

CODA – REMEMBERING THE BLITZ:
Coventry and Southampton over sixty years on[1]

Introduction: perpetuating, if not myths, flawed conclusions
What is most remarkable about the Blitz is that, for all the efforts of
historians to secure greater public awareness as to what actually took
place - maximising reliable information about the impact and
consequences of the bombing without minimising the heroism and
the suffering - the power of popular mythology is so great that most
people in Britain retain a remarkably stereotyped view of what
actually took place. Notwithstanding the herculean efforts of Mark
Connolly's 'sensationalist revisionists' (among whom Clive Ponting
boasts pride of place), the popular notion of a 'people's war' survives
intact, with yet another commemorative anniversary offering a timely
boost just at the point when fascination with the travails of a passing
generation start to flag. Equally potent is the commercial imperative,
witness the readiness of provincial newspapers such as the *Coventry
Evening Telegraph* [CET] and the *Southern Daily Echo* [SDE] to
publish special editions whenever a fall in circulation or advertising
demands guaranteed sales: all 32 pages of the CET's 1977
supplement on 'The spirit that was Coventry '39-45' depicts a
community indifferent to rank and status, pulling together,
maintaining a stiff upper lip, and demonstrating a remarkable
capacity to endure the worst efforts of the *Luftwaffe* with fortitude
and humour so long as daylight can bring a nice hot cup of tea and
the promise of RAF retaliation - in other words a microcosm of the
British people as a whole. Here, needless to say, is an untarnished
portrayal of national resilience carefully cultivated from that moment

in June 1940 when it became shockingly obvious Britain now stood alone. The elevation of Churchill to leadership of a genuine coalition, the evacuation from Dunkirk, and the fall of France together forged a fresh image of the British at war, conveniently drawing a line under the appeasement years, the inertia and false optimism of the 'phoney war', and the debacle of the Norway campaign. The winter of 1940-41 remains central to our overall impression of the nation at war, even for those born long after the last bomb sites had been reclaimed and the final few Anderson shelters grassed over. In *The Myth of the Blitz* Angus Calder saw this apparently defiant response to nightly bombardment as reinforcing a 'consensual memory of 1940' moulded even as events were unfolding. For all its early hiccups here was a fine-tuned propaganda machine impressive in its capacity to boost morale at home and cultivate outrage abroad, not least in the United States. Even as the fires burned, 'the Myth accorded Britain, standing alone, a moral victory over Germany.' For many – and not solely unforgiving *Sun*-satiated football fans – that moral victory still stands the test of time. A vicarious self-congratulation over an assumed mass heroic response to the bombing is of course only one element in what has become a peculiarly English infatuation with the Second World War, which shows no sign of abating. Even after six decades of remorselessly recycling, rediscovering, and reinterpreting the events of 'our finest hour', there is at best only restrained soul-searching whenever 'reality' jars with individual reminiscence and communal folklore, let alone national mythology. Notwithstanding the occasional broadsheet revelation (in recent years often courtesy of the National Archives' impressive capacity for self-promotion), among consumers of 'public history' there is a curious absence of reflection and a continued reluctance to contest popular assumption. Indeed, it could be argued that the growth of public history, whether via the 'heritage industry' or through individual initiative, has served only to reinforce the status quo. Professional historians should acknowledge more fully the contribution of those once dismissively labelled 'antiquarians', and yet many of us can testify to a mystified response when suggesting to a thriving local history society or a Stakhanovite website enthusiast that they might consider fresh interpretations and different lines of inquiry.[2]

Academics have the luxury of advising a less cautious, less respectful approach to such seemingly hallowed topics as individual and communal endurance of the Blitz: the response may be scorn, but there is scant prospect of serious discrimination. Thus, the worst I have experienced is a thinly veiled insult in a mature student's final year dissertation, my sin having been to point out that, for all Supermarine's speed establishing dispersal factories after the destruction of its Woolston plant in September 1940, the proud and widely-held belief that assembly of Spitfires continued without interruption was simply not true. Furthermore, I had pointed out that, while Southampton might feel justified in its much-trumpeted claim to be 'The Home of the Spitfire', Castle Bromwich had a legitimate claim to fame given that from November 1940 production of Reginald Mitchell's legendary aircraft was based in the West Midlands. To be fair, most recent histories of wartime Southampton acknowledge this to be the case, with the passage of time facilitating a more detached, and thus more accurate (more honest?), treatment of events. Nevertheless, community historians working for publicly-funded bodies, most especially those operating under the auspices of the local authority, need to display a level of tact rarely demanded of their campus-based colleagues. Thus, since its inception in 1983 Southampton City Council's Oral History Unit has endeavoured to commemorate the dead and to celebrate the 'strength, humour and resilience' of the survivors, while at the same time contextualising controversy in a frank, unequivocal, yet sensitive fashion.[3] Borrowers across the city queuing to return or renew library books are urged to contact an assortment of local history organisations, almost all of which have a particular fascination with 1939-45; but always prominent are details of the Oral History Unit's 'Blitz Collection'. Here is a seemingly endless discourse: elderly residents eager to tell or retell their story are complemented – and indeed, complimented - by younger scions of the city seeking via numerous pre-recorded evocations of all too powerful memories an empathetic experience of the Home Front under sustained attack. Clearly this is not a parochial story frozen in time, with information technology confirming a national, even transnational, appeal, witness the contribution of the Civic Centre's historians to the *PortCities* website. Treatment of the Blitz is enviably concise and admirably balanced, the authors paying tribute to the courage of the local population while at the same time noting how: 'Propaganda of the time and fond recollection have created the idea of people facing with fortitude whatever bombs and horrors the enemy could inflict. In Southampton accusations of failing in this have caused great hurt and controversy.'[4]

Evidence that within the academe there exists a similar recognition of the extent to which open – global - access reinforces the case for sensitivity, albeit without compromising intellectual honesty, is seen in the inter-university on-line project *Rebuilding Coventry in the post-war era*. In this case earlier recordings of Blitz survivors, made as in Southampton on the initiative of local government, were in 2001 complemented by a fresh wave of interviews. Given the project's roots in human geography and town planning, here is a conceptual framework demonstrably different from that familiar to most 'traditional' oral historians. In commenting upon the immediate and longer-term impact of 'Coventration', the authors demonstrate a two-fold intention: to comprehend how and why an emotional response is perhaps at variance with events; and to place recorded experience in the context of a relatively new trans-disciplinary discourse re the memories and testimonies of those traumatised, however briefly, by intense aerial bombardment.[5]

For Southampton and Coventry revisiting familiar events and long-held assumptions is long over-due. Rarely has the phrase 'the fog of war' been more appropriate. Both cities, and Southampton in particular, have had to contend with unduly concise accounts of how they responded to intense and incessant bombing. Textbooks invariably rely on the recycling of narrative and interpretation, with editorial constraints forcing their authors in to making painful decisions of synthesis and excision. In such circumstances anecdotal evidence is rarely tested, and ostensibly authoritative documentary sources assumed to be reliable; careful qualification is at a premium. Historiographical debate may not be ignored, but the reputation of the author, and the overall quality of the text, gives credence and credibility to her/his exposition and explanation. Consequently, key texts take their place in the pantheon of scholarship, granted the hallowed status of 'recommended reading' by tutors happy to see this secondary (tertiary?) literature digested by their students and then all too often incautiously regurgitated – in other words, at whatever level, from undergraduate to post-doctoral, perpetuating a version of events which is for all intents and purposes an unchallenged orthodoxy. Two examples will suffice. In the highly readable, rightly prize-winning *Never Again: Britain 1945-51*, Peter Hennessy described the burning cities of 1940 with characteristic humanity and imagination (what did wartime Walthamstow *smell* like?). While tempering his judgement with a reminder that, 'the spirit of the Blitz could and did prevail even in the most shattered circumstances', he nevertheless depicted Southampton as 'broken in spirit'. This had been the conclusion of the Bishop of Winchester in early December, his tour of the port's devastated parishes revealing that 'morale has collapsed...and everywhere there was fear.' Dr Garbett's oft-quoted appraisal of the situation derives from Tom Harrisson's *Living Through the Blitz*. With Charles Madge, and to a lesser extent Humphrey Jennings, Harrisson had been the driving force behind Mass Observation (MO), an organisation which in 1940 was only three years old and yet was a key source of information and advice for the Home Intelligence Division within the Ministry of Information. The reliability of MO reports, not least with regard to Southampton, will be considered at greater length. At present suffice it to say that the methodology underpinning the observers' intelligence gathering was seriously flawed – if it existed at all. Drawing heavily upon Harrisson's personal experience as project director, and with extensive use of the MO archive, *Living Through the Blitz* is an admirable, informative, and genuinely illuminating book. But the frequency with which it is quoted gives the impression that here is the definitive text, which it quite clearly is not. To be fair to Harrisson, over three decades later he did endeavour to qualify any judgement made at the time ('The strongest feeling in Southampton today is the feeling that Southampton is finished.'), offering a more measured conclusion, which Hennessy quoted at length in *Never Again*. Nevertheless, the overall image of Southampton in the aftermath of 'Blitz weekend', with ferocious attacks on successive nights (30 November and 1 December 1940), remains negative. At least Hennessy noted Harrisson's retrospective view that, even if there was a prevailing sense of Southampton being 'finished', the same did not necessarily apply to many local residents, even those keenest to seek shelter in the surrounding countryside. While Mark Donnelly was similarly cautious in his succinct account of *Britain in the Second World War*, Robert Mackay's rival textbook stated baldly that in both Coventry and Southampton 'there was a similar failure of civic leadership'. Without a hint of extenuating circumstances, Mackay painted an unflattering picture of traumatised city dwellers flooding out in to the rural hinterland – although, to be fair, the term 'trekking', which, as we shall see, still retains pejorative connotations, was used in a wholly neutral fashion.[6]

At the end of the day Mackay's depiction of the Blitz may be largely accurate, but selective use of a solitary source, namely Harrisson's MO reports minus the retrospective commentary, does present a very crude picture of a highly complex sequence of events. In such circumstances it is understandable why communities boasting a proud civic culture take umbrage at the perpetuation of an unqualified, too often uncontested, negative image. It is actually very easy to perpetuate a set of only partially correct or at worst wholly erroneous assumptions, and here I must confess my own guilt: for too long the general impression I gave my students was that on the whole local government in Coventry had responded pretty well to the Blitz, in contrast to generally inept crisis management in Southampton. One possible explanation, I suggested, was that the strength and organisation of the Coventry Labour Party, particularly after it embarked on thirty years of municipal control in 1937, was such as to ensure a relatively resilient response to the cataclysmic raid of 14-15 November 1940; perhaps the much looser political machine of Southampton's governing Ratepayers Party, notwithstanding the towering presence of Alderman Sir Sidney Kimber, undermined the efficiency of the emergency administration following the first heavy raid, on 23 November 1940. This analysis revealed a lot more about me, not least my place of birth and political leanings, than it did about the comparative performances of each local authority in the maelstrom of 1940-41. The first – embarrassingly late - seeds of doubt were sown when Andrew Motion's biography of Philip Larkin revealed that Sidney, the poet's father, was an open admirer of Hitler pre-war, and that, despite being Town Clerk, with the first bombs he quickly vacated the family home for temporary accommodation in Warwick.[7] If the 'real' history of the Blitz in Coventry did not always conform to the version I had been schooled in, and which my parents' generation – the survivors – had with the passage of time mythologised, then might the reverse be the case? Might Southampton's experience in the Blitz not be as bleak as depicted in a succession of undergraduate textbooks re Britain at war, each of which either fed off the others or drew upon only one or at most two primary sources, the reliability of which remained open to question.

Britain throughout 1940-41 suffered around 43,000 civilian casualties, with the remaining four years of the war witnessing a further 17,000 deaths as a result of rocket or air raids. In addition 86,000 were seriously injured, and 149,000 less so. For every civilian killed, 35 were rendered homeless, and by May 1945 roughly two and a half million were in urgent need of secure accommodation. The speed with which Germany secured victory in France and Japan in the Far East, and the relatively small scale of the Mediterranean theatre compared to the Eastern Front, meant that it was not until late 1942 that the attrition rate for the British Army finally overtook that of civilians at home. Admittedly, the total number of air raid victims is dwarfed by the loss of nearly 700,000 German civilian casualties, albeit not all as a result of strategic bombing. Neither do the losses in any way match the Air Staff's pre-war projections, the worst of which predicted a quarter of a million Londoners dead or wounded inside the first two weeks. Yet the fact that Whitehall planners' doomsday scenarios had not come about must have provided scant relief to the literally hundreds of thousands of people the length and breadth of the country who in one way or another found themselves caught up in the Blitz. The prospect of worst things happening to the Germans and the Japanese was both distant and irrelevant – in the spring of 1941 the level of destruction and the loss of life were unprecedented, and they were truly shocking. Consider the fact that in the final four months of 1940, when the capital was bombed on a total of 57 nights, with precious respite, no less than 17,937 Londoners were injured and 13,339 killed. Given the collective or individual terror and trauma generated by such losses – and the material devastation that accompanied them - is it that astonishing to discover in the spring of 1945 around 12,000 people still queuing nightly to shelter in the tube stations? I wonder if, despite the saliency of the Blitz within our national psyche, familiarity has bred contempt. In other words that too often now we shake our heads when confronted with the pictorial evidence, and rapidly move on – a sub-conscious compassion fatigue that, if articulated at all, can be reduced to 'well that was then, and this is now'. But to state the all too obvious, many of those who survived 'then' are here 'now'. As already suggested, a large number have a very positive strategy for dealing with their more painful memories of the Blitz, one which is in accord with what might be termed the dominant discourse (my father was filled with shrapnel and temporarily blinded when putting out an incendiary early on the night of 14 November, but he always joked about it whenever we walked past the house he 'saved'). Others quite clearly do not, suggesting that long-term post-traumatic stress is by no means the preserve of the uniformed veteran. Closely scrutinising photographs of wartime Southampton and Coventry in advance of writing this paper it was almost as if I was seeing them for the first time – I was genuinely shocked by the scale of destruction, not least because it was so concentrated, and yet many of these photographs I had scanned countless times previously. I am after all of an age that ensures childhood memories of bomb-damaged buildings awaiting final demolition and prefab shops at the heart of the city centre. This of course raises a subsidiary question as to whether children of the 1950s and 1960s were so eager to embrace the new that we airbrushed any lingering evidence of a war on our doorsteps out of our mental landscapes – as young boys, when the Second World War was an anaesthetised concoction of comics, Airfix kits, and films starring Kenneth More or Richard Todd, did we switch off whenever our parents recalled events which to them must have seemed like only yesterday but which for us seemed aeons ago? And was this the same for girls of my generation?

The major raids on Coventry and Southampton, winter 1940-41
It is no exaggeration to suggest that my parents, their relatives, their friends, their neighbours, and indeed every other 'Coventry kid' who lived through the night of 14-15 November 1940 were to some degree or other emotionally scarred by the ferocity and the intensity of the raid. In many cases those scars healed quickly - sometimes, as with my dad, faster than the physical ones. With no less than 23 raids since mid-August aerial bombardment had become a familiar phenomenon, killing or seriously injuring 448 people and inflicting damage across the city. However, the scale of 'Operation Moonlight Sonata' reflected the *Luftwaffe*'s intention to eliminate a key centre of manufacturing industry, crucial to the war effort. Literally from

dusk to dawn around 400 aircraft dropped 503 tons of high explosive, with delayed-action bombs creating havoc for days afterwards. Even more deadly were the thousands of incendiary canisters which rained down throughout the night, and which in the initial onslaught had set the medieval heart of the city ablaze. The cathedral was gutted, although desperate fire-fighting saved the neighbouring church of Holy Trinity – twelve months later a vindicated vicar bewailed the diocesan authorities' costly failure to emulate his own contingency planning. By morning little remained of Broadgate, the focus of pre-war redevelopment, and the rest of the city centre lay in ruins. Despite its rapid growth between the wars Coventry remained unusually compact, and no district could claim to have escaped lightly. With so many buildings and residents concentrated in such a small area the damage and loss of human life was that much greater, and the psychological shock that much more profound – to quote Tom Harrisson, who within 24 hours was personally directing two separate teams of MO reporters, there was an 'unprecedented dislocation and depression'. Over 50,000 residences and 500 shops were destroyed or damaged, with 21 key production plants and numerous smaller factories temporarily put out of action. For once the civilian loss of life matched pre-war predictions, with 568 killed and 863 seriously hurt. Power supplies were disrupted from the outset, and the two hospitals were hit early on, but it was the loss of water and the rapid breakdown in telecommunications which most severely disrupted fire-fighting and rescue operations. The pathfinders' deliberate targeting of public utilities - by dropping the biggest bombs in the first wave - ensured that the incendiary fires would spread rapidly, and that the emergency services would be stretched to breaking point at a very early stage. In this respect the *Luftwaffe* was spectacularly successful. That success was repeated twice, albeit thankfully not on the same scale, in early April 1941. The relative severity of these later raids can be measured by the fact that they averaged around five hours in duration and resulted in 451 killed and 723 seriously hurt; major civic buildings and four factories were seriously damaged, as well as over 30,000 houses. Nor were these by any means the last occasions on which the sirens wailed.[8]

Angus Calder and Malcolm Smith have noted how the attack on Coventry not only signalled a fresh phase in the bombing of

Britain, but was projected to a wider world as being unprecedented, with the Germans intentionally maximising the degree of collateral damage. Yet earlier raids had already demonstrated this to be the case, not least in Southampton where the autumn of 1940 brought significant casualties, extensive damage to housing, especially around the wrecked Supermarine works, and at least two deliberate attacks on the newly-constructed Civic Centre: daylight bombing of such a prominent building confirmed that collateral damage was no longer the regrettable price of war, and the consequent killing of art school tutors and their pupils had a harrowing effect upon the local community. The extent to which these deaths were not overshadowed by subsequent events is reflected in the prominence still given to the raid in recent accounts of Southampton at war, and the dedication of a memorial chamber within the Civic Centre as late as 1994 – the deliberately jarring juxtaposition of artificial and natural light within such a tiny space, and the bold calligraphy of survivors' terse recollections in sharp relief upon the white stone surface, at first glance suggest a demonstrably postmodernist response to the demands of commemoration and mourning, but on further reflection recall the contribution of Eric Gill and the arts and crafts movement to inter-war memorialisation. Located in the foyer of the Civic Centre, this highly original reminder of the art school bombing is easy to find; yet one has to make a conscious effort to do so, and therefore the memorial does not actually fulfil its role. Far more prominent, and yet equally invisible, are other memorials scattered around Southampton, for example the plaque in Houndwell Place where a public shelter was directly hit, or even for 364 days of the year the massive cenotaph in Watts Park. The most recent chronicler of the Southampton Blitz neatly summed up their dilemma: 'They are reminders of the past sitting in the present and time has mischievously blurred the connection. They therefore remain physically present but somehow divorced from modern day relevance.' Perhaps unintentionally echoing the work of Jay Winters, Alex King, and Adrian Gregory, let alone Roland Barthes, local journalist Andrew Bissell observed the way in which memorials are imbued at the point of creation with a clear semiotic relationship, shared and understood across the community, and that, while 'those who follow inherit the earlier meanings but also add new ones of their own', these 'once special places' become literally meaningless for successive generations deprived of the necessary cultural capital – they have a half-life, as most Victorian statues and reliefs readily demonstrate. Incidentally, Bissell, a senior editor with the *Southern Daily Echo*, wrote his glossy, fully illustrated, well-packaged history of wartime Southampton with the full cooperation of his employer. A quarter of a century earlier literary editor Tony Brode had enjoyed full access to the newspaper's archives in compiling a photographic record of events across the winter of 1940-41. Ten years later, Anthony Kemp produced a similar gift book, republished in 1994 with the SDE logo prominent on the cover. As indicated at the outset, for largely commercial reasons the local newspaper works actively to counter what might be termed 'the memorial effect', in other words the Blitz becoming ever more obscured within the everyday physical - and the shared mental - landscapes. The SDE may form a heritage-conscious alliance with the local tourist information office, but to be fair the paper retains a genuine sense of its own place in history, not least the total destruction of its editorial and printing works in late 1940. This raises an interesting question as to how succeeding generations perceive their local newspaper, the loyalty of older readers a legacy of an era when the *Echo* or the *Telegraph* was a key conduit of civic, community, and crucially, family news.[9]

Given later complaints over poor communications, silencing the local newspaper proved an unforeseen bonus when the *Luftwaffe*'s strategy of obliterating provincial city centres quickly extended to Southampton. Principal targets remained the docks and factories, but the damage to housing and the loss of 77 lives incurred on 23 November signalled a renewed focus upon undermining civilian morale, with the deliberate destruction of homes compounded by the complete disruption of services and public utilities. The crippling six hour raids of 30 November and 1 December left 137 dead, nearly 250 seriously injured, and 1,169 properties wholly destroyed. Yet mere statistics scarcely capture the scale of devastation: several thousand incendiaries and nearly 300 tons of high explosive rendered the town, in the words of one observer, 'a blazing furnace in which every living thing seemed doomed to perish.' Given the destruction of so many familiar landmarks, including the two oldest churches, we need an almost impossible leap of imagination to picture what faced the emergency services and the general population on 2 December 1940. The commercial centre above and below the medieval Bargate, which remarkably had survived intact, was a barren, smoking landscape; the wreckage spread out in to the terraced streets of deprived inner-city areas such as St Mary's and Northam, while less central districts such as Portswood and Shirley bore witness to the geographical spread as well as the intensity of each night's bombardment. Supplies of electricity, gas, and water had all ceased, with scant prospect of early repairs; similarly, it would be several weeks before even the most essential telephone lines could be fully restored. Attention must naturally focus upon the aftermath of this cataclysm, but it should be noted that raids continued intermittently for a further 18 months, leaving a final tally of 630 civilians killed, 898 seriously wounded, and 979 slightly injured.[10]

Painful memories: lingering controversies in both Southampton and Coventry

Setting aside any conspiracy theory that Churchill 'sacrificed' Coventry in order to protect the Enigma secret, the city shares with Southampton several sensitive issues regarding civilian morale and control of the emergency services. Yet there is evidence of an initial resentment on the part of Southampton residents, MO noting complaints that Fleet Street had devoted more attention to the aftermath of the bombing in Coventry than to the ostensibly far worse conditions on the south coast. The claim was largely correct, but only because what had happened in Coventry was so unique, and both the Air Ministry and the Ministry of Information had seen propaganda value in frankly acknowledging the scale of destruction. In succeeding weeks events moved so rapidly that Southampton was quickly competing for coverage with other ports in the south under attack, notably Plymouth, Bristol, and Portsmouth. Ironically, while people in Coventry soon came to appreciate their city's status as a provincial symbol of suffering and defiance – as we have seen, memorably captured in *Heart of Britain* - MO noted an initial suspicion of the popular press's 'ballyhooing of morale'.[11]

One of the biggest shocks for survivors in Southampton was that the emergency services had failed to deal with the conflagration, notwithstanding the 2000 extra fire-fighters drafted in from as far north as Nottinghamshire. The absence of compatible kit, and the consequent lack of water, let alone the paralysis of authority at the centre, ran counter to a popular assumption that over three years of ARP planning, a healthy supply of shelters, and a well-run evacuation scheme, together signalled a community unusually well prepared to deal with the worst Hitler could deliver. A generous explanation is that the system collapsed simply because it was never designed to handle one attack on such a scale, let alone two. Yet this fails to account for very obvious failings once it became clear the *Luftwaffe* would not return for a third consecutive night. The same question pertains to conditions in Coventry, but here evidence suggests that, notwithstanding the ferocity of the assault, ARP fell well short of the Ministry of Home Security's minimum standards, witness inadequate shelters, an acute shortage of volunteers, and the authorities' reluctance to put pressure on parents to evacuate their children from a likely target. Again, in the absence of a national fire service, an appalling situation was made worse as a result of equipment failure or incompatibility and an absence of adequately trained fire-crews. The survival of Holy Trinity simply highlighted the absence in most key buildings of adequate fire-fighting facilities and of fire-watchers trained to deal with incendiaries. Local residents were forced to confront these inadequacies while still in shock, the then *Midland Evening Telegraph* urging a more co-ordinated response whenever the raiders returned. Yet the real soul-searching focused, and continues to focus, upon the inadequacies of the War Emergency Committee both during the raid (for example, Sidney Larkin's belated arrival at the Council House) and afterwards. Why were no less than 13 out of 15 rest centres destroyed because of their vulnerable locations? Why, despite an impressive road-clearing effort, was transport provision so poor? Where was the material and manpower to render lightly damaged accommodation habitable? Why was information so hard to come by, and why were national and local support services so slow to make themselves available? The list of questions was long and painful, with MO sensing a general impression of impotence and ineptitude. The authorities' sluggish response was rooted in shock and inertia, but it also reflected a lack of genuine power (for example, reluctant bus and tram crews could not be compelled to work), as well as the very real tension that existed between local and central government: probably the only reason Labour councillors withstood pressure to surrender control to the Regional Commissioner was the arrival in Coventry of the Home Secretary, Herbert Morrison, a pillar of municipal socialism. The presence within the Coventry Labour Party of strong personalities such as George Hodgkinson and the WVS co-ordinator Pearl Hyde, both of whom emerged with credit from the war, and crucially, the council's high profile record of reconstruction after 1945, meant that with the passage of time the authorities' response to the Blitz was seen in a more generous light. In other words, they benefited from a broader desire to focus upon the best and ignore the worst. Even while the arguments raged, propagandists were already encouraging what might be termed 'the phoenix mentality', with George VI's visit on 16 November initiating the rehabilitation process. Ironically, very few actually saw the King, the boost to morale deriving from newspaper and newsreel coverage. Churchill, although keenly interested in relief activities, waited ten months before finally inspecting the damage. The premier's visit further convinced him that Communist malevolence on the shopfloor had seriously undermined productivity prior to June 1941, and had exacerbated the allegedly low level of morale evident from the earliest raids. Only a week before the 14-15 November attack Churchill had been briefed on Coventry's vulnerability given a transient population that lacked 'civic patriotism'; and at the end of the year MO contrasted recent immigrants into the city placing a strain on the social fabric with Southampton's surprisingly stable population's communal cohesion and keen sense of identity. Whatever his reservations, once Russia was in the war Churchill insisted that Coventry be properly rewarded for all it had endured: a reluctant Morrison raised the mayoral status to that of lord, but, as a stickler for municipal protocol, baulked at doing the same for Southampton, still then technically a town.[12]

The King attracted large crowds in Southampton on 5 December, as did a defiant prime minister at the end of January: on the steps of the Civic Centre Churchill asked an enthusiastic crowd, 'Are we downhearted?', to which the answer was a resounding 'No!'. Much was made of these two visits in *Southampton The English Gateway*, an official history commissioned in 1950 by the 'War History Committee' and authored by the secretary to the chamber of commerce, Bernard Knowles. Knowles was a disciple of Arthur Bryant, offering a heroic Tory vision of the past which at the

same time endorsed the very Whiggish G.M. Trevelyan's dictum that
'history is governed by geography'. In his treatment of the Blitz
Knowles portrayed everybody doing their bit in a cool, unflustered,
phlegmatic, insistently *English* fashion – for all the chaos of war, the
system had stood the test and the community met the challenge. As
befits the era, the book's tone is one of understatement and dignified
celebration, not least in its tribute to the local worthies who either
commissioned it or had advised the author. *Southampton The
English Gateway* and its popular spinoffs provided the authorised
version of events for the next twenty years. While unable to bask in
the reflected glory of the first pedestrian precinct and a new, ultra-
modern cathedral symbolising international reconciliation, in the
1950s and 1960s the residents of Southampton followed the example
of Coventry in depicting the Blitz as a crucible of fire out of which
the local population had emerged proud in the face of adversity. For
both cities the availability of MO records from 1973 raised testing
questions, not only about the performance of the emergency services
in late 1940, but also the fragile state of civilian morale. In May
1972 a carelessly worded newspaper article by Paul Addison had
generated furious correspondence in the *Sunday Times* and the
Coventry Evening Telegraph over the level of panic following the
worst raids. Yet there was very little reaction once it was possible to
read all the relevant MO report, even though it contained remarks
such as, '"Coventry is finished", and "Coventry is dead" were the
key phrases in fishless Friday's talk.' Perhaps this was because the
reporters' comments had already been quoted in Angus Calder's
1969 *The People's War*. The MO criticism of Southampton made
public by Calder was not all that contentious - unlike the material
quoted at length in an MA thesis written at the University of Hull
four years later but largely ignored at the time. When the views of
MO's young south coast reporter, Leonard England, did at last
become more widely available then local feelings ran high. England
had noted 'a fairly general feeling that Southampton was done for',
and no doubt this was an opinion expressed by some or perhaps
many of the shocked survivors he spoke to. Needless to say these
views were rubbished when given front page coverage by the
Southern Daily Echo on 14 February 1973: correspondents were
largely united in the view that this was 'a slander on the town'. The
knee-jerk reaction of indignant aldermen and civic patriots is

understandable, and indeed some criticism was wholly valid: what is obvious from close scrutiny of Len England's initial report is that he was unfamiliar with the area, as confirmed by misspelt place names, and that during his stay he scarcely ventured beyond the town centre. His recordings are random, and lack the depth and detail of the experienced Harrisson's observations in Coventry a fortnight earlier. The Home Secretary/Minister of Home Security's advisers were sceptical of England's conclusions, while Morrison himself accused MO of an alternative, implicitly defeatist, agenda. More recently, Malcolm Smith has speculated that MO assessments of morale were more pessimistic than the upbeat and optimistic Home Intelligence reports because of 'preformed assumptions...of a gap between governors and governed on which MO had been founded.' Calder goes further, suggesting that it was in Harrisson's financial interest to demonstrate his organisation's unique ability to delve into public opinion 'below the surface'. MO's judgement that, 'the human and morale problems of Southampton are being left to local resources, and local personalities which are, in this case, inadequate' not only contradicted Bernard Knowles' by now familiar 'finest hour' version, but chimed with the views of the Inspector General of Air Raid Precautions, Wing Commander E.J. Hodsoll, who had visited Southampton on 5 December 1940 and whose subsequent indictment of the local authority also entered the public domain in 1973. While dismissive of MO's bleak assessment, Morrison responded immediately to Hodsoll's insistence that the regional organisation intervene. That swift response was largely because Hodsoll was so damning, and was unafraid to attribute the blame. It was this readiness to name names, notably the Mayor, 'a poor creature' whose 'sole concern was to be out of town as soon as possible in the afternoon', the conveniently ill Chief Constable, and the Town Clerk who was 'entirely unsuited' to crisis management, which generated so much local anger in March 1973.[13]

While paying tribute to the emergency services' heroism and remarkable capacity for improvisation, Hodsoll painted a depressing picture of organisational chaos during, between, and after the two raids. In his view not only were senior personnel not up to the job, but emergency planning and implementation had been severely impaired by petty internal rivalries, as well as the Civic Centre's reluctance to seek help from the Regional Controller of ARP. By the time the latter took over from the Town Clerk, at Whitehall's insistence, morale had plummeted as a consequence of elected and non-elected officials' demonstrable failure to offer practical advice and provide material comfort. In this respect Hodsoll's criticism endorsed England's initial impressions, and ran wholly counter to Knowles' subsequent version of events. The force of Hodsoll's argument was undermined by his well-known antipathy towards local government, and demonstrable errors (witness a genuinely incapacitated Chief Constable); but his credibility was enhanced by a readiness to acknowledge competence where appropriate, as in the contribution of both the Medical Officer and the Water Engineer. In March 1973 critics highlighted the mistakes and insisted that Hodsoll himself was party to the personality clashes which had allegedly proved so fatal. Whereas reaction to the MO revelations was largely spontaneous and unco-ordinated, the response to the Hodsoll report was carefully orchestrated, with letters to the SDE from pillars of the community, not least veteran aldermen such as Sir James Matthews, whose civic credentials had been established in the course of the war. The few dissenting voices in the correspondence columns were drowned out by the howls of protest from the great and the good. The Town Clerk was induced to recall his own experience of waging war on the municipal Home Front, paying tribute to his maligned predecessor's patience and resilience. A former mayor from later in the war drafted a lengthy denunciation of the decision to declassify the report, and insisted the Government place all corrections and counter-claims on the record. This prompted the formation of a Defence of Southampton Committee, and eventual agreement on a statement which condemned a prejudiced and ill-informed Inspector General's 'panic report', insisting that wartime problems were invariably due to extenuating circumstances. Remarkably, in March 1975 the Home Office agreed to local MP Bob Mitchell's request that the Public Records Office place this statement of rebuttal in the same file as Hodsoll's original report.[14]

A quarter of a century later one is struck by the degree to which Leonard England's conclusions correlate and correspond with Hodsoll's. Yet while the latter drew the fiercest response in 1973, it is the MO report which has cast the longer shadow over Southampton's communal view of the Blitz. As suggested at the outset, response to the raids remains a more sensitive topic among older residents than appears to be the case in Coventry. While in recent years much attention has focused upon wartime crime, and how much looting took place during the Blitz, a residual area of contention is 'trekking', a term commonly applied to spontaneous as opposed to organised evacuation once the bombing was finally over. Not that organised evacuation was free from controversy, with RAF officers based in the port wrestling control from council officials simply overwhelmed by the scale of the task. Much later came the suggestion that too many of the 'refugees' bussed out of Southampton in early December 1940 had been, in the words of one liberal, rarely judgemental evacuation officer, 'doubtful both as to cleanliness and honesty': schoolteacher Eric Gadd's diary, published over forty years later, detailed the wasteful and insanitary habits of around 450 inner city residents relocated to New Milton.[15]

Trekking was, in Calder's memorable phrase, 'a fissure in the body of a provincial city'; Londoners rarely lived close to the countryside, and instead sought sanctuary underground.   MO reported large numbers escaping the destruction and carnage in Coventry: 'the small size of the place makes people feel that the only thing they can do *is get out if it altogether.*' In Southampton what might after all be seen as a sensible, collective instinct of self-preservation became tainted by the failure of the Mayor, William Lewis, to lead by example, follow established ARP advice, and not abandon 'his key post around 3 p.m. each afternoon to trek to his rural hideout'. Young Len England was simply noting what was common knowledge across the town, but by 1973 Lewis' implicit cowardice was seen as reflecting upon the steadfastness under fire of *all* Sotonians. Hodsoll estimated that in the first instance about 2,000 fled, but actually far higher numbers either made their own way or left via the relief centres – a week after 'Blitz weekend' MO speculated that only 20 per cent were 'sleeping in old parts of the city'.   Advice was confusing in that, contrary to government guidelines, on 2 December the council's only loudspeaker van toured the town encouraging evacuation.   In consequence many ARP wardens left with their families, and, to add to the rescue services' problems, there was scant manpower available to clear the roads of rubble. Throughout December 1940 large numbers either remained in barracks-style accommodation provided by the authorities, as in the example of New Milton, or fended for themselves. The latter were not necessarily homeless, and often travelled back in to the town to work and to use their normal accommodation during the day. By early 1941 some trekkers did sleep at home during the week, believing that most *Luftwaffe* raids were on Saturdays or Sundays. In Coventry 'sleeping out' was a well established practice even prior to 14-15 November, but the numbers rose dramatically in the final weeks of 1940. A Home Office assessment twelve months later estimated that between 70,000 and 100,000 (out of a population of 194,000) had left the city in the aftermath of its worst raid, dropping back in the New Year to 15-20,000 permanent evacuees. It is difficult to see how the latter figure squares with Tom Harrisson's later conclusion that in Coventry trekking was a temporary phenomenon and not, as in Southampton, 'a way of life'. At the time Harrisson and his colleagues in the Midlands had noted within 48 hours evidence of initial shock subsiding, and 'out of the rubble began to grow local pride'. Interestingly, in the light of subsequent events in Southampton, MO registered 'a complete absence of scape-goating', as well as a readiness to get back to work. Whether or not this was wishful thinking, the regional commission also observed how sheer panic had been replaced by a range of strategies for dealing with the demands of home, work, and above all, travel. Rather than the negative *trekking*, many workers were in fact *commuting*, hence Tony Mason quoting Midland Red's 1941 estimate that 5,000 more passengers were carried in to Coventry every morning in time to clock on. Among them was my father, living with his parents in Braunstone, but proud that he never missed a shift at Armstrong Whitworth until the day he was called up. Travelling by bus or motorcycle out into the Northamptonshire countryside at the end of a twelve hour shift was tiring and tedious, but at least he was guaranteed a decent night's sleep. The key reason why Coventry's factories were slow to resume full production was a lack of power and water, not labour: by mid-December 80 per cent of the workforce was back on the shopfloor. Raids the following April saw a similar rate of recovery. The biggest problem, not surprisingly, was persuading workers to resume the night shift. Coventry, like other industrial centres in the winter of 1940-41, demonstrated that, whatever the immediate impact, the morale of workers would not be broken by raids of the scale undertaken by the *Luftwaffe* (or even the far greater aerial assault of the RAF and

USAAF later in the war), and that production depended upon operational machinery and not the buildings that housed them.[16]

Conclusion
In 1940 and again in 1976 Tom Harrisson drew an important distinction between Coventry and Southampton. In the case of the former the *Luftwaffe* did not return the following night, thereby ensuring the survival of a surprising proportion of industrial plant. Equally crucially, the resolve of the local population was given a vital breathing space in which to recover. Over Coventry's 'Blitz weekend' the level of fear and panic eased as it became clear the bombers were not coming back. The emergency infrastructure could not match the level of control and ARP/fire-fighting provision which had painfully evolved over 57 nights in the capital, and residents had not made the psychological adjustment Londoners found necessary to tolerate and survive nightly danger and disruption – but neither had residents in Southampton, and they needed to. Throughout 2 December those still in Southampton had every reason to suspect the bombers would be back for a third consecutive night, and when they failed to appear the fear still remained: after all there had been a week's gap between the first major raid and the next two. The uncertainty of 'episodic blitzkrieg' was psychologically *very* debilitating Thus, it is scarcely surprising Harrisson warned the Ministry of Information a week later that, in the absence of comfort and distraction, morale continued to deteriorate: 'Nine-tenths of all talk was still about the damage and the raids of a fortnight ago. The topic remains an obsession, and among many people is becoming dangerously near neurosis. There are apparently no official attempts to provide any antidote or to make any attempt to extrovert these feelings.' Dissatisfaction was compounded by concern that Southampton's plight was being overlooked, and that Coventry was benefiting from the publicity awarded to the first major victim of the *Luftwaffe*'s switch from London to the provinces. Such resentment was understandable, and there is evidence to suggest that the Midlanders' morale during, and after, the war was indeed boosted by the level of national *and* international attention given to their city, its charred, burnt-out cathedral, and its capacity to rebuild the centre along lines that would have horrified the ultra-cautious rate-paying shopkeepers of Southampton. Comparison of experience was

actually a short-lived phenomenon, but a senior citizen on the south coast would be entitled to point out the irony that thousands more Coventrians fled their city than left Southampton. Yet for too many historians of the Home Front, what was no more than a basic survival instinct is still seen in a negative light whenever 'trekking' is depicted as an integral part of Southampton's response to intense – and repeated - aerial bombardment. The emergency authorities clearly failed to rise to the occasion, but in such circumstances would any untested organisation have succeeded in retaining effective control of events? In any case, during and after Coventry's worst raid its War Emergency Committee performed only marginally better; the Labour leadership's real success lay in later avoiding close scrutiny, with members utilising peacetime success to camouflage wartime failure. The left-leaning MO, although initially harsh in condemning a manifest absence of adequate preparation, soon mellowed in its judgement. In Southampton, by comparison, the strictures became ever harsher.[17]

Andrew Bissell, entitled by profession to claim some local knowledge, portrayed survivors of the Blitz in Southampton today as largely indifferent over which community responded most positively and most courageously: the simple answer is that there were no winners and losers, and all can feel proud that they lived through such a frightening and yet life-enhancing experience. For those who can remember, the Blitz remains very much a shared experience, as well as a defining moment in the history of both the town and the docks. Similar sentiments would be expressed by my mother and her friends in Coventry, although any suggestion that in November 1940 not everything went to plan is invariably treated as a thinly veiled insult and brusquely dismissed. Nevertheless, these Midlands veterans of the Home Front would wholeheartedly endorse the lament of Bissell's interviewees that the biggest difference between 1940 and the present day is 'community friendliness and camaraderie'. It is easy to dismiss such views as over-sentimental and unduly nostalgic, but here is a generation who came through a test most of us can scarcely envisage. Thus they deserve our close attention as to their memories of war, but above all, they deserve our respect.[18]

NOTES

1. Introduction

---

[1] Regrettably, I had to bow to my mother's wishes and have not recounted in this volume her experience of the Blitz, and her remarkable support for my father after he was severely injured on 14 November 1940, the night of the *Luftwaffe*'s most severe raid on Coventry.

[2] Most recently, J. Hinton, *Women, Social Leadership, and the Second World War – Continuities of Class* (Oxford, Oxford University Press, 2002). Although focusing upon the work of the WVS across Britain, Hinton draws upon his specialist knowledge of 1940s Coventry.

[3] On 25 August 1939 an IRA bomb in the basket of a tradesman's bicycle killed five and injured many more. There was strong anti-Irish feeling, and 2000 workers from Armstrong Whitworth, my father's employer, marched in to the city centre to attend a protest meeting.

[4] Coventry's 'post-1992 university' was originally Lanchester Polytechnic, the name consciously acknowledging the city's industrial heritage. The polytechnic's first director was commissioned to write an official history, which remains the first point of reference: K. Richardson, *Twentieth-Century Coventry* (Coventry, Coventry City Council, 1972). Warwick, a mid-1960s 'plateglass university', has always seemed physically and psychologically remote from Coventry, witness the number of staff and students who prefer to live in the county town or its near neighbours, Leamington and Kenilworth. The Centre for the Study of Social History was a flagship initiative headed by E.P. Thompson for a brief and turbulent period, which, despite its undoubted influence, was closed down in the mid-1990s.

[5] T. Mason and P. Thompson, '"Reflections on a Revolution"? The political mood in wartime Britain' in N. Tiratsoo (ed.), *The Attlee Years* (London, Pinter, 1991), pp. 54-70; B. Lancaster and T. Mason an (eds.), *Life and Labour in a Twentieth Century City: The Experience of Coventry* (Coventry, Cryfield Press, 1986); N. Tiratsoo, *Reconstruction, Affluence and Labour Politics: Coventry 1945-60* (London, Routledge, 1990). See also N. Tiratsoo, 'The Reconstruction of Blitzed British Cities, 1944-55: Myths and Reality', *Contemporary British History* 14 (2000), pp 27-44. On the historiographical debate re Coventry and reconstruction, see N. Tiratsoo, J. Hasegawa, T. Mason and T. Matsumura, *Urban Reconstruction*

in Britain and Japan, 1945-1955: Dreams, Plans and Realities (Luton, University of Luton Press, 2002), p. 17.

[6] See for example G. Hodgkinson, *Sent to Coventry* (Bletchley, Maxwell, 1970). Hodgkinson movingly summarised his life and political beliefs in J. Seabrook, *What Went Wrong? Working People and the Ideals of the Labour Movement* (London, Victor Gollancz, 1978), pp. 167-72. Edelman was better known as a political novelist than as a backbench fixer. Dick Crossman's influence in Whitehall 1940-45 was limited by his maverick reputation, but from Bevanite dissent he moved in to the party mainstream, his courting of Harold Wilson ensuring a tempestuous ministerial career from 1964 to 1970, after which he licked his wounds back in his natural home, the editorial offices of the *New Statesman*. On his pre-ministerial relations with the Coventry Labour Party, see J. Morgan (ed.), *The Backbench Diaries of Richard Crossman* (London, Jonathan Cape, 1981).

[7] Audit Commission, *2002 Comprehensive Performance Assessment*, quoted in P. Hetherington, 'Driven to the limits', *Guardian*, 12 March 2003.

[8] For example, only Plymouth matched Coventry in erecting 8,000 new permanent dwellings between 1945 and 1953, but the target set at the end of the war had been 30,000 new units (7% of the 1938 housing stock was irreparable) and the council waiting list over a decade later exceeded 10,000 names. Tiratsoo *et al*, *Urban Reconstruction in Britain and Japan, 1945-1955*, pp. 13, 18 and 21.

[9] Seabrook, *What Went Wrong?*, pp. 167-201.

[10] Tiratsoo, *Reconstruction, Affluence and Labour Politics*, passim. Tiratsoo *et al*, *Urban Reconstruction in Britain and Japan, 1945-1955*, p. 25.

[11] J. Hasegawa, *Replanning the Blitzed City Centre: A Comparative Study of Bristol, Coventry and Southampton 1941-1950* (Buckingham, Open University Press, 1992), pp. 23-4 and 52-64; Tiratsoo *et al*, *Urban Reconstruction in Britain and Japan, 1945-1955*, pp. 20-22.

[12] For example, Arnold Wesker's *Roots* fresh from the Royal Court. My parents, no doubt for the best of reasons, took me to see this production, and needless to say I didn't have a clue as to what was going on.

[13] The wheel would come full circle when Mumford wrote approvingly of the new Coventry in *The City in History* (London, Secker & Warburg, 1961), and at greater length in *The Highway and the City* (New York, 1963/Greenwood, 1981).

[14] John Hewitt, 'New Jerusalem 1' in F. Ormsby (ed.), *The Collected Poems of John Hewitt* (Dublin, Blackstaff Press, 1994), p. 151.

[15] The layout of the seven-section exhibition, and the format of the illustrated guide, placed a heavy emphasis upon visual, non-technical, explanation and instruction, and *A City Reborn* was shown at regular intervals in a screening room adjacent to the main hall. Tiratsoo *et al*, *Urban Reconstruction in Britain and Japan, 1945-1955*, pp. 22-3.

[16] On the critical and public reception given to *Never Had It So Good*, see Tiratsoo, *Reconstruction, Affluence and Labour Politics*, p. 100. Shooting script of *Face of England*, Central Office of Information film files, September 1960, National Archives/Public Records Office.

[17] Ibid.

[18] See, for example, John Hewitt, 'Godiva Rides Again' in a New Coventry', in *Belfast Telegraph*, 20 September 1957.

[19] F. MacCarthy, 'Humanising History', *Guardian*, 8 February 2003.

[20] Coventry Cathedral was consecrated in 1962. On its construction and decoration see Louise Campbell, *Coventry Cathedral: Art and Architecture in Post-War Britain* (Oxford, Clarendon Press, 1996). The 1941 Leeds exhibition, in which Kenneth Clark juxtaposed Henry Moore's sculptures and shelter drawings alongside the early sketches and paintings Sutherland and Piper produced under the War Artists' Scheme, 'may well have marked the English acceptance of a subdued native modernism at the national level' – as endorsed twenty years later in the two painters' epic contributions to the new cathedral. P. Stansky and W. Abrahams, *London's Burning: Life, Death and Art in the Second World War* (London, Constable, 1994), p. 58.

[21] On Jennings' cinematic and Larkin's fictional representations of Coventry in the aftermath of the *Luftwaffe*'s 'Operation Moonlight Sonata' on 14-15 November 1940, see the relevant essays

[22] MacCarthy, Humanising History'. A less visible contribution to the Festival was the proposal for a 'live exhibition' of urban regeneration [the Lansbury estate in Poplar] made by Coventry's most distinguished designer, Frederick Gibberd, the architect of Heathrow and Harlow New Town. Tiratsoo *et al*, *Urban Reconstruction in Britain and Japan, 1945-1955*, p. 29.

[23] Broadgate also boasted the council's flagship hotel, the ultra-modern 'Leofric' and above the entrance from Hertford Street a mechanical clock which on the hour produced the naked lady and the dastardly Peeping Tom, struck blind for his impertinence at not remaining indoors while the first lady of Mercia made her famous protest over her husband's rapacious taxes. It sounds kitsch, but it's not, and until the novelty wore off everyone in Broadgate would stop just prior to the hour in order to watch the protagonists appear. While Lady Godiva's equestrian statue is today back in Broadgate, only a few years ago civic planners seemed to find it something of an embarrassment, shifting both plinth and sculpture around the city centre to a relentless chorus of disapproval from old and young alike.

[24] M. Remy, *Surrealism in Britain* (London, Ashgate, 1999) pp. 198-9; exhibition notes for 'Curiouser and Curiouser: A Surrealist Sensation', Southampton City Art Gallery, 18 October-15 December 2002.

[25] Wallnotes on restored Cullen ceramic mural, Lower Precinct. The fact that few complained when the mosaic tableau of medieval maps was irrevocably damaged by council workmen in the 1970s speaks volumes about municipal and public indifference to the 'townscape' at the time.

[26] On Hewitt's early idealism re Coventry, see the relevant essay.

[27] Immediately adjacent, in Donegall Street, is the John Hewitt Bar and Restaurant, owned by the Unemployed Resource Centre next door. Hewitt opened the support centre in 1985, hence the decision in 2001 to name the pub after him. Appropriately, the bar has a great atmosphere, looks good (framed poems, obituaries, etc., plus modern art), and boasts several awards for the quality of its food. Highly recommended for all visitors to Belfast!

[28] Tiratsoo, *Reconstruction, Affluence and Labour Politics*, pp. 88-100; Tiratsoo *et al*, *Urban Reconstruction in Britain and Japan, 1945-1955*, pp. 24-5. Tiratsoo makes the point that because of poor organisation the Conservatives after the war failed to recover at the rate their local membership justified, hence the marginal status of the newly created seat of Coventry South. 'The result was a party that promised much but delivered little, and something of a breathing space for Labour.' By the 1960s, however, the Conservatives were attracting a better calibre of parliamentary candidate (for example, future favourite of Mrs Thatcher, Ian Gow) and placing ward/constituency organisation in the hands of efficient middle managers drawn from local industry and commerce, including my father. Carrying little ideological baggage, but attracted by an organisational rather than an overtly political challenge, Dad masterminded the election and re-election of his Tory friends in council wards at the heart of Dick Crossman's constituency. Disillusion with Edward Heath and an undisguised loathing of Mrs Thatcher ended a decade-long flirtation with a party which was never his natural home.

[29] Sir Terry Frost quoted in D. Lewis et al, *Terry Frost* (Aldershot, Lund Humphries), pp. 28-9; obituaries, *Guardian* and *Daily Telegraph*, 3 September 2003.

[30] R. Dorment, 'The dark side of suburbia', *Daily Telegraph*, 26 August 2003. George Shaw, 'What I Did This Summer', exhibition, Ikon Gallery, Birmingham, August-September 2003.

[31] P. Bailey, 'Jazz at the Spirella: Coming of Age in Coventry in the 1950s' in B. Coneckin, F. Mort and C. Waters (eds.), *Moments of Modernity Reconstructing Britain 1945-1964* (London, Rivers Oram Press, 1999), p. 22.

[32] Ibid., pp. 23-4. On affluent workers' changing family dynamics in Midlands and southern cities even prior to the Second World War, see R. McKibbin, *Classes and Cultures: England 1918-1951* (Oxford, Oxford University Press, 1998), pp. 188-98.

[33] Bailey, 'Jazz at the Spirella', p. 23. The majority of grammar school boys and girls in the 1950s pursued careers within the city; it took the advent of the Robbins Report to facilitate – permanent -movement elsewhere in the country, as described in the first essay on Coventry Rugby Club.

[34] As Bailey acknowledges, Larkin is the role model here even if he was never mentioned at King Henry VIII School in the 1950s – as opposed to my experience a decade later. Ibid., p. 32.

[35] Funding for the Festival was from the rates and an Arts Council grant. Festival director John Lowe was a friend of Britten, who accepted the commission for a £1000 fee. The 1963 recording of the *War Requiem* was a great critical and commercial success, the boxed double album selling over 200,000 copies in five months. M. Oliver, *Benjamin Britten* (London, Phaidon, 1996), pp. 174-80; M. Cooper (ed.), *Britten: War Requiem* (Cambridge, Cambridge University Press, 1996).

[36] Duke Ellington, 22 February 1966, in Coventry Cathedral, quoted in A.H. Lawrence, *Duke Ellington and his World* (London, Routledge, 2001), p. 368.

[37] The NJO, led by Neil Ardley from 1963 to 1970, recorded two albums during that time. According to one-time member Ian Carr, 'It was a band of player-

composers, its express purpose to perform the works of new writers, and so it became a crucible for the strongest talents of the British scene.' I. Carr, *Music Outside Contemporary Jazz in Britain* (London, Latimer New Divisions, 1973), p. 6.

[38] At Robert Wyatt's instigation, an eight-piece line-up, including composer Keith Tippett's horn section, recorded *Third* in January 1970 before playing select dates, including the Lanchester Polytechnic. S. Nicholson, *Jazz-Rock A History* (Edinburgh, Canongate, 1998), pp. 23-4.

[39] Jon Hiseman quoted in Carr, *Music Outside*, p. 64. Both the NJO and Soft Machine performances attracted more respectful audience reaction than rock bands usually did (and provided me with my first – exhilarating - experiences of a full brass section at maximum volume).

[40] The Specials, *In The Studio* (2-Tone, 1984). '...this inspired, non-ska mire of lounge-jazz musak and dub-reggae', famous for the anthemic 'Nelson Mandela', took Dammers three years to record. J. Irwin (ed.), *The Mojo Collection The Greatest Albums of All Time* (Edinburgh, Mojo Books, 2000), p. 543; interview with Jerry Dammers in A. Petridis, 'Ska for the Madding Crowd', *Guardian*, 8 March 2002. On the Midlands roots of Two Tone, see R. Eddington, *Sent From Coventry: The Chequered Past of Two Tone* (London, IMP, 2004).

[41] But sadly not for Wood End, a 1950s council estate out on the north-eastern fringe of Coventry and miles from the city centre. Parts of Wood End, one of England's 39 most deprived communities and notorious for widespread social behaviour, looks like Grozny. With £34 million invested since 1987, the estate is to be partially or wholly demolished under the New Deal for Communities scheme. Statement by the Office of the Deputy Prime Minister quoted in A. Gillan, 'Where the law abiding live in fear', *Guardian*, 11 November 2002. 'A Sense of Place – Coventry', BBC Radio 4, 28 September 2002 offered a radio portrait of contemporary Coventry, including life on the Wood End estate.

[42] For a summary of Hill's contribution to modern football, see R. Holt and T. Mason, *Sport in Britain 1945-2000* (Oxford, Blackwell, 2000), pp. 80-82 and 99-100.

[43] There have been several histories, of varying quality, with the Hill era adequately covered in D. Brassington, *Singers to Sky Blues: The Story of Coventry City Football Club* (London, Sporting and Leisure Publications, 1986). As with most other clubs, the success of Nick Hornby's *Fever Pitch* prompted similar pitches at a mass market, including Joycean scholar Rick Gekoski's witty and revealing record of a season spent with the Sky Blues. Clearly inspired by Hunter Davies's veil-lifting *homage* to Tottenham Hotspur, *The Glory Game*, this American academic turned bookseller overcame manager Gordon Strachan's initial suspicion to produce the best book so far on Coventry City. R. Gekoski, *Staying Up Behind the Scenes in the Premiership* (London, Little, Brown and Company, 1998).

[44] Most notably, A. Smith, 'Civil War in England: the clubs, the RFU, and the impact of professionalism on rugby union, 1995-99' in A. Smith and D. Porter, *Amateurs and Professionals in Post-war British Sport* (London, Frank Cass, 2000), pp. 146-88.

---

[45] Howling Sky Blue fans note: notwithstanding a first loyalty to rugby union, I feel wholly qualified to make such a claim having supported Coventry City through thick and thin since attending my first match in a pre-Jimmy Hill era.

[46] J. Hill, *Sport, Leisure and Culture in Twentieth-Century Britain* (Basingstoke, Palgrave, 2002).

[47] McKibbin, *Classes and Cultures*, p. 332; M. Polley, *Moving the Goalposts: a History of Sport and Society Since 1945* (London, Routledge, 1998), pp. 4-5.

[48] For a profile of Pearl Hyde, see Hinton, *Women, Social Leadership, and the Second World War*, pp. 86-8.

[49] Comments noted by Mass Observation representative in Southampton, November 1940, in T. Harrisson (ed.), *Living Through The Blitz* (London, Collins, 1972), pp. 150-1. See this volume's final essay.

2. Cars, cricket and Alf Smith

[1] This essay originally appeared in the *International Journal of the History of Sport*, 19 (March 2002), pp. 137-50.

[2] M. Smith, *Britain and 1940 History, Myth and Popular Memory* (London, Routledge, 2000), p. 1.

[3] D. Edgerton, *England and the Aeroplane An Essay on a Militant and Technological Nation* (London, Macmillan, 1991), p. xv.

[4] On works-based sport before the First World War see R. Munting, 'The games ethic and industrial capitalism before 1914: the provision of company sports', *Sport in History*, 1 (2003), pp. 45-63; and re literature on company paternalism see J. Hill, *Sport, Leisure and Culture in Twentieth-Century Britain* (Basingstoke, Palgrave, 2002), pp. 189-80, ft. 22.

[5] J. Crump, 'Recreation in Coventry Between the Wars' in B. Lancaster and T. Mason (eds.), *Life and Labour in a Twentieth Century City: The Experience of Coventry* (Coventry, Cryfield Press, 1986), pp. 261-287. The paper upon which part of this essay is based – given on 7 January 2001 to the Social History Society's annual conference, 'Cultures and Sub-Cultures: Rethinking Histories of Culture' – noted with appreciation Crump's extensive research in to the origins and interwar activities of Coventry's workplace clubs.

[6] Ernie Bevin was of course General Secretary of the Transport and General Workers Union until accepting office in the Churchill coalition in May 1940. The TGWU was particularly well organised in wartime Coventry, recruiting aggressively and targeting female employees. D. Thoms, *War, Industry and Society The Midlands 1939-45* (London, Croom Helm, 1989), p. 69. See also J. Hinton, 'Coventry Communism: a study of factory politics in WW2', *History Workshop Journal*, 10, pp. 90-118.

[7] The Warwickshire coalfield, which survived until the 1970s, was located north of the city, and most of the colliery sides were based around the then separate village of Bedworth, halfway between Coventry and Nuneaton. Midlands coalfields,

especially Nottinghamshire, tended to have broader seams, facilitating easier working conditions, higher output, and marginally better pay. Miners had, in relative terms, more disposable income than their counterparts further north, hence their greater participation in organised sport. England's most famous and controversial fast bowler between the wars, Harold Larwood, had been a Nottinghamshire miner, and the coalfield boasted cricket leagues solely composed of colliery teams. J. Williams, *Cricket and England A Cultural and Social History of the Inter-war Years* (London, Frank Cass, 1999), p. 51.

[8] For someone who had been such a fluent batsman, my father was remarkably successful at stifling childhood enthusiasm, encouraging me to treat every ball as if I was Trevor Bailey or at best Geoffrey Boycott, i.e. play an endless succession of defensive shots à la England's two best-known postwar exponents of the long and dogged innings.

[9] For an overview of 'the summer game' in the 1930s, see Jack Williams' *Cricket and England.*

[10] R.E.S. 'Bob' Wyatt was an amateur captain of both Warwickshire and England (on sixteen occasions) in the 1930s, who could afford to be generous in his praise of the less privileged county professionals: 'as fine a lot of fellows as anyone could wish to meet'. Wyatt was the antithesis of my father, fostering his skills at the city's best-known private school, King Henry VIII, and the then very select cricket club, Coventry and North Warwickshire. R.E.S. Wyatt, *The Ins and Outs of Cricket* (London, Bell,1936), p. 255.

[11] Although not himself a miner, kit would have been paid for out of the Miners Welfare Fund, based on a levy on each pit's output. Keresley, another Warwickshire colliery side, were funded directly by the pit owners, and could afford to employ two Yorkshire professionals as part-time coaches. Williams, *Cricket and England*, p. 51; Crump, 'Recreation in Coventry Between the Wars', p. 275.

[12] Griff and Coton was a joint colliery side located on the northern outskirts of the city. Most English cities of course still publish a Saturday evening edition of the local newspaper, which focuses upon sport and gives all that afternoon's results. 'The Pink' is the *Coventry Evening Telegraph*'s sports edition.

[13] T. Buchanan, *Britain and the Spanish Civil War* (Cambridge, Cambridge University Press, 1997), pp. 126, 23-24. The debate on the level of awareness of events in Spain and of active support remains ongoing, not least via the work of Jim Fyrth and Tom Buchanan. For a very different view of Midlands car workers, from the perspective of a militant shop steward who migrated from Wales to the Cowley plant at Oxford, see A. Exell, 'Morris Motors in the 1930s, Part I', *History Workshop Journal*, 6 (1978), pp. 52-78, and 'Morris Motors in the 1930s, Part II', ibid., 7 (1979), pp. 45-65. G. Orwell, 'Looking Back on the Spanish War' in S. Orwell and I. Angus (eds.), *The Collected Essays, Journalism and Letters of George Orwell: Volume 2 My Country Right Or Left 1940-1943* (London, Penguin, 1969), p. 299.

[14] Thus my father played for St Margaret's, a grim looking turn of the century Anglican Church, its worshippers imbued with a strong evangelical mission.

[15] For example, R. McKibbin, *Classes and Cultures: England 1918-1951* (Oxford, Oxford University Press, 1998), pp. 188-198.

[16] With 184.1 private cars per thousand population, it is not surprising that density of traffic was a key driver in pre-war initiatives to rebuild the city centre. Between 1928 and 1938 Coventry gained 26,000 more houses, of which around 22,500 were privately built. The local building society's assets rose to an astonishing £4 million. J. Hasegawa, *Replanning the Blitzed City Centre: A Comparative Study of Bristol, Coventry and Southampton 1941-1950* (Buckingham, Open University Press, 1992), pp. 22-23.

[17] For evidence that this was by no means the smooth process of reconstruction popularly assumed, see ibid., pp. 30-46, 95-100, 122-125 and 132-133.

[18] Ibid., pp. 42-52 and 100; K. Richardson, *Twentieth-Century Coventry* (Coventry, Coventry City Council, 1972), pp. 310-343. For profiles of Hodgkinson and Stringer, see ibid., pp. 204-206.

[19] Herbert donated £100, 000 towards the cost of the gallery, but with a number of conditions. J. McG. Davies, 'A Twentieth-century Paternalist: Alfred Herbert and the Skilled Coventry Workman' in Lancaster and Mason (eds.), *Life and Labour in a Twentieth-century City*, p. 124.

[20] See the relevant essay on John Hewitt.

[21] The strength of grassroots rugby is reflected in what was then the relatively modest size of local football's senior league, the Coventry and District League, which in 1938 comprised of three divisions and 30 teams: Papers of the Coventry and District Football League, 1912-76, Coventry Records Office, ref. 617.

[22] Both clubs retain their reputations as hard sides, as evidenced by two of England's most combative players in recent years, ex-Barkers Butts forwards, Neil Back and Richard Cockerill.

[23] 1928 signalled the start of local industry's sustained growth: Courtaulds significantly increased rayon production, William Lyons established his SS car company (the forerunner of Jaguar), Morris increased output to over 50,000 cars per annum, and Alfred Herbert embarked on a major programme of investment in 1928; the complementary activities of A.C. Wickman and Coventry Gauge and Tool ensured Coventry's centrality to machine tool production (for a damning indictment of the industry's record before and during the war, see C. Barnett, *The Audit of War The Illusion and Reality of Britain as a Great Nation* (London, Macmillan, 1986), pp. 133-136 and 159.). By 1931 there were 11 car manufacturers in Coventry, and by 1941 seven 'shadow' munitions factories, the first four dating from 1936-7.

[24] Crump, 'Recreation in Coventry Between the Wars', pp. 270-271; Davies, 'A Twentieth-century Paternalist', p. 120. An influx of at least 30,000 armaments workers and their dependants by the autumn of 1939 raised the city's population above 250,000. Hasegawa, *Replanning the Blitzed City Centre*, p. 35.

[25] Despite the demise of the aircraft industry, the unemployment rate in 1968 stood at 3.3 per cent. Richardson, *Twentieth-Century Coventry*, pp. 40-42, 141 and 337.

[26] Crump, 'Recreation in Coventry Between the Wars', Thoms, *War, Industry and Society*, pp. 269-270.

[27] Richardson, *Twentieth-Century Coventry*, pp. 99-102; pp. 13, 60 and 101.

[28] Crump, 'Recreation in Coventry Between the Wars', pp. 268-269 and 272

[29] In the 1960s the Courtaulds works team fostered the Warwickshire (later Somerset) and England spin bowler, Tom Cartwright.

[30] Crump, 'Recreation in Coventry Between the Wars', pp. 269, 276-277, and 284; Papers of the Coventry Sports Assocation, 1953-80, Coventry Records Office, ref. 847.

[31] Davies, 'A Twentieth-century Paternalist', pp. 98-132.

[32] By the late 1930s up to 800 dancers were packing in to the Connor on Wednesday and Saturday nights and for special events. This popularity carried on in to the war, and beyond, not least because the GEC boasted the best dance band in the city. Interview with Mrs Frances Smith, 4 August 2001. The financial collapse of GEC's successor, Marconi, has meant that the Allard Way pitches and pavilion have now been sold to property developers. The closure of Massey Ferguson in 2003 leaves Sphinx as the only ex-works side with its own ground still playing football in the Midland Combination. Within the city, surviving works-based teams play in the Coventry Alliance. As syndicated columnist Steve Field has pointed out, ironically one of the few genuine works teams still playing football, albeit never able to field the same side twice, is the West Midlands Police. S. Field, 'Playing the Field', Worcester City v. Aldershot Town match programme, 30 November 2002. My thanks, as always, to Dil Porter for that particular tit-bit.

[33] My father had played for a rival colliery club, Bedworth, but accepted an invitation to play for Griff and Coton simply because it was a superior side.

[34] Crump, 'Recreation in Coventry Between the Wars', pp. 276-276.

[35] Bristol [formerly Armstrong] Siddeley's merger with Rolls Royce compounded the loss of approximately 11,000 jobs in the aircraft industry between 1962 and 1968. This increased the city's dependence upon vehicle manufacture, and by the second half of the 1970s ensured that a national pattern of deindustrialisation would prove especially damaging in Coventry.

[36] *AWA Affairs*, December 1959.

[37] J. Castle 'Factory Work for Women: Courtaulds and GEC between the Wars' in Lancaster and Mason (eds.), *Life and Labour in a Twentieth-century City*, pp. 141-142; Crump, 'Recreation in Coventry Between the Wars', p. 274; interview with Mrs Frances Smith, 4 August 2001; Richard Holt, *Sport and the British A Modern History* (Oxford, Clarendon Press, 1990), pp. 128-129; J. Hargreaves, *Sporting Females Critical Issues in the History and Sociology of Women's Sports* (London, Routledge, 1994), pp. 123-124. On the popularity of the Women's League of Health and Beauty (166,000 members in England by 1939), see ibid., pp. 135-136.

[38] *AWA Affairs*, December 1959, February 1960, and April 1960.

[39] Ibid., April 1955.

[40] *AH News*, all issues 1965.

[41] *Jaguar Journal*, August 1960, and September 1960. The magazine was a revival of an earlier initiative, which had ceased publication in the early 1950s, ironically at the very time that Lyons agreed to the establishment of the Jaguar Social Club, and Sports Field. On Jaguar's poor industrial relations, 1959-63, see S. Tolliday, 'High Tide and After: Coventry Engineering Workers and Shopfloor Bargaining,

1945-80' in Lancaster and Mason (eds.), *Life and Labour in a Twentieth-century City*, pp. 220-221.

[42] *Jaguar Journal*, September 1960.

[43] A further example of research in this field is P. Thompson, 'Playing at Being Skilled Men: Factory Culture and Pride in Work Skills among Coventry Car Workers', *Social History*, 1 (1988), pp. 45-69.

[44] For example, the work of Stephen Tolliday. Tolliday, 'High Tide and After', pp. 204-243.

[45] On 'Our Finest Hour' and the power of the popular/national myth, see Smith, *Britain and 1940*, and A. Calder, *The Myth of the Blitz* (London, Jonathan Cape, 1991).

3. Temporary Gentleman

[1] This essay was published in its original form as '"Temporary gentleman" My father and World War II', *Encounter* (July-August 1990), pp. 28-32.

[2] On a peculiarly English obsession with the Second World War see A. Smith, 'Doubts about D-Day', *Times Higher Education Supplement*, 10 June 1994.

[3] Information imparted by my father some time in the 1970s as I scanned the photographs decorating his office walls.

[4] On direct combat experience and morale see D. French, *Raising Churchill's Army The British Army and the War against Germany 1919-1945* (Oxford, Oxford University Press, 2000), pp. 135-46; D. French, '"You cannot hate the bastard who is trying to kill you…" Combat and ideology in the British Army in the war against Germany, 1939-45', *Twentieth Century British History*, 11 (2000), pp. 1-22; D. French, '"Tommy is no soldier": the morale of the Second British Army in Normandy, June-August 1944', *Journal of Strategic Studies*, 19 (1996), pp. 154-78.

[5] The same man, who by 1947 was invariably drunk, had the temerity to test to the limit the hospitality of my impoverished parents: he arrived in Coventry 'just for the day', and stayed for a week.

[6] J.Ellis, *The Sharp End of War The Fighting Man in World War II* (Newton Abbott, David & Charles, 1980), pp. 226-7.

[7] Ibid., p. 192.

[8] French, *Raising Churchill's Army*, pp. 49, 61-3.

[9] I. Beckett, 'The British Army, 1914-18: the illusion of change' in J. Turner (ed.), *Britain and the First World War* (London, Unwin Hyman,1988), pp. 114-16.

[10] Ellis, *The Sharp End of War*, pp. 226-7; French, *Raising Churchill's Army*, p. 65, 74-5.

[11] M. Petter, '"Temporary gentlemen" in the aftermath of the Great War: rank, status and the ex-officer problem', *The historical Journal*, 37 (1994), pp. 127-52.

[12] Berlin's principal mess for British occupying forces was in the Olympic Stadium, and remained so for much of the Cold War. Dad won the 100 yards 'dash' when the Army staged an athletics tournament there in 1946. When I told

the stadium supervisor this on a visit in August 1982 he let me make a commemorative jog around the track.

[13] I suspect my father's personal misery was compounded by regular invitations to have lunch at the House of Lords, all of which he politely declined: Lord Mancroft finally got the message that wartime companionship could not always survive a return to peacetime normality.

[14] Sebastian Faulks [column], *Independent on Sunday*, 11 March 1990.

[15] The cramped central library became for all intents and purposes permanent, and the council canteen differed little from its glory days as a British Restaurant. I spent much of what today would be labelled a 'gap year' gaining either mental or physical sustenance in these two relics of 1940s austerity.

[16] On the differing attitudes of British troops towards SS POWs, see French, '"You cannot hate the bastard who is trying to kill you..."', pp. 17-18.

[17] A second challenge in Algiers to de Gaulle's authority no doubt confirmed Dad's low opinion of the French Army; a prejudice rooted in his wartime inability to comprehend why the Free French chose to place smart uniforms and snappy drill so far down the priority list.

[18] 'I couldn't say anything more then, because I had a funny choke in my throat and I had to clean my glasses because there now, below us, grey and always beautiful, was spread the city I love best in all the world.' E. Hemingway, 'How we came to Paris', *Collier's*, 7 October 1944, in *By-Line* (London, Penguin, 1970), p. 354.

[19] Until casualty replacements and dispersal in July-August 1944 transformed 1/7th Battalion, it largely comprised of 'Coventry kids'. 'War Diary of 1/7th Battalion The Royal Warwickshire Regiment', WO171/1388, PRO.

[20]'First D-Day tribute is recalled', *Coventry Evening Telegraph*, 6 June 1984. J. Charmley, *Duff Cooper The Authorized Biography* (Weidenfeld and Nicholson, 1986), pp. 210-11.

[21] M. Hastings, *Overlord D-Day and the Battle for Normandy 1944* (London, Michael Joseph, 1984), p. 303. The battalion had initially come up against one of the Germans' most ideologically driven fighting units: 12th SS Panzer (Hitler Youth). This was the division which took a key role in holding open the neck of the Falaise pocket for so long. WO171/1388, PRO; J. Keegan, *The Second World War* (London, Pimlico, 1997), p. 342.

[22] Allied land casualties in the battle for Normandy totalled 209,672, of which 36,976 died; Anglo-Canadian losses were two-thirds those of the United States. A daily casualty rate of 2000+ exceeded that of the BEF (including the Royal Flying Corps) at Passchendaele in the autumn of 1917. British and Canadian battalions matched the 1914-18 monthly average of 100 casualties, and in many cases significantly exceeded it. A disproportionate number of those killed or wounded were front-line riflemen waging static attritional warfare not that dissimilar from the experience of their fathers and grandfathers. Infantry rifle companies sustained 70 per cent of all casualties. There was a steep learning curve, and evidence suggests an improvement in combat performance, as well as a diminution of resistance, when surveying the campaign in north-west Europe through to May 1945: 13.5 men per 1000 per month, compared with 28.1 men per 1000 per month 1914-18. Hastings, *Overlord*, p. 313; G.D. Sheffield, 'The shadow of the Somme:

the influence of the First World War on British soldiers' perceptions and behaviour in the Second World War' and T. Copp, "'If this war isn't over, And pretty soon, There'll be nobody left, In this old platoon...'": First Canadian Army, February-March 1945' in P. Addison and A. Calder (eds.), *Time To Kill The Soldier's Experience of War in the West 1939-1945* (London, Pimlico, 1997), pp. 35-6, and 148-9; French, '"Tommy is no soldier"', p. 170.

[23] French, *Raising Churchill's Army*, pp. 77, 147. On total German losses, and on the debate surrounding the Allied, and in particular the British, failure to seal the Gap a fortnight earlier, see Hastings, *Overlord*, pp. 313-15.

[24] Address to 59th Division by CO, Major General L.O. Lyne, 21 August 1944, and to senior battalion officers by Field Marshal Sir Bernard Montgomery, 22 August 1944, WO171/1388, PRO; Copp, '"If this war isn't over"', pp. 148-9; French, *Raising Churchill's Army*, pp. 188-9, 244-7, 255-6, 275-7, 277-9. The infantry constituted less than 25 per cent of 21st Army Group, but accounted for 71 per cent of its casualties. The collapse of the regimental system even prior to D-Day, and the undermining of unit cohesion with the transfer in of troops, had a detrimental impact upon morale. Ironically, Lyne had pioneered induction and orientation for new arrivals in the 59th. On the other hand, of the 'green' divisions his had the second highest number of deserters (42 in August 1944). French, '"Tommy is no soldier"', pp. 159, 168, and 173.

[25] By which time, it should be noted, he had been Mentioned in Despatches. *London Gazette*, 8 November 1945.

[26] Keegan, *The Second World War*, pp. 344-5.

[27] The Benn-style belated radicalism came later, fuelled by a loathing of Mrs Thatcher – to my astonishment Dad became a unilateralist, and in 1982 he privately opposed the Falklands campaign on the grounds that he had seen too many young men sacrificed for their country.

[28] By the time those final words first appeared in print it was clear to me that with old age the nightmares would come back to haunt the survivors of Britain's last great citizen army.

4. Sent to Coventry

[1] This essay was first published as 'Humphrey Jennings' *Heart of Britain* (1941) – a reassessment', *Historical Journal of Film, Radio and Television*, 23 (June 2003), pp. 133-54.

[2] *London Can Take It* (Humphrey Jennings/Michael Watt, GPO Film Unit/MOI; UK, 1940), released in an edited form in the UK as *Britain Can Take It*.

[3] On the contribution of Quentin Reynolds ['I am a neutral reporter. I have watched the people of London live and die.'] to the propaganda success of *London Can Take It!*, see A. Calder, *The Myth of the Blitz* (London, Jonathan Cape, 1992), pp. 223-7 and 232-3, and M. Smith, *Britain and 1940 History, Myth and Popular Memory* (London, Routledge, 2000), pp. 82-4.

[4] Humphrey Jennings to Cicely Jennings, 3 November 1940, in K. Jackson (ed.), *The Humphrey Jennings Film Reader* (Manchester, Carcanet Press, 1993), p. 8.

[5] Humphrey Jennings to Cicely Jennings, 12 and [?] November 1940, *ibid.*, p. 9.

[6] Public Record Office (PRO) INF 5/77, 'HARD WORK AND HIGH JINKS– The backbone of Britain' film proposal, [?] 1940.

[7] *Heart of Britain* (Humphrey Jennings, GPO Film Unit; UK, 1941), released in a slightly longer form overseas as *This Is England*.

[8] See, for example, N. Reeves, *The Power of Film Propaganda Myth or Reality?* (London, Continuum, 1999), pp. 147-61, and J. Chapman, *The British At War Cinema, State and Propaganda, 1939-1945* (London, I.B. Tauris, 1998), pp. –57.

[9] The authorised biography is Kevin Jackson, *Humphrey Jennings The definitive biography of one of Britain's most important film-makers* (London, Picador, 2004). A less satisfactory life is A. W. Hodgkinson and R.E. Sheratsky, *Humphrey Jennings More Than a Maker of Films* (Hanover/London, University Press of New England, 1982). A 1982 exhibition of Jennings' work at the Riverside Studios in London generated a catalogue and collection of essays edited by his daughter: M. Jennings (ed.), *Humphrey Jennings Film-Maker/Painter/Poet* (London, British Film Institute, 1982). Other essays include J. Richards' 'England, Their England: *Fires Were Started*' in A. Aldgate and J. Richards, *Britain Can Take It: The British Cinema in the Second World War* (Oxford, Basil Blackwell, 1986), pp. 218-45, G. Nowell-Smith, 'Humphrey Jennings Surrealist Observer' in C. Barr (ed.), *All Our Yesterdays 90 Years of British Cinema* (London, British Film Institute, 1986), pp. 321-33, Calder, *ibid.*, pp. 228-44, Peter Stansky and William Abrahams, *London's Burning Life, Death and Art in the Second World War* (London, Constable, 1994), pp. 71-125, and more recently, a lightweight profile in C. Drazin, *The Finest Years: British Cinema of the 1940s* (London, Andre Deutsch, 1998), pp. 148-61. See also a BFI Film Classics volume: Brian Winston, *"Fires Were Started –"* (London, British Film Institute, 1999), which contains the most up to date bibliographical guide.

[10] Humphrey Jennings season, NFT, January 2000; 'Humphrey Jennings 1907-1950 Film Director, Painter and Poet', Imperial War Museum, 20 September 2000; *Humphrey Jennings: The Man Who Listened to Britain*, Channel 4, 24 December 2000 [the second television documentary, following 'Heart of Britain', *Omnibus*, BBC1, 20 September 1970].

[11] *Listen to Britain* (Humphrey Jennings/Stewart McAllister, Crown Film Unit; UK, 1941); *Fires Were Started* [originally titled *I Was A Fireman*] (Humphrey Jennings, Crown Film Unit; UK, 1943); *Diary for Timothy* (Humphrey Jennings, Crown Film Unit; UK, 1945). Essays on Jennings largely indifferent to *Heart of Britain*, include Richards, *ibid.*, and Nowell-Smith, *ibid.*.

[12] D. Vaughan, *Portrait of an Invisible Man: The Working Life of Stewart McAllister Film Editor* (London, British Film Institute, 1983), pp. 72-4.

[13] The *Documentary News Letter* was founded in 1940, to promote 'films of democracy on the social offensive', and unenthusiastically reviewed *Heart of Britain* [under its American title, *This is England*] in March 1941. R. Manvell, *Films and the Second World War* (London, Dent, 1974), p. 77, and Vaughan, *ibid.*, pp. 38-9 and 72-3.

[14] Richards, *ibid.*, pp. 225-7.

[15] *Words for Battle* (Humphrey Jennings, Crown Film Unit; UK, 1941).

[16] The exhibition attracted 57,500 visitors over two weeks in October 1945: 1 in 4 of Coventry's entire population. J. Hasegawa, *Replanning the Blitzed City Centre: A Comparative Study of Bristol, Coventry and Southampton 1941-1950* (Buckingham, Open University Press, 1992), p. 45.

[17] Assuming of course that one subscribes to the widely shared view that Jennings' four completed films, 1945-50, are a pale shadow of his finest wartime documentaries.

[18] Humphrey Jennings to Cicely Jennings, 21 September and 20 October 1940, *ibid.*, p. 7.

[19] Clark saw a clear role for documentaries within the second of the three propaganda themes identified by the MoI Policy Committee in December 1939: 'What Britain is fighting for', 'How Britain fights', and 'The need for sacrifice if the fight is to be won'. Pronay, *ibid.*, pp. 152-3; Chapman, *ibid.*, pp. 53-5.

[20] For lively profiles of Beddington, Cavalcanti, Watt, and Dalrymple, see Drazin, *ibid.*

[21] Ian Dalrymple, 'The Crown Film Unit, 1940-43' in N. Pronay and D.W. Spring (eds.), *Propaganda, Politics and Film, 1918-45* (London, Macmillan, 1982), p. 212.

[22] Humphrey Jennings to Cicely Jennings, 3 November 1940, *ibid.*, p.8.

[23] Vaughan, *ibid.*, p. 69; Tom Harrisson, 'Films and the Home Front – the evaluation of their effectiveness by 'Mass Observation' in Pronay and Spring, *ibid.*, p. 241; Chapman, *ibid.*, pp. 98-9.

[24] Reeves, *ibid.*, pp. 167-8.

[25] PRO INF6/328: press handout by Hugh Findlay, quoted in Chapman, *ibid.*, p. 98.

[26] Humphrey Jennings to Cicely Jennings, 20 October 1940, *ibid.*, p.7. Correspondence with Coventry Employment Exchange confirmed Jennings was filming from late summer: PRO INF 5/77, R.B. Hutchinson to Humphrey Jennings, 10 September 1940. *Ibid.*, 'HARD WORK AND HIGH JINKS– The backbone of Britain' film proposal, [?] 1940.

[27] *Spare Time* (Humphrey Jennings, GPO Film Unit; UK, 1939) has been labelled Jennings' 'Mass Observation film', but his direct involvement ceased after completion of *May the Twelfth*, the compilation of reports from over 200 observers on Coronation Day, 12 May 1937, which he co-edited with MO pioneer Charles Madge. Nevertheless, co-founder Tom Harrisson recalled Jennings seeking Mass Observation's advice on morale when making *Heart of Britain*. H. Jennings and C. Madge, eds., *May the Twelfth: Mass Observation Day Surveys 1937* (London, Faber & Faber, 1937); Anthony W. Hodgkinson, 'Humphrey Jennings and Mass-Observation: a conversation with Tom Harrisson', University Film Association Journal, 4 (1976), p. 33.

[28] PRO INF 5/77, 'HARD WORK AND HIGH JINKS– The backbone of Britain' film proposal, [?] 1940.

[29] *Ibid.*, two untitled treatments, 29 October 1940, and 'Backbone of Britain – tentative schedule 1.11.40.'. Humphrey Jennings to Cicely Jennings, 20 October 1940, *ibid.*, p. 8.

[30] PRO INF 5/77, two untitled treatments, 29 October 1940.

[31] *Ibid.*

[32] *Ibid.*, 'Backbone of Britain – tentative schedule 1.11.40.'. Humphrey Jennings to Cicely Jennings, 12 and [?] November 1940, *ibid.*, p. 9.

[33] Neither Pearl Hyde's and the Coventry WVS's papers at the University of Warwick's Modern Records Centre, nor the Coventry City Record Office's council records from 1940-41, contain any reference to Jennings' three visits to the city. Similarly, an appeal to elderly readers of the *Coventry Evening Telegraph* for any recollection of meeting the film crew in late 1940 drew a blank.

[34] For data re the raid, see A.W. Kurki, *Operation Moonlight Sonata: The German Raid on Coventry* (Westport, CT, Greenwood Press, 1995), pp. 15-19 and 116-27, and N. Longmate, *Air Raid: The Bombing of Coventry, 1940* (London, Hutchinson, 1976), pp. 180-90.

[35] Mass Observation reports culled from Kurki, *ibid.*, pp. 130-132, and T. Harrison, *Living Through The Blitz* (London, Collins, 1976), p. 138-40.

[36] On Coventry's initial recovery, and George VI's visit on 16 November 1941, see Longmate, *ibid.*, pp. 190-207.

[37] Drazin reproduces Gerry Bryant's caustic 'wartime rhyme' as an illustration of Jennings' capacity to generate a mixture of deep loyalty and intense loathing, noting that his 'tantrums and his biting tongue were notorious within the unit. To be asked to work with him was like being sent to the Russian Front.' Drazin, *ibid.*, pp. 148-9.

[38] After Dalrymple left Crown, Jennings was his own producer. In 1945 Basil Wright, Dalrymple's eventual successor, headed the production team on *A Diary for Timothy*.

[39] Humphrey Jennings to Cicely Jennings, 14 December 1940, *ibid.*, p. 10.

[40] PRO INF 5/77, Humphrey Jennings to Sidney Bernstein, 22 January 1941, and 'MoI Weekly Release for Monday, February 10th, 1941'. On Murrow's close collaboration with the MoI, for whom his wife worked, see Calder, *ibid.*, pp. 211-22

[41] *Ibid.* 'The Heart of Britain'; PRO INF 5/79 'This is England [American & Empire version]'. At the same time Reynolds was asked to write the commentary for a second film, *Christmas Under Fire*, in which he spoke to camera

[42] *Heart of Britain.*

[43] The roof-spotter was Frank Halliwell, 'mill-foreman at Farnsworth in Lancashire'. PRO INF 5/77, two untitled treatments, 29 October 1940.

[44] Vaughan, *ibid.*, p. 74.

[45] Recorded in Manchester's Odeon Theatre on 1 December 1940, and not in the Free Trade Hall as is popularly assumed. Sargent received a 'nominal fee of 25 guineas', and complained when he had not been paid after two months. PRO INF 5/77, financial correspondence.

[46] *Heart of Britain.*

[47] '…there is an extraordinary frisson about this juxtaposition [Hyde and the Huddersfield Choral Society], as if the massed ranks of people were rising in homage to the woman's shy smile.' Vaughan, *ibid.*, p. 73. The first part of the

statement is undoubtedly correct, but not for the reason given: the viewer simply thrills to the power of the music and the size of the choir.

[48] *Heart of Britain.*

[49] 'Back and forth go these contrasting, conjunctive images, until the music broadens out to its conclusion, the roar of engines joins in, and the bombers take off.' L. Anderson, 'Only Connect: some aspects of the work of Humphrey Jennings', *Sight and Sound*, 23 (1954), reprinted as appendix in Winston, *ibid.*, p. 72.

[50] *Heart of Britain.*

[51] Humphrey Jennings to Richard Winnington, quoted in Hodgkinson and Sheratsky, *ibid.*, p. 82.

[52] Vaughan, *ibid.*, p.73;

[53] Chapman, *ibid.*, p. 100.

[54] Note how in the course of the film 'Jerry' transmogrifies into 'the Nazis'. Christopher Frayling, speculating that the final sequence 'must have packed a huge punch' with cinema audiences, suggested that *Heart of Britain* is unique in being the only Jennings film to make direct reference to striking back at the enemy. *Humphrey Jennings: The Man Who Listened to Britain*, Channel 4, 24 December 2000.

[55] *The Silent Village* (Humphrey Jennings, Crown Film Unit; UK, 1943).

[56] Dalrymple, *ibid.*, p. 217.

[57] Anderson, *ibid.*, p. 72.

[58] Jeffrey Richards, 'Listening to Britain: Humphrey Jennings and Music', IWM conference, 20 September 2000; Humphrey Jennings to Cicely Jennings, 25 January 1941, *ibid.*, p. 11; Dalrymple, *ibid.*, pp. 219-20. Ironically, Paul Rotha in his review of *Heart of Britain* accused Jennings of 'going religious' by incorporating *The Messiah*. Humphrey Jennings to Cicely Jennings, Easter Monday 1941, *ibid.*, pp. 16-17; *Documentary News Letter*, 2/3 (March 1941), p. 48.

[59] Unlike the mid-eighteenth-century 'Rule Britannia', with its much cruder connotations of an expansionist Protestant Great Britain. According to his assistant director on *Listen to Britain*, Joe Mendoza, Jennings' musical tastes were rooted in the late Stuart and Hanoverian court's response to the Baroque: his two favourite composers were Handel and Purcell. The Handel Male Voice Choir performed the [Anglo-]German composer's *Largo* in *Spare Time*. Drazin, *ibid.*, p. 154

[60] *Heart of Britain.*

[61] R. Aldous, *Tunes of Glory The Life of Malcolm Sargent* (London, Hutchinson, 2001), pp. 102-7.

[62] On these 'Baroque moments', and Jennings's cinematic equivalents of the Metaphysical conceit, see Winston, *ibid.*, pp. 35-7.

[63] Hodgkinson and Sheratsky, *ibid.*, p. 57; J. Richards, 'England, Their England: *Fires Were Started*' in Aldgate and Richards, *ibid.*, p. 222.

[64] Account of recording the LPO at the Queen's Hall in: Humphrey Jennings to Cicely Jennings, 8 March 1941, *ibid.*, pp. 13; PRO INF 5/79 Proposal for 'In England Now' and 'In Germany Now', 12 February 1941.

[65] Vaughan, *ibid.*, p.75;

[66] Hodgkinson and Sheratsky, *ibid.*, p. 54.

[67] Winston, *ibid.*, pp. 32-3.

[68] A pillar of the Coventry Labour Party, the glamorous Alderman Mrs Hyde served a term as Lady Mayoress, and always generated plentiful local gossip about her private life. Her greatest moment was on 25 May 1962 when, arriving at the Council House prior to the consecration of Coventry Cathedral, she attracted more cheers from the crowd than the Queen. Personal recollection.

[69] Humphrey Jennings to Cicely Jennings, 10 May 1941, *ibid.*, pp. 28-9.

[70] 'In a Jennings film each strip of celluloid had its own intrinsic value. His faith in the texture of reality meant that a person laughing was always that…[he] was at his best when he was showing the audience a world and teaching them to see it anew.' Drazin, *ibid.*, p. 158.

[71] The view of Paula Rotha, Edgar Anstey, and other acolytes of John Grierson writing for the *Documentary News Letter*. Jackson and Richards in *Humphrey Jennings: The Man Who Listened to Britain*, Channel 4, 24 December 2000.

[72] Gerald Noxon quoted in Stansky and Abraham, p. 123.

[73] See in particular Richards, *ibid.*, pp. 225-8.

[74] Yet both men were constrained by education, accent, and upbringing from experiencing any genuine shared experiences with ordinary working-class people – as Orwell acknowledged in *The Road to Wigan Pier*, and Tom Harrisson identified as a real problem for Mass Observation's pioneers. See Tom Harrison 1975 interview quoted in Stansky and Abrahams, *ibid.*, pp. 84-5.

[75] '…a family with the wrong members in control': G. Orwell, 'The English Revolution' in *The Lion and the Unicorn: Socialism and the English Genius* (London, Warburg, 1941/Penguin, 1988), p. 54. On both men's nation/family analogies see *ibid.*, pp. 227-8; and on Jennings' increasingly inclusive view of national identity, embracing ethnicity as well as class, see Winston, *ibid.*, pp. 52-3.

[76] '…the people who feel at home in the radio and ferro-concrete age': Orwell, *ibid.*, pp. 112-13. 'Your remarks about Wellington and Waterloo and the last twenty years very good. Excellent analysis of same thing in George Orwell's *Lion and the Unicorn*: still quite a bunch of "intellectuals" here who are afraid of becoming patriots.' Humphrey Jennings to Cicely Jennings, 10 May 1941, *ibid.*, p. 29. The same faith in 'expertism', at the expense of a reactionary and irrational amateurism that had prevailed for far too long, was articulated by the specialists contributing to *Picture Post*'s much-publicised 'Plan for Britain', 4 January 1941; see Smith, *ibid.*, pp. 98-9.

[77] A hostile Ministry of Town and Country Planning could not ignore Labour's municipal by-election success, nor support for an ambitious rebuilding of the city centre expressed by the two local newspapers, both of which were normally critical of council intentions. Hasegawa, *ibid.*, pp. 30-46 and 106-7. Council discussion of Donald Gibson's radical plan for the city centre coincided with the first serious national debate on postwar reconstruction, prompted by *Picture Post*'s multi-authored 'Plan for Britain'.

[78] 'A memorial in the ashes – New Yorkers look to Coventry as a model', *Guardian*, 25 September 2001. Commentating on the three minute silence at 11am on 14 September 2001, the BBC's David Dimbleby used the twinned cities of

Dresden and Coventry as a familiar point of reference for British viewers mourning those killed three days earlier in New York.

[79] On initial national reporting as to how 'Coventrification' was unique and unprecedented, see Smith, *ibid.*, pp. 84-5.

[80] Harrisson, *ibid.*, pp. 150-1.

[81] Smith, *ibid.*, p. 102.

[82] Harrison, *ibid.*, pp. 150-1.

[83] H. Forman, 'The non-theatrical distribution of films by the Ministry of Information' in Pronay and Spring, *ibid.*, pp. 223-30; Roger Manvell, regional Films Officer 1940-45, Foreword, in Hodgkinson and Sheratsky, *ibid.*, p. xiii.

[84] Re debate on effectiveness, see Reeves, *ibid.*, p. 171, and Chapman, *ibid.*, pp. 112-13. Review of *Heart of Britain*, *Documentary News Letter*, 2/3 (March 1941), p. 48. The Grierson-inspired view of Jennings as being 'too self-consciously artistic' was echoed in the *Spectator*, where Edgar Anstey freelanced as occasional film critic. Chapman, *ibid.*, p. 169.

[85] T. Harrisson, 'Films and the Home Front – the evaluation of their effectiveness by 'Mass Observation' in Pronay and Spring, *ibid.*, pp. 241 and 243. On MO's 1940-41 research findings for the MoI, which were generally favourable towards the short documentaries, see Chapman, *ibid.*, pp. 106-7.

[86] Ian Dalrymple quoted in Richards, *ibid.*, pp. 218-19.

[87] Calder, *ibid.*, pp. 9-13.

5. The Coventry factor

[1] I am grateful to Sarah Ferris, research student at the University of Newcastle Department of English Literary and Linguistic Studies for a copy of her paper, 'John Hewitt's disciples and the 'kaleyard provincials'', and for her comments on my original essay; published in *Literature and History*, 8 (1990); and also to Nicola McNee, archivist of the John Hewitt Collection at the University of Ulster, for additional information and photocopied material. At King Henry VIII School, Jeff Vent was characteristically helpful and effusive, even providing a previously unpublished photograph of Philip Larkin in the sixth form. My thanks also to Noel Hughes for his 'insider's' comments on an early draft.

[2] Adrian Henri, Roger McGough & Brian Patten, *Penguin Modern Poets 10: The Mersey Sound* (London, Penguin, 1967), had been reprinted six times by 1971.

[3] P. Larkin, *The Whitsun Weddings* (London, Faber, 1964).

[4] Larkin had little time for the old school tie, but even in middle age he could not resist a dig at the old rival, Bablake School; see Philip Larkin to Colin Gunner, 19 November 1973, in A. Thwaite (ed.), *Selected Letters of Philip Larkin 1940-1985* (London, Faber, 1992), p. 493.

[5] F. Ormsby (ed.), 'Introduction', *The Collected Poems of John Hewitt* (Belfast, Blackstaff Press, 1992), pp. lxii & lxviii; J. Hewitt, forward to a 1970 unpublished history of Cushendall, quoted in ibid., p. lx. Hewitt's disenchantment with

management by 1971 inspired a short and witty celebration of technocratic Luddism, which has a curiously 1990s feel about it ('that maze of programme budgeting/input analysis and cost effectiveness'): 'Executives Third Tier', ibid., pp. 359-60.

[6] J. Hewitt, *Ulster Reckoning* (Belfast, privately published, 1971) and *Out Of My Time: Poems 1967-1974* (Belfast, Blackstaff Press, 1974). Attempts to halt the early marches of the Civil Rights Association left Hewitt questioning a permanent return: 'Going back would mean being involved in the feuds. I mean I would have to take a stand against Paisley, as my friends have done'; Hewitt quoted in J. Evans, 'Profile of John Hewitt', *Coventry Evening Telegraph*, 29 August 1968. That feeling prevailed even after the purchase of the Hewitt's retirement home, witness a late warm tribute to Coventrians and their symbol of reconstruction:

> These people I now live among
> are friendly in the street
> and quiet in the evenings
> around their own hearths.
> And I grown old
> do not wish to shuffle
> through the rubble of my dreams
> and lie down in hope's ashes:
> the Phoenix is a fabulous bird.

J. Hewitt, 'Exile', 1969, *Collected Poems*, pp. 141-2. Hewitt nevertheless felt uncomfortable with that stance, witness 'A Belfastman argues with himself', written only a month earlier, and acknowledging that, 'You should have spoken when that evil man [Paisley]/first raised his raucous shout', ibid., p. 142.

[7] J. Hewitt, 'Variations on a Theme', ibid., pp. 320-1. As early as 1963 Hewitt's chosen theme for the annual John Shelton Memorial Lecture was 'The Continuing Crisis in Art'.

[8] The Hewitts entertained modestly in their Belfast flat during and after the war. As well as Larkin, they hosted E. M. Forster when he visited Northern Ireland in October 1952, renewing contact when the latter became a frequent visitor to mutual friends in Coventry, Bob and May Buckingham. Hewitt would read and chat to the blind Forster, 'gripped by the marvel that we still could find/an edge of sharpness in that gentle mind'. R. McFadden, 'No Dusty Pioneer: A Personal Recollection of John Hewitt' in G. Dawe and J. Wilson Foster (eds.), *The Poet's Place: Ulster Literature and Society Essays in Honour of John Hewitt* (Belfast, Institute of Irish Studies, Queens University, 1991), p. 172; J. Hewitt, 'With E.M.F. on 28th December 1965' and 'An Hour With E.M.F. at Ninety', *Collected Poems*, pp. 108 & 167.

[9] See P. Larkin, 'Posterity', *High Windows* (London, Faber, 1974), p. 27, and J. Hewitt, 'Dissertation I & II', *Collected Poems*, pp. 364-5. Both men also had in common their first poems being published in the *Listener*, Hewitt with 'Ireland', 18 May 1932, and Larkin with 'Ultimatum', 28 November 1940.

[10] P. Larkin, 'I Remember, I Remember', 1955, in A. Thwaite (ed.) *Collected Poems*, (London, Faber, 1988), p. 81, and *Jill* (London, Faber, 1946, second edition, 1964), pp. 218-28; J. Horder, 'Poet on the 8.15', *Manchester Guardian*, 20 May 1965.

---

[11] A. Motion, *Philip Larkin A Writer's Life* (London, Faber, 1993), pp. 33-5.

[12] Philip Larkin to Charles Monteith, 30 November 1984, quoted in ibid., p. 4.

[13] The Larkin family arrived in Coventry in 1919 when Philip's father, Sydney, was appointed Deputy Treasurer. Three years later he was promoted to City Treasurer, and by 1927 he could afford to purchase a house in the part-industrial, part-middle-class residential Parkside, close to the Council House, and appropriately the railway station.

[14] Ormsby (ed.), 'Introduction', in Hewitt, *Collected Poems*, p. lxiv.

[15] Most notably in J. Hewitt, 'From chairmen and committee men, Good Lord deliver us', *Honest Ulsterman*, 6, (1968), pp. 16-22, reprinted in T. Clyde (ed.), *Ancestral Voices: The Selected Prose of John Hewitt* (Belfast, Blackstaff Press, 1987), pp. 48-55, & 'The family next door', *Threshold*, 23 (summer 1970), pp. 14-19, reprinted in *Evening Press*, 17 August 1970, and presumably quoted with Hewitt's approval in A. Warner (ed.), 'Introduction', *The Selected John Hewitt* (Belfast, Blackstaff Press, 1981), p. 5.

[16] 15 Sarah Ferris provides several examples of Hewitt's growing uneasiness in 'John Hewitt's disciples and the 'kaleyard provincials'', unpublished paper, University of Newcastle Department of English Literary and Linguistic Studies, p. 10; D. Casey, 'The doyen: a *Quarto* interview with the Belfast poet John Hewitt, December 4 1980, the New University of Ulster', *Quarto*, 7 (1980-1), pp. 1-14.

[17] Heaney in 1969 was one of the first to describe Hewitt setting 'his lonely present against a rooted past, in terms of a lost community and family'; a view later developed by Edna Longley in arguing the significance of Hewitt's premature assault upon Unionist philistinism. S. Heaney, 'The poetry of John Hewitt', *Preoccupations: Selected Prose 1968-1978* (London, Faber, 1980); E. Longley, 'Writing, Revisionism and Grass-seed: Literary Mythologies in Ireland' in G. Dawe & E. Longley (eds.), *Across a Roaring Hill: the Protestant Imagination in Modern Ireland Essays in Honour of John Hewitt* (Belfast, Blackstaff Press, 1985), pp. 11-21.

[18] McFadden, 'No Dusty Pioneer', pp. 178-9. Kirkland's assertion that the over-riding pattern of Hewitt's 'intellectual life ... is one in which methodology seeks to restrict the chaos of sensory impression' is quoted in Ferris, 'John Hewitt's disciples and the 'kaleyard provincials'', p. 3; E. Longley, 'Progressive Bookmen: politics and Northern Protestant writers since the 1930's', *Irish Review*, 1:1 (1986), pp. 50-7, and D. Kibberd, *Anglo-Irish Attitudes*, Field Day Pamphlet, 6 (Londonderry, Field Day, 1984), p. 22 - my thanks to Ms Ferris for these references. Hewitt's vision that regional loyalties might one day transcend sectarian division in Northern Ireland is a major theme in his work, and a central preoccupation of most critical studies since the early 1980s: 'Hewitt embraced the concept on every level - intellectual, emotional, imaginative and practical', Ormsby (ed.), 'Introduction', in Hewitt, *Collected Poems*, p. l. Three key essays are: J. Hewitt, 'Regionalism: the last chance', 1947, and 'No rootless colonist', 1972, in *Ancestral Voices*, pp. 122-5 and 90-5; and less easily accessible, 'The bitter gourd: some problems of the Ulster writer', *Lagan*, 3 (1945), pp. 93-105.

[19] J. Hewitt, 'Godiva Rides Again in a New Coventry', *Belfast Telegraph*, 20 September 1957.

[20] T. Mason and B. Lancaster, 'Society and Politics in 20th Century Coventry' in T. Mason and B. Lancaster (eds.), *Life and Labour in a Twentieth Century City: The*

Experience of Coventry (Coventry, Cryfield Press, 1986), pp. 355-9; N. Tiratsoo, *Reconstruction, Affluence and Labour Politics* (London, Routledge, 1990), pp. 88-100.

[21] For the city council's unease by the time construction of the new art gallery and museum began in 1954 over the terms of machine tool magnate Sir Alfred Herbert's 100,000 gift, see J. McG. Davies, 'A Twentieth Century Paternalist: Alfred Herbert and the Skilled Coventry Workman' in Mason and Lancaster (eds.), *Life and Labour in a Twentieth Century City*, p. 124. For sanitised profiles of Stringer and Hodgkinson, see K. Richardson, *Twentieth-Century Coventry* (Coventry, Coventry City Council, 1972), pp. 204-6.

[22] Tiratsoo, Reconstruction, Affluence and Labour Politics, p. 120.

[23] J. Hewitt, 'Godiva Rides Again in a New Coventry', and 'Poets on Poetry: Hewitt', Radio Éireann, 18 February 1975, quoted in Ormsby (ed.), 'Introduction', in Hewitt, *Collected Poems*, p. xlii.

[24] For Morris's continuing influence upon Hewitt, see: ibid.; introduction to *The Rain Dance: Poems New and Revised* for *The Poetry Book Society Bulletin*, 99, (Christmas 1978) reproduced in ibid., pp. 610-11 (which also mentions recent 'nourishment in the English Philip Larkin ... '); and 'No rootless colonist'. On discovering Mumford and Geddes in the early 1940s, see Ormsby (ed.), 'Introduction', in Hewitt, *Collected Poems*, p. l.

[25] Hewitt, 'Godiva Rides Again in a New Coventry'.

[26] J. Hewitt, 'Coventry, the tradition of change and continuity' in Coventry Corporation, *COVENTRY The Tradition of Change and Continuity* (Coventry, Coventry Corporation, 1966), pp. 11 and 10. For the importance of the 'utility churches' to both the diocese and the architect, see L. Campbell, *Coventry Cathedral Art and Architecture in Post-war Britain* (Oxford, Clarendon Press, 1996).

[27] Hewitt quoted in 'Proposals for Coventry Art Collection', *Coventry Evening Telegraph*, 1 November 1957.

[28] Tiratsoo, Reconstruction, Affluence and Labour Politics, pp. 46-52 and 100; Richardson, Twentieth-Century Coventry, pp. 310-43.

[29] Hewitt, 'Coventry, the tradition of change and continuity', p. 10.

[30] Ibid., p. 1

[31] Larkin, 'I Remember, I Remember', *Collected Poems*, p. 81.

[32] Ibid.; Hewitt, 'Coventry, the tradition of change and continuity', pp. 13 and 9.

[33] Hewitt, 'No rootless colonist'; K. Levine, 'A tree of identities, a tradition of dissent: John Hewitt at 78', *Fortnight*, 213, 4-17 February 1985, pp. 16-17. For a critique of Hewitt's insistence to Levine that his radicalism has 'strong British roots' ('my intellectual ancestry goes back to the Levellers') with little to draw upon from Gaelic culture, see S. Hillan King, 'The Note of Exile: Michael McLaverty's Rathlin Island' in Dawe and Foster (eds.), *The Poet's Place*, pp. 215-217.

[34] Hewitt, 'Coventry, the tradition of change and continuity', pp. 3-7. On why you can still tell Coventry was a parliamentary stronghold and a setting for George Eliot novels (that 'moral explicitness, an earnestness ... '), see Paul Barker's pen portrait of the city that 'best embodies the postwar socialist ideal' in 'Observations', *New Statesman*, 17 January 1997.

[35] Ibid., p. 6; Ormsby (ed.), 'Introduction', in Hewitt, *Collected Poems*, p. lxiv.

[36] Hewitt, 'Coventry, the tradition of change and continuity', pp. 12-13; John Hewitt interview in the *Standard*, 5 June 1959, quoted in Ormsby (ed.), 'Introduction', in Hewitt, *Collected Poems*, p. lxiii.

[37] Hewitt, 'Coventry, the tradition of change and continuity', p. 9.

[38] Hewitt quoted in Evans, 'Profile of John Hewitt'. Larkin painted a similarly gloomy picture of Coventry twenty years earlier: 'I never knew anyone ... who was interested in writing. There may have been little groups who met and discussed each other's work, but I never came across them'. P. Larkin, 'Not the Place's Fault', *Umbrella*, 1:3 (1959), p. 112. In later years Larkin was unhappy about this 'rather rambling' essay on his childhood, which, 'said just a little more about myself than I really want known'. *Umbrella* was an obscure arts magazine circulating around Coventry in the late 1950s, and Larkin was insistent that his article should not become more widely known by being included in the 1983 prose selection *Required Writing*. Philip Larkin to Blake Morrison, 22 October 1982, quoted in Motion, *Philip Larkin*, p. 500.

[39] 'An Ulsterman in England Remembers' and 'The Dilemma', Hewitt, *Collected Poems*, pp. 133 and 132.

[40] 'Lines on the Opening of the Belgrade Theatre, ibid., pp. 513-15. The same year saw a further (not very impressive) example of Hewitt the public - yet this time discreet - poet: his anonymous 'To the memory of John B. Shelton, Antiquarian', *Coventry Evening Telegraph*, 5 Dec. 1958; ibid., p. 196.

[41] Ibid., and 'Prologue for an Evening at the Whitefriars', ibid., pp. 531-4.

[42] 'Suburban spring in Warwickshire', 'The Burnt Post', and 'Compton Wynyates, Warwickshire, 1968', ibid., pp. 165, 175 and 166.

[43] 'An Irishman in Coventry', 1958, ibid., pp. 97-8.

[44] John Hewitt interview in the Standard, 5 June 1959, quoted in ibid., p. 588; Hewitt quoted in Evans, 'Profile of John Hewitt'.

[45] 'The Search', 1966, Hewitt, *Collected Poems*, p. 160.

[46] Ibid. The poem contains an oblique reference to the Hewitt family in medieval and early modern Coventry, one of whom, 'I would like to imagine ... came with the Planters and settled in Co. Armagh'; Hewitt's notes on 'The Search' quoted in *Collected Poems*, p. 600.

[47] 'The Coasters', ibid., pp. 135-7.

[48] 'The Tribunes', 'The Well-intentioned Consul' and 'Parallels Never Meet', ibid., pp. 138, 138-9 and 139-40.

[49] 'The Colony', ibid., p. 79.

[50] Ibid.

[51] 'The Roman Fort', ibid., pp. 175-6.

[52] 'Bogside, Derry', 1971, ibid., pp. 176-7.

[53] Heaney, 'The Poetry of John Hewitt', p. 209; Ormsby (ed.), 'Introduction', in Hewitt, *Collected Poems*, p. lxiv.

[54] 'The King's Horses', ibid., p. 185.

[55] For Hewitt's tribute to his schoolteacher father, 'a just and kindly man', see 'Freehold II The Lonely Heart', ibid., pp. 373-9. Contrast with P. Larkin, 'This Be The Verse', *High Windows*, p. 30!

[56] Motion, *Philip Larkin*, p. 35.

[57] Ibid., pp. 54 and 11-12; P. Larkin, 'An Interview with the *Observer*', *Required Writing Miscellaneous Prose 1955-1982* (London, Faber, 1983), p. 47. Noel Hughes insists that Larkin told him his father was a member of The Link, and that he never categorically denied it: 'He merely claimed that he had no knowledge of it and that search of his father's papers produced no evidence for it'. N. Hughes to the author, ? April 1997. For a detailed study of The Link, see R. Griffiths, *Fellow Travellers of the Right British Enthusiasts for Nazi Germany 1933-39* (Oxford, Oxford University Press, 1980).

[58] N. Hughes, 'The Young Mr Larkin' in A. Thwaite (ed.), *Larkin At Sixty* (London, Faber, 1982), pp. 17-22. One wonders how Larkin felt about the repeated assertion that, 'There is much in Philip that is reminiscent of his father', ibid., p. 21.

[59] 'He [Larkin] said once he despised people committed to music (meaning classical music). When I [Sutton] said, "What about jazz then?", he said, "That's different!".'. J. Sutton, 'Early Days' in G. Hartley (ed.), *Philip Larkin 1922-1985 A Tribute* (London, Marvell Press, 1988), p. 78. On Sutton and Larkin's mutual passion for trad jazz, see Motion, *Philip Larkin*, pp. 21-2.

[60] 'I [Larkin] wrote ceaselessly, however: now verse, which I sewed up into little books, now prose, a thousand words a night after homework.' Larkin, 'Not the Place's Fault', p. 112. Anthony Thwaite included 19 poems written prior to October 1940, of which 6 were published in the *Coventrian*, King Henry VIII's school magazine and one ('Ultimatum') in the *Listener*; Larkin, *Collected Poems*, pp. 225-52.

[61] Larkin [& N. Hughes], 'Last Will and Testament', ibid., pp. 250-2. Peter Porter has suggested that Auden's 'love of gossip is put to therapeutic use' in 'this richly reverential poem', but his alternative description of 'Their Last Will and Testament' as a 'cod document' seems far more apposite: P. Porter, 'Wonder of Wystan', *Guardian*, 20 March 1997.

[62] W.H. Auden, 'Chapter V Letter to Lord Byron Part II', in W.H. Auden and L. MacNeice, *Letters From Iceland* (London, Faber, 1937/1967), p. 49. A further West Midlands connection is Auden's 'Letter to R.H.S. Crossman, Esq.', ibid., pp. 89-96, Crossman having been chosen as Labour's parliamentary candidate for Coventry East well before the outbreak of war.

[63] With characteristic crudity Larkin discussed the importance of Auden to his sixthform poems in Philip Larkin to J.B. [Jim] Sutton, 16 April 1941, in Larkin, *Selected Letters*, pp. 11-12.

[64] For a recollection of that twice-daily journey see Larkin, 'Not the Place's Fault, p. 109.

[65] Motion provides a very full portrait of the schoolboy Larkin, who as an undergraduate labelled pre-sixth form generalist secondary education 'Evil Incarnate': 'Each man (generally) has one talent. Education should help him to find it - should make the child say 'of course" as it recognises with delight what it has always potentially known'. There speaks, not the voice of Wordsworth or Rousseau, but a man who has has suffered double-period Physics, with antique textbooks and ancient tutors (*plus ça change*)! Motion, *Philip Larkin*, pp. 15-25 and 28; Philip Larkin to Norman Iles, 17 April 1941, in Larkin, *Selected Letters*, p. 14.

[66] Larkin [& N. Hughes], 'Last Will and Testament', *Collected Poems*, pp. 250-2. 'French master' F.J. Liddiard was still teaching (me) 30 years later, and advising Andrew Motion over fifty years later.

[67] Philip Larkin to Norman Iles, 7 April 1942, in Larkin, *Selected Letters*, p. 24; Motion, *Philip Larkin*, pp. 32-3.

[68] In 1939 King Henry VIII was a 'neutral school' in that it was located within neither an evacuation nor a reception area. Attendance was thus voluntary once adequate shelter provision had been made. Larkin continued fire-watching at Oxford, where he was also obliged to join the Student Training Corps. G.L. Marson, F.H. Metcalf and A.A.C. Burton, *King Henry VIII School 1545-1945* (Coventry, King Henry VIII School, 1945), p. 46; Motion, *Philip Larkin*, pp. 33 and 38.

[69] P. Larkin, *Jill* (London, 1946, 2nd. edn. 1964), pp. 11-20, 52, 54 and 56-7. Noel Hughes believes that Kemp's adventures owe more to Larkin's personal experience than is usually acknowledged, for example, the hero's initial discomfort travelling south from Huddlesford recalls his stammering school friend's horror of being trapped in a crowded LMS railway compartment where peacetime English reserve had been abandoned: 'I [Hughes] do not think that Philip ever stuffed sandwiches down a loo, but I feel sure that the story reflected a searing experience that he once had on a train journey'. Noel Hughes to the author, ? April 1997.

[70] Ibid., p. 83; Larkin, 'Not the Place's Fault', pp. 111-12.

[71] Larkin, *Jill*, pp. 90-95, and 'Not the Place's Fault, p. 110; Motion, *Philip Larkin*, p. 20.

[72] Larkin, *Jill*, p. 203. Postmodernists and students of irony can have a field day with *Jill*, for example, when Whitbread speculates on the bombers' targets he asks Kemp, 'Do you live anywhere near the station?' ; Kemp awaits a train south from 'Kilbury Holt' in a pub called the 'Brandon Arms', and after Coventry railway station was put out of action on 14-15 November 1940 trains from the south terminated at Brandon, then a village outside the city boundaries; ibid., pp. 204 and 216.

[73] There had been 24 raids on Coventry since late August, but the 500 tons of high explosive dropped on the night of 14-15 November devastated the city centre, including the cathedral; destroyed or damaged 56 per cent of the total housing stock (42,904 houses); disabled 27 munitions and engineering factories; and killed or injured well over 2,000 people (the official death figure of 506 is considered far too low given that so many missing were never accounted for). Figures quoted in T. Lewis (ed.), *Moonlight Sonata: the Coventry blitz, 14/15 November 1940* (Coventry, Coventry City Council, 1990), pp. 31, 80, 144 and 167.

[74] N. Hughes, 'Going Home With Larkin', *London Magazine*, 29, 1/2 (April/May, 1989), pp. 115-119; Motion, *Philip Larkin*, pp. 48-9.

[75] *Jill* suggests Larkin and Hughes walked up King William's Street, as Kemp is instructed 'to go round Swanmill Park way', which must be a reference to Swanswell, the small park separating Hillfields from the city centre. Also, the civil defence workers, whose 'interest did not extend outside the particular district', tell Kemp that, "They had it badly round the hospital": the Coventry and Warwickshire Hospital, badly damaged because of its close proximity to the Royal Ordnance Works, was/is adjacent to Swanswell. However, Noel Hughes insists they took a different route

(Bishop's Street plus bus to Foleshill), and 'It would surprise me a great deal if he [Larkin] ever visited Hillfields. He was not interested in his fellow man'. Larkin, *Jill*, pp. 213-14; Lewis, *Moonlight Sonata*, p. 121; Noel Hughes to the author, April 1997.

[76] Larkin, *Jill*, pp. 213-15; Hughes, 'Going Home With Larkin, pp. 117-19; various descriptions of the centre of Coventry in the aftermath of the Blitz in Lewis, *Moonlight Sonata*, pp. 131-41, 144, 148-9, 158 and 174. 'Did you ever read JILL? Frightful piss, but has a flashback to Coventry that might amuse you'. Philip Larkin to Colin Gunner, 13 October 1971, in Larkin, *Selected Letters*, pp. 447-8.

[77] Motion, *Philip Larkin*, pp. 49-50. Motion suggests that not just 'A Stone Church Damaged by a Bomb' (1943), but even 'Church Going' and 'The Explosion', are poems directly or indirectly indebted in their imagery to Larkin's blitz experience.

[78] Larkin, *Jill*, pp. 218-19. Crouch uses a strained train analogy when advising Kemp of the need to network, having first revealed that the grammar school sustained a direct hit in the Huddlesford raid. Although forced to close, King Henry VIII escaped damage on 14-15 November 1940, but the main building was gutted on the night of 8-9 April 1941. Larkin no doubt had this in mind later in the war when first drafting Crouch's description of the extent of the (almost identical) damage. Larkin, *Jill*, pp. 228 and 226; Mason et al, *King Henry VIII School 1545-1945*, pp. 46-7.

[79] 'New Year Poem', 31 December 1940, Larkin, *Collected Poems*, pp. 255-6.

[80] Ibid. For evidence of cynicism and immaturity, albeit tempered by the odd good joke, see P. Larkin to J. B. Sutton, 9 & 20 December 1940, in Larkin, *Selected Letters*, p. 3-10. The latter poem gives some insight into the gestation of 'New Year Poem'.

[81] Philip Larkin to Barbara Pym, 14 February 1978, ibid., pp. 579-80. The other leading award winners were Bishop Cuthbert Bardsley, Chief Education Officer Robert Aitken, and TGWU General Secretary (and wartime union leader in Coventry) Jack Jones.

[82] Ibid. Admittedly there was a downside for Larkin in that he had to listen to Jack Jones monopolise the speech-making.

[83] Ibid.

6. An oval ball and a broken city, part 1

[1] This essay first appeared in the *International Journal of the History of Sport*, 11 (1994), at a particularly low point in the fortunes of the Coventry Rugby Club. By the time the article appeared 'Cov' had won the 1993-4 Division Three title, and were back in the then Courage Championship Division Two after only a season's absence. The final footnote asked if this was the first step on the long and painful path back to greatness. As the following essay makes clear, the answer to that was no. My thanks to sports history doyen Dick Holt for his enthusiastic response to the original piece, and his encouragement to write more about rugby union.

[2] For the uninitiated, in the British Isles rugby union players can be selected for their home countries, and for overseas tours with the British and Irish Lions.

[3] When the original essay was written, Matrix Churchill, a Coventry factory bought by and Iraqi-backed consortium, was at the heart of the arms smuggling scandal investigated in the 1995 Scott Report.

[4] Although injured for the whole of the 1993-4 season Jeremy Guscott was one of England's most exciting and glamorous threequarters; while of course 'Gazza' was the tabloid newspapers' nickname for English football's 1990s working-class hero, Paul Gascoigne.

[5] In the early 1990s England's regular back row forwards were unashamedly working-class, even if they played for fashionable clubs. Neither was ethnic background a bar to success, witness two Nigerian-born forwards in the then England pack. A decade later Bath remains a surprisingly genteel spa town, while south London's Harlequins have never wholly shaken off their public school, Oxbridge image. Orrell, once memorably described by Harlequins' very superior Will Carling as no more than a 'layby on the M6', was a remarkably successful Lancashire side in the final years of the amateur game. After elite rugby union went professional in the mid-1990s Orrell's fortunes swiftly faded.

[6] Workers in car factories such as Humber had Saturday afternoons off, and the football match would kick off at the Highfield Road ground fifteen minutes later than elsewhere in the country so that supporters of the 'Bantams' a chance to eat after the morning shift.

[7] The 1971 British Lions pulled off the rare feat of winning a test series against New Zealand. Duckham was also present on the first occasion the All Blacks lost at home to a national side from the British Isles: 10-16 at Eden Park, Auckland, on 15 September 1973. Four other Coventry players were in the England side that day.

[8] Bablake and King Henry VIII were Coventry's independent grammar schools for boys (now mixed). In the 1950s and 1960s fee-paying students were outnumbered by 'direct grant' students who had passed the Eleven-Plus and whose fees were paid by central government via the local education authority (LEA). Coventry's girls grammar schools were both LEA-controlled. The Roman Catholics had their own 'voluntary-aided' grammar and secondary modern schools, jointly funded and administered with the LEA under the 1944 Education Act. Post-1970 and the end of selection Coventry's LEA and RC schools all became comprehensives, while Bablake and King Henry VIII each reverted to its privately-funded status.

[9] Let's name names – anyone who ever saw Steve Tyrell play fly-half for Warwickshire Under-19s would know exactly what I mean.

[10] After writing this essay I very belatedly read *Dai for England: The Autobiography of David Duckham*, (London, Pelham Books, 1980). This remarkably prescient book was predicting the decline of Coventry nearly fifteen years before relegation to Division Three. Duckham lamented the absence of a permanent coach and an effective youth policy, and warned against complacency. The original essay assumed that the absence of any close involvement with the club since his retirement meant that Duckham's advice was not well received by the then committee. I suggested that the same might well have been true of Duckham's club colleagues in the England squad. After all between 1967 and 1976, eighteen Coventry players gained international recognition, and yet by the early 1990s only two of them - Peter Rossborough and Ian Darnell – were involved in coaching senior rugby [even in a

pre-professional era, Rossborough at a remarkably high level given his 'day job' as a secondary head teacher - of Woodlands School, which incidentally provided two members of the 2003 World Cup squad]. I later discovered that the RFU restriction on Duckham's involvement in the game was so draconian that it's a miracle he was even allowed in to the Coundon Road clubhouse. Securing royalties from his book was deemed to infringe Duckham's amateur status, and the ban was only rescinded in December 1995 following the International Rugby Board's decision to make the game open.

7. An oval ball and a broken city, part 2

[1] My thanks for their help in researching the original essay, which first appeared in the *International Journal of the History of Sport*, 17 (March 2000), to John Wilkinson (*Coventry Evening Telegraph*), Huw Richards (*Financial Times*), Peter Bills (*Sunday Times*), and Ian Malin (*Guardian).*

[2] Over twenty years and £60 million later Twickenham became a hi-tech temple of international sports unmatched elsewhere in the UK, and the inspiration for [much delayed] redevelopment of Wembley and of the Welsh RFU's Millenium Stadium in Cardiff.

[3] On the postwar history of Coventry FC [now RFC] see the preceding essay, and J.R. Barker-Davies (ed.), *Coventry Football Club (R.U.) 1874-1974* (Coventry, Coventry FC, 1974). For a brief and colourful insight into the strength and reputation of the Coventry club in the 1960s see D. Green, 'A celebration of the club game', in S. Barnes and M. Seabrook, (eds.), *Nice Tries A Collection of New Rugby Writing* (London, Vista, 1996), p. 146.

[4] Description of Coventry's 1973 and 1974 cup finals and March 1998 fixture based on author's recollection.

[5] English First Division Rugby Ltd., 'English Rugby Charter', *Allied Dunbar Premiership Weekly Update*, I, 14-15 March 1998, p. 17.

[6] See the preceding essay. Leading clubs already employed administrators/commercial managers; their sponsorship income in 1994-95 was boosted by tranches of £100,000 each from BSkyB. Bristol was probably not alone in depending on these payments to remain viable. D. Plummer, 'All the clubs have to do now is find some way of paying the bill', *Guardian*, 28 August 1995.

[7] A. Smith, 'Civil War in England: the clubs, the RFU, and the impact of professionalism in rugby union, 1995-99' in A. Smith and D. Porter, (eds.), *Amateurs and Professionals in Post-war British Sport* (London, Frank Cass, 2000), pp. 146-88.

[8] The annual Five Nations Championship involved the four 'home nations' of England, Wales, Scotland, and Ireland, plus France. It became the 'Six Nations' in 1999-2000 when Italy joined the competition. The second World Cup was in the UK and France in 1991 and the third in South Africa in 1995.

[9] M. Polley, *Moving the Goalposts: A History of Sport and Society Since 1945* (London, Routledge, 1998), p. 69; I. Malin, *Mud, Blood and Money English Rugby Union Goes Professional* (Edinburgh, Mainstream Publishing, 1997), p. 76.

[10] S. Barnes, *Rugby's New Age Travellers* (Edinburgh, Mainstream Publishing, 1997), pp. 1 and 14; Malin, *Mud, Blood and Money*, pp. 110-11.

[11] Malin, *Mud, Blood and Money*, p. 34. Private information. Rugby attracted successful businessmen in other sports: Gloucester's Tom Watkinshaw (F1 motor racing - Arrows team owner), Bedford's Frank Warren (boxing promoter) and Wasps' Chris Wright (football – Queens Park Rangers chief shareholder).

[12] 'Attendance figures for Allied Dunbar matches 1997-98', *Rugby World*, August 1998, p. 32. Adult tickets were in the £14-20 price range, itself a disincentive given a traditional assumption that rugby union is cheaper to watch compared with professional football. For the wide range of marketing ploys then used by market leaders Saracens and other Premiership One clubs, see P. Nichols, 'Counter culture: your rugby club needs you', *Guardian*, 7 November 1998.

[13] P. Bills, 'Players pay price as family silver sold off', *Sunday Times*, 15 March 1998; I. Malin, 'Moseley left on rugby's back burner', *Guardian*, 14 March 1998; 'Club Guide – Midlands', *Rugby World*, June 1997, p. 92.

[14] Figures quoted in R. Bates, 'Shattered Dreams', *Rugby World*, October 1998, pp. 44-7.

[15] 'The decline and fall of once ship-shape Bristol is a sorry saga of arrogance, self-delusion and unerring foot-shooting': Frank Keating, 'From local gods to downright clods', *Guardian*, 23 May 1998. The irony is that Bristol proved the exception to the rule in that it did attract a multimillionaire, Malcolm Pearce, who as the principal shareholder in Bristol Rugby Ltd., was prepared to buy success. He secured the services of top Australian coach Bob Dwyer to ensure Bristol returned to Premiership One in May 1999, and then paid for top players from the southern hemisphere to emulate Newcastle Falcons and win the championship at the first attempt. Pearce pointed out that, unlike Sir John Hall, he was a rugby enthusiast (albeit a lifelong supporter of Bath, Bristol's neighbour and in recent years far more successful rival), and that unlike the north-east rugby union had a tradition of being the premier sport in the West Country, i.e. success and superstars, fresh from the World Cup, would bring back old fans and attract new ones. Bristol imploded for a second time after relegation in 2003, and yet returned to the Guinness Premiership at the first attempt..

[16] Between 1997-98 at least two other players earned over £50,000 (plus bonuses and a car), with less established squad members negotiating contracts of £20-30,000 basic. Account of Coventry's experience 1995-99 based upon regular reports in the *Coventry Evening Telegraph*, and private information.

[17] Three Coventry-born forwards were in the England team which beat South Africa 13-7 on 6 December 1998, including Richard Cockerill and British and Irish Lion Neil Back, who both still live locally. The 2003 World Cup squad included two 'local boys', the ever-present Back and Danny Grewcock. As noted in the previous essay, both were educated at Woodlands School, with former England full-back and Coventry coach Peter Rossborough as head teacher.

[18] The final straw for Sugrue seems to have been the city planning committee's conclusion that the stadium proposals were 'totally unacceptable', prompting two councillors to withdraw from the club's steering committee. Neither Gerry Sugrue nor Bryan Richardson, chairman of Coventry City FC, acknowledged the author's requests for an interview.

[19] A five-man board was headed by wholesale Keith Fairbrother, former Coventry and England prop forward, and one-time wholesale grocer turned rugby league professional. Various club stalwarts alienated by Sugrue returned to assist the club, while others who had felt it necessary to stick with him until the bitter end, now bowed out.

[20] The first phase of the new stadium staged its first rugby match in August 2004.

[21] J. Wilkinson, 'Unveiled ... plans for new Cov stadium' and 'We want to be successful - and solvent', *Coventry Evening Telegraph*, 12 and 23 March 1999.

[22] M. Wilson, 'Stadium's future is sky blue', *Coventry Evening Telegraph*, 23 January 1999. The text remains as written in 1999, if only to expose the dangers of writing contemporary history. The following three years in fact proved to be a planning nightmare for both projects, with final planning permission for the football stadium still on a knife-edge in October 2003. Eventually approval was granted, and the Sky Blues celebrated their departure from Highfield Road in May 2005 by thumping Derby County 6-1 – remarkably repeating the feat on 21 January 2006 in their first season at the Ricoh Arena.

[23] Saracens successfully moved from north London to ground-share with Watford FC. Wasps and Queens Park Rangers FC were jointly owned until 2001, both playing at QPR's ground in south-west London. Since then Wasps have shared the Causeway Stadium with Wycombe Wanderers.

[24] Coventry and Barkers Butts initiated a player-share scheme in late 1998, with members of the former's Emerging XV gaining experience in the Midlands One League. Barkers Butts could play at Coundon Road when the pitch was available, and the scheme was intended to prevent future talent following the example of ex-Barkers Butts players such as Neil Back and moving on to Leicester; 'Club Guide: Midlands', *Rugby World*, January 1999, p. 99.

[25] For profiles of Worcester and Newbury as 'rugby's new middle classes', see Malin, *Mud, Blood and Money*, pp. 121-5, and for Worcester's own publicity see *Gold'n'Blues*. The All Blacks used Worcester as a training base during the 1999 World Cup.

[26] Eager to reduce the Premiership One from 14 to 12 clubs, EFDR took advantage of Richmond's bankruptcy and the availability of a stake in ailing London Scottish to force through a 'merger' in south-west London that resulted in both clubs being subsumed into London Irish. For a summary of conflicting views, see S. Barnes, 'Saint or Sinner?', *Rugby World*, August, 1999, pp. 53-6.

8. "Back, Moody, Kronfeld?   We don't need those lads at Treize Tigers"

[1] This essay was originally written for the *International Journal of the History of Sport*, 21 (January 2004), pp. 99-110.

[2] H. Trevor-Roper, 'History and Imagination' in V. Pearl, B. Worden and H. Lloyd-Jones (eds.), *History and Imagination: Essays in Honour of Hugh Trevor-Roper* (London, Duckworth , 1981), pp. 363ff.

[3] Rugby league's elite clubs have historically been concentrated in Lancashire, Yorkshire, and Cumbria, i.e. the traditional industrial heartland of England. The only exception is the capital's London Broncos, which has a hard core of metropolitan supporters, many originally from the north, but until 2005 endured a peripatetic existence moving from one temporary home to another. The Broncos' survival as a missionary for professional rugby league in the south depended heavily upon the continued support of the club's sponsor, Virgin. However, the 2006 season saw the renamed team form part of a joint operation with NEC Harlequins. Past initiatives in south Wales have failed, but plans are always ongoing to establish an elite side in the Principality, i.e. a team with a mass fan base playing at the highest level of the game in Great Britain, and with its matches covered by Sky Sports. France saw its relaunch of the Super League in 2006, but this time in Perpignan not Paris.

[4]Thompson actually used the hybrid German term, '*Geschichtenscheissenschlopff*'. My thanks to Tony Mason for confirming his former colleague's total disinterest in rugby, when this article was delivered as a short paper at the annual conference of the British Society of Sports History, 12 April 2003. E.P. Thompson, 'The Poverty of Theory: or an Orrery of Errors' in *The Poverty of Theory and other essays* (London, Merlin Press, 1978), p. 300.

[5] On the opprobrium attracted by counterfactual history see N. Ferguson, 'Introduction' in N. Ferguson (ed.), *Virtual History Alternatives and Counterfactuals* (London, Papermac, 1997), p. 5-7.

[6] Ibid., pp. 4-8; M. Oakeshott, *Experience and its Modes* (Cambridge, Cambridge University Press, 1933), pp. 128-145.

[7] R.J. Evans, 'Telling it like it wasn't', *BBC History* (December 2002), pp. 23-25, and *In Defence of History* (London, Granta, 1997), notably pp. 103-128. Within modern British history Evans' 'young fogey' historians would include Roberts and, perhaps above all, John Charmley, trenchant critics from a 'New Right' perspective of what they perceive to be an all-pervasive liberal consensus across the academic community ('neo-conservative' would be an inappropriate description given the term's present almost uniquely American connotations). G.M. Trevelyan, 'If Napoleon had won the Battle of Waterloo' in *Clio, a Muse and Other Essays Literary and Pedestrian* (London, Longmans, Green and Co., 1913), pp. 184-200. Macaulay's nephew reaffirmed in 1922 that Britain's defeat of Bonaparte guaranteed 'a hundred years of progress in liberty and high civilization'. D. Cannadine, *G.M. Trevelyan A Life in History* (London, Fontana, 1993), p. 107.

[8] Ironically, Ferguson's personal contributions are most open to such a charge, particularly his insistence that the European Union represents a German domination of Europe which the Allies' victory in 1918 merely postponed. N. Ferguson, 'The Kaiser's European Union: What if Britain had 'stood aside' in August 1914?' in Ferguson (ed.), ibid., pp. 228-280.

[9] Ferguson, 'Introduction' in ibid., p. 18.

[10] The 1894-95 schism in English rugby which led to the creation of the Northern Union [the original name for what became rugby league] was not over the fundamental issue of professionalism - or over changes in the rules, as 13-man rugby league only evolved as a manifestly different game in succeeding decades. The dispute focused upon 'broken time payments' to compensate for loss of wages. In London the staunchly amateur gentlemen-legislators of the Rugby Football Union rejected the popularly supported northern clubs' request to reimburse working-class players financially penalised as a consequence of taking time off from their jobs to train and to play, i.e. their entitlement 'to compete on the same basis as the sons of the liberal professions and the landed'. R. Holt, *Sport and the British A Modern History* (Oxford, Clarendon, 1992), p. 105. For the definitive history of the early Northern Union see T. Collins, *Rugby's Great Split: Class, Culture and the Origins of Rugby League Football* (London, Frank Cass, 1998).

[11] '... what is called realism (as opposed to fancy or ignorance of life or utopian dreams) consists precisely in the placing of what occurred (or might occur) in the context of what could have happened (or could happen), and in the demarcation of this from what could.' Isaiah Berlin, 'Determinism, Relativism and Historical Judgements', quoted in Ferguson, 'Introduction' in ibid., pp. 83-84.

[12] See extracts from Berlin's 'Concept of Scientific History' quoted in ibid. pp. 84-85, notably the claim that, 'When the historian asks himself about the probability of a past event, he actually attempts to transport himself, by a bold exercise of the mind, to the time before the event itself, in order to gauge its chances, as they appeared upon the eve of its realisation. Hence probability remains properly in the future.'

[13] This works both ways, i.e. political leaders (or even sports administrators!) may act rationally four times out of five, but the exception can rarely if ever be accurately predicted; and even the most unpredictable autocrat may suddenly, for whatever reason, appear to be dictated by reason rather than mere calculation or incipient megalomania (Stalin is perhaps a case in point).

[14] Ferguson, 'Introduction' in ibid., p. 86.

[15] 'For, in considering only the possibility which was actually realised, he [the – solely male? – historian] commits the most elementary teleological error.' Ibid., p. 87.

[16] Ibid., p. 88; Evans, ibid., p.24.

[17] Trevor-Roper, ibid.

[18] This section relies heavily on G. Williams, 'Midland Manoeuvres A History of Northern Unionism in Coventry', *Code 13 The Journal of Rugby League Heritage*, 2 (1986), pp. 9-14, kindly provided by Tony Collins. My thanks also for information provided by a former student, Peter Mills, whose 1997 undergraduate

dissertation drew attention to the Leicester rugby club's prewar brush with the RFU.

[19] On the Coventry club's success in cutting across class divisions, see the preceding 'An Oval Ball and a Broken City: Coventry, Its People and Its Rugby Team, part 1'.

[20] Collins, ibid., pp. 183 and 69.

[21] Coventry provided five of the Midlands and South team that played the Australians. Ironically, most of the matches played by the 1909-10 'Kangaroos' touring side were marred by rain. The tour attracted poor attendances, and made a loss. Ibid., pp. 223-4.

[22] The final fixture, against Wakefield Trinity, was cancelled by mutual consent, hence the odd number of matches played. Williams, ibid., pp. 13-14.

[23] Collins, ibid., p. 183.

[24] Strictly speaking Northern Union, as the term 'rugby league' was only formally adopted in the 1920s.

[25] Williams, ibid., pp. 11-12. Playing the inaugural final of the Works League Challenge Cup at the Griff and Coton collieries' sports grounds in Bedworth symbolised the collective involvement of both the traditional and the rising – manufacturing – industries.

[26] Smith, ibid.

[27] The Great War effectively forced communities to decide which code would predominate for the foreseeable future. Wartime division between the two games, plus postwar class polarisation ensured that henceforth there was minimal transfer of allegiance [Darnall in Sheffield was the only club between the wars to abandon union for league]. My thanks to Tony Collins for these observations. See also T. Collins, 'English Rugby Union and the First World War', *The Historical Journal* 45 (2002), pp. 797-817.

[28] In the late 1920s and early 1930s my father played representative rugby union for Frederick Bird's [elementary] School in Coventry from the age of 11. Nearly 40 years later, having passed the selective Eleven-Plus to attend one of the city's two grammar schools for boys, I played a full game of rugby on my first afternoon of 'games'.

[29] The secondary modern schools taught pupils aged 11 to 14, and from 1948, 15. Younger children were henceforth taught at 5-11 primary schools.

[30] The 1920s witnessed a flood of public and grammar schools abandoning football and adopting rugby union because of its positive association with 'all that was best' about the British war effort. Collins, 'English Rugby Union and the First World War', pp. 815-16.

[31] The two flankers, or wing forwards, are missing from rugby league's six-man scrum.

[32] In actuality Coventry beat Bristol 27-15 at Twickenham to win the 1973 RFU National Knockout trophy. At that point the club boasted 13 current or recent internationals.

[33] Castle claimed that for financial reasons he turned down an invitation to tour with England, but in 1954 played for Great Britain in Australia because he was guaranteed a share of the proceeds. 'Yesterday's Heroes: Frank Castle (Barrow &

Great Britain)', *Open Rugby* (March 1998), p. 31. *Cov Centenary Souvenir Special* (Coventry, Coventry Newspapers, 1974); J.R. Barker-Davies (ed.), *Coventry Football Club (R.U.) 1874-1974* (Coventry, Coventry Football Club, 1974). Personal recollection of Ron Tilbury silent on the touchline.

[34] D. Duckham, *Dai For England The Autobiography of David Duckham* (London, Pelham Books, 1980); interview with David Duckham, autumn 1996.

[35] On the club's long run of success since the late 1980s and its future plans, see www.tigers.co.uk.

[36] Collins, 'English Rugby Union and the First World War', pp. 815-17.

9. Coda – Remembering the Blitz

[1] Paper given (in summary) at the Oral History Society's annual conference, 'Using the War: Changing Memories of World War Two', King's College London, 2 July 2005

[2] M. Connolly, *We Can Take It! Britain and the Memory of the Second World War* (London, Routledge, 2004), pp. 1-25; A. Calder, *The Myth of the Blitz* (London, Jonathan Cape, 1991), pp. 1-19.

[3] Most demonstrably in Adrian Rance's introduction and 'historical foreword' to C. Frankland, Donald Hyslop and Sheila Jemima (eds.), *Southampton Blitz The Unofficial Story* (Southampton, Southampton Local Studies Section, 1990), pp. 1-13.

[4] *PortCities*, www.plimsol.org/Southampton/Southamptonatwar

[5] K.D. Lilley at al, *Rebuilding Coventry in the post-war era*, www-staff.lboro.ac.uk/~gypjh/Coventry

[6] P. Hennessy, *Never Again: Britain 1945-51* (London, Jonathan Cape, 1992), pp. 34-5; T. Harrisson (ed.), *Living Through the Blitz* (London, Collins,1976), pp. 143-81; M. Donnelly, *Britain in the Second World War* (London, Routledge,1999), pp. 36-8; R. Mackay, *The Test of War: Inside Britain 1939-45* (London, UCL Press, 1999), p. 131.

[7] A. Motion, *Philip Larkin A Writer's Life* (London, Faber, 1993), pp. 11-12, 36 and 49-51.

[8] A.W. Kurki, *Operation Moonlight Sonata: The German Raid on Coventry* (Wesport CT., Greenwood Press, 1995); T. Lewis (ed.), *Moonlight Sonata The Coventry Blitz 14-15 November1940* (Coventry, Tim Lewis/Coventry City Council, 1990); N. Longmate, *Air Raid: The Bombing of Coventry, 1940* (London, Hutchinson,1976); T. Mason, 'Looking Back on the Blitz' in Bill Lancaster and Tony Mason (eds.), *Life and Labour in a 20th Century City The Experience of Coventry* (Coventry, Cryfield Press, 1986), pp. 321-341; Vicar of Holy Trinity [G.W. Clitherowe], *Coventry Under Fire* (Gloucester, The British Publishing Company,1941), pp. 31, 50 and 53; Harrisson (ed.), *Living Through the Blitz*, pp. 133-42.

[9] A. Calder, *The People's War: Britain 1939-45* (London, Jonathan Cape,1969), pp. 203-5 ; M. Smith, *Britain and 1940: History, Myth and Popular Memory* (London, Routledge, 2000), pp. 84-5; A. Bissell, *Southampton's Children of the Blitz* (Bournemouth, Red Post, 2001), pp. 8-8; T. Brode, *The Southampton Blitz* (Winchester, Barry Shurlock,1977); A. Kemp, *Southampton at War* (Southampton, Ensign Publications,1994).

[10] B. Knowles, *Southampton The English Gateway* (London, Hutchison,1951), pp. 154-80 and 201-2; Harrisson (ed.), *Living Through the Blitz*, pp. 143-81.

[11] Harrisson (ed.), *Living Through the Blitz*, p. 340.

[12] Mason, 'Looking Back on the Blitz', pp. 321-341; J. Hinton, *Women, Social Leadership, and the Second World War Continuities of Class* (Oxford, Oxford University Press, 2002), pp. 86-9; G. Hodgkinson, *Sent to Coventry* (Bletchley, Maxwell,1970), p. 156; M. Gilbert, *Winston S. Churchill Volume VI Finest Hour 1939-1941* (London, Heinemann,1983), pp. 912-16 and 1941. On pro-Soviet sentiment in Coventry, especially post-June 1941, see S.O. Rose, *Which People's War National Identity and Citizenship in Britain 1939-1945* (Oxford, Oxford University Press, 2003), pp. 503. On the relative success of the CP (led locally by Bill Alexander, former commander in Spain of the International Brigades' British Battalion) in exploiting post-raid popular discontent, see James Hinton, 'Coventry Communism A study of factory politics in the Second World War', *History Workshop Journal*, 10 (1980), pp. 90-118.

[13] Knowles, *Southampton,* passim.; Harrisson (ed.), *Living Through the Blitz*, pp. 327-9; Mason, 'Looking Back on the Blitz', pp. 329-33; Frankland et al (eds.), *Southampton Blitz*, pp. 8-12; Brode, *The Southampton Blitz*, pp. 12-27; Calder, *Myth of the Blitz*, pp. 131-4; Smith, *Britain and 1940*, pp. 32-4.

[14] Brode, *The Southampton Blitz*, pp. 12-27; Frankland et al (eds.), *Southampton Blitz*, pp. 8-12; Harrisson (ed.), *Living Through the Blitz*, pp. 327-9.

[15] E. Wyeth Gadd, *Hampshire Evacuees The War Time Diary 1939-1945 of Eric Wyeth Gadd* (Southampton, Paul Cave Publications,1982), pp. 32-3, 62-3 and 66-7.

[16] Calder, *The People's War*, p. 219; Harrisson (ed.), *Living Through the Blitz*, pp. 327-9; Mason, 'Looking Back on the Blitz', pp. 326-8; Lewis, *Moonlight Sonata*, pp. 144-9; Bissell, *Southampton's Children of the Blitz*, pp. 102-4 and 149-50.

[17] Harrisson (ed.), *Living Through the Blitz*, pp. 133-42 and 143-81; K.D. Lilley, *Rebuilding Coventry in the post-war era*, www.staff.lboro.ac.uk/~gypjh/Coventry.

[18] Bissell, *Southampton's Children of the Blitz*, pp. 151-2.

INDEX